Elizabeth Kirkland

A short history of England for young people

Elizabeth Kirkland

A short history of England for young people

ISBN/EAN: 9783337204402

Printed in Europe, USA, Canada, Australia, Japan

Cover: Foto ©ninafisch / pixelio.de

More available books at **www.hansebooks.com**

A SHORT HISTORY OF ENGLAND

FOR

YOUNG PEOPLE

BY

MISS E. S. KIRKLAND

AUTHOR OF "A SHORT HISTORY OF FRANCE," "SIX LITTLE COOKS,"
"DORA'S HOUSEKEEPING," "SPEECH AND MANNERS," ETC.

CHICAGO
A. C. McCLURG & COMPANY
1891

To My Classes in English History:

You already know something of American history. For two hundred years it was closely connected with that of England, and it is but little more than a century since we began to have a history exclusively our own. England is our mother-country; her past belongs to us as much as it does to the English, and ought to be equally interesting to us and them. After reading what was done and thought by our ancestors, you will understand all the better how the separation came about which made us an independent Nation.

E. S. K.

Chicago, October, 1891.

CONTENTS.

CHAPTER.		PAGE.
I.	Ancient Britain and the Romans,	7
II.	The Saxons and the Heptarchy,	16
III.	From Egbert to the Six Boy-Kings,	25
IV.	Six Boy-Kings to Norman Conquest,	33
V.	The Norman Conquest,	42
VI.	Norman England. William II. Henry I.,	50
VII.	White Ship. Death of Henry. Stephen,	56
VIII.	The First Plantagenet,	63
IX.	Richard I. and the Third Crusade,	73
X.	John Lackland and the Magna Charta,	82
XI.	Henry III. Simon de Montfort. First House of Commons,	90
XII.	Edward I., Conqueror of Wales,	98
XIII.	The War with Scotland,	106
XIV.	Edward II. Bannockburn,	113
XV.	Edward III. The Hundred Years' War,	120
XVI.	The Black Prince,	129
XVII.	Richard II. Wat Tyler. Bolingbroke,	137
XVIII.	Henry IV. Shrewsbury. Henry V.,	147
XIX.	Agincourt. Treaty of Troyes. Death of Henry V.,	154
XX.	Henry VI. War in France. Jack Cade,	162
XXI.	The Wars of the Roses,	170
XXII.	Edward IV. Little Princes in the Tower,	178
XXIII.	The Last Plantagenet. The First Tudor,	185
XXIV.	The Sixteenth Century. Henry VIII.,	193
XXV.	Henry the Tyrant; also "Defender of the Faith,"	201
XXVI.	Henry's Wives. English Bible. Edward VI.,	209
XXVII.	Lady Jane Grey. Bloody Mary. Calais,	217
XXVIII.	Elizabeth. Mary Queen of Scots,	225
XXIX.	Plots. The Navigators. Mary Stuart,	233
XXX.	The Armada. Ireland. Queen's Death,	240

CONTENTS.

XXXI.—	Sixteenth Century Summary. James I.,	249
XXXII.—	The Bloody Hand. Raleigh. Translation of the Bible,	257
XXXIII.—	Charles I. The Long Parliament,	264
XXXIV.—	Civil War. Marston Moor. Naseby,	273
XXXV.—	Pride's Purge. Execution of Charles I. Dunbar and Worcester,	279
XXXVI.—	The Protectorate. The Restoration,	287
XXXVII.—	Charles II. Triple Alliance. Treaty of Dover,	295
XXXVIII.—	Plots. Habeas Corpus. Death of Charles,	302
XXXIX.—	James II. Sedgemoor. Seven Bishops. Flight of the King,	310
XL.—	Revolution of 1688. William and Mary,	317
XLI.—	Glencoe. Death of Mary. Peace of Ryswick. Death of William III.,	323
XLII.—	Anne. Act of Settlement. War of the Spanish Succession. Union with Scotland. Death,	330
XLIII.—	George I. Invasion of the Pretender. South-Sea Bubble. George II.,	337
XLIV.—	War with Spain. Austrian Succession. Young Pretender. Quebec,	345
XLV.—	Seven-Years' War. India. Death of George II. Stamp Act,	353
XLVI.—	War with America. Peace of Versailles. Warren Hastings,	361
XLVII.—	The French Revolution. Napoleon in Egypt. Ireland,	370
XLVIII.—	Union with Ireland. Trafalgar. Orders in Council. Peninsular War. War of 1812. Waterloo. St. Helena,	378
XLIX.—	Death of George III. George IV. Catholic Emancipation. William IV.,	386
L.—	Parliamentary Reform. Abolition of Slavery. Victoria,	392
LI.—	Boundary Treaties. Corn-Laws Repealed. Crimean War,	399
LII.—	Treaty of Berlin. Egypt. The Queen's Jubilee,	407
List of Sovereigns,		414

A SHORT HISTORY OF ENGLAND

FOR

YOUNG PEOPLE.

CHAPTER I.

ANCIENT BRITAIN AND THE ROMANS.

THE earliest name for the country now called England was Albion, which we find in the works of Greek writers more than three hundred years before Christ. When the Romans went there it bore the name of Britain, and as such it was known for many centuries. Then it gradually became Angle-land, or England; and in modern times the inhabitants have given to the whole island, including England, Scotland, and Wales, the name of Great Britain.

There are many stories told about the Britons, going back as far as eight or nine centuries before Christ; and although there is reason to think that these stories were invented by writers who lived long afterward, and that we really know nothing about the old Britons, yet it is well to know something of the fables.

The first person to settle in Britain, we are told, was one Brutus, (called "Brut" by the early story-tellers), who was a great-grandson of Æneas, a Trojan warrior and the hero of Virgil's Æneid. This Brutus is said to have conquered a race of giants who dwelt in the country, and to have built on the River Thames a city which he called "New Troy."

Some hundreds of years after this we hear of a certain Prince Bladud, who, being afflicted with leprosy, was obliged to leave his father's palace and wander about the country. By a lucky accident he discovered near the River Avon some hot springs in which he bathed himself and was completely cured. In gratitude for this, he built a city around the magic waters, the modern successor whereof is known by the name of Bath.

The son of this prince was the unhappy King Lear who lives for us in Shakspeare's pages. The old story makes Cordelia's husband, a French king, help poor Lear to his throne again, driving away the wicked sisters; but Shakspeare has altered it into one of the grandest of his tragedies, and the king and his lovely daughter both die as a consequence of the father's over-trustfulness.

After several centuries there comes a king called Lud, who improved the city of New Troy and built walls around it. It was then called after him Lud's Town, or whatever answered to that name in Celtic, (the language of the Britons); the Romans called it Londinum, and it has now settled down into London.

The son of this King Lud was named Caswallon, (Latin, Cassivelaunus), and as he was the king or chief reigning in Britain when it was invaded by the Romans, he belongs to the period of authentic history. So much for fable.

The first people who visited the shores of Britain from

southern countries were undoubtedly the Phœnicians and Carthaginians, who went to the south-western part of the island (now called Cornwall), to obtain a supply of tin. They made no settlements, nor did they leave any account of what they saw there, so we may pass on at once to the invasion by Julius Cæsar, which took place 55 B.C.

The Britons whom Cæsar attacked were fierce and warlike savages, using javelins and arrows when they fought, as well as shields to defend themselves. They had, besides, a kind of blunt sword, which does not seem to have done much harm. They rode furiously to battle in chariots with sharp scythes sticking out on either side, managing their well-trained little horses with wonderful skill. In winter they dressed themselves in the skins of animals; in summer, when Cæsar first saw them, they painted or tattooed their bodies with the blue juice of a plant called woad, which must have been somewhat like indigo. They had learned so much of civilized ways as to make rough, round houses of sticks and clay, with a hole at the top to let out the smoke; and those who lived near the sea-shore had little boats called coracles, made of basket-work covered with leather.

The most interesting thing to us about the Britons is their religion. They were heathens, and their priests, who directed all their affairs, were called Druids. Among these Druids were the bards, or song-makers, who told in verse the stories of chiefs and heroes. These songs the people learned by heart and shouted them out before they went to battle, or when they returned after a victory. Other poets composed hymns, which the priests used in their worship. But as none of these were written down, the Druids having made it unlawful to keep any record of what was done on these occasions, the memory of them soon faded away.

All oak trees were considered sacred by the Druids; and where the mistletoe plant was found growing upon one, it was made the occasion of a magnificent festival. The Druids also built for their worship a kind of open-air temple, formed by enclosing a large space of ground with stones so immense that we wonder to this day how they were able to set them up in their present position.

These Druids had everything their own way; they were not only priests and poets, but law-givers, teachers, judges, and physicians; and they took care to keep up the idea of their power by surrounding themselves with mystery. The most ancient of their temples is at Stonehenge, near the city of Salisbury; but another, better preserved and more nearly perfect in form, is near Keswick in Cumberland.

Besides the harmless ceremonies already mentioned, the Druids had another kind of worship which fills our minds with horror; the sacrifice of human beings. Fearful tales are told of their burning alive hundreds of persons at once, usually criminals, in great wicker cages; and what are called "sacrificial stones" are still standing, on which we can imagine the victim laid, while fierce faces looked eagerly on, waiting for the death-stroke. The remembrance of these terrible scenes blots out the more innocent and pleasing parts of the picture; and we are glad to learn that about a hundred years after the invasion of Britain by Julius Cæsar, Druidism was abolished forever.

This great general was engaged in a war in Gaul, (the modern France), a country occupied by a race of men much like the Britons, when it occurred to him that there was an island just across the Channel which he might as well add to his other conquests. He crossed with his army over the narrowest part of the sea, now known as the Straits of Dover, and landed at a place called Deal, not far from the present city of Dover, in Kent. The poor Britons, naked savages though they were and armed only with miserable weapons, fought so hard with their dull swords and weak arrows that Cæsar's soldiers were driven back more than once. At last, however, Roman discipline and Roman steel got the better of ignorant bravery, and after the loss of many men, Cæsar managed to encamp on British ground.

The summer of the year 55 B. C. was now drawing to a close, and as Cæsar was afraid of the equinoctial gales he decided to go back to Gaul and leave the Britons alone; but the next year, 54 B. C., he came again, for he was not easily turned from his purposes. (Remember, that in counting the years *before* the birth of Christ, the number grows less and less as it gets nearer to our own time). The Britons were not in Cæsar's day one solid nation, governed by a king or chief; they were divided into many tribes, which were always quarreling with one another, and scarcely ever acted together; being, like most savages, ignorant of the fact that "union is strength." It happened just at this time, however, that the brave and spirited Caswallon, who has been already mentioned, was chosen general over several of the tribes in the south-eastern part of Britain, and under his direction they agreed to combine against the intruders. Caswallon was driven back by Cæsar's large and well-trained army, and then the British union melted away. Deserted by his neighbors, he was at last obliged to beg for peace, which Cæsar granted on very easy terms. He demanded a tribute, which was probably never paid, and a few hostages, of whom we hear nothing further; then, getting into their boats with all convenient speed, the Romans sailed away.

Such was the so-called "Conquest of Britain." Cæsar took no towns, left no garrisons, carried away no spoils, and marched into the country only a few miles from the sea-coast. It is true that he defeated the Britons in several battles, but this was all; and for a hundred years after he left the island they were as independent of the Romans, except for some commercial intercourse, as they had been before he came. His invasion was of some advantage to them, however; they sent the products of their country to Rome, getting valuable commodities in return; and, what was more important, some of their young men went there to be educated, and brought back with them a knowledge of Roman civilization.

In the year 43 A. D., a British traitor advised the emperor Claudius to send an army to conquer his native country, and a general named Aulus Plautius was sent to Britain. This time the Britons were really vanquished, but it took long years to accomplish the conquest; and many a Roman soldier found a grave on British soil before the fierce patriots would give up the struggle. A very able British chieftain named Cynobelin, (called by Shakspeare "Cymbeline," in his play of that name), had died just before Aulus Plautius came to the island, but even though he had lived it would have made little difference; Rome was too powerful for the Britons.

Another prince about whom many romantic stories are

told was Caradoc, (Latin, Caractacus). This fine soldier made a brilliant defence among the mountains of Wales, but was finally overcome, taken prisoner, and carried to Rome with his family. When he was taken before Claudius, after being marched through the streets in the train of the victorious general, he made an address to the emperor so noble and touching that the latter set him at liberty.

It was next the Druids' turn to suffer. They had gradually retired to their sacred island of Mona, now called Anglesey, at the north-western extremity of Wales, and there they were practising their religion, feeling quite safe from any interference. But the Roman general Suetonius, suspecting that this stronghold of the Druids afforded a refuge to rebels, pursued them into their retreat, defeated them in battle, and, if we may believe the hideous story, burned them alive in their own wicker cages.

While these dreadful things were taking place in Anglesey, others, different but also terrible, were going on elsewhere. A native tribe called the Iceni had been left by their chief at his death under the command of his queen, Boadicea, in the hope that even the Romans would respect her position as a woman. But he did not know them. She and her daughters were shamefully treated, and the queen was scourged, according to the cruel Roman practice, by the hard-hearted conquerors. As was natural, her people determined to avenge these insults, and a battle followed where Boadicea, standing up in her chariot, her long yellow hair streaming behind her and her royal robes displayed in their utmost splendor, fought like a tigress; but the Britons were no match for their enemies. They broke their ranks and fled, and the unhappy queen ended her life by poison. Cowper's poem of "Boadicea," beginning:

> "When the British warrior-queen
> Bleeding from the Roman rods;"

presents a thrilling picture of her heroism and her sufferings.

A pleasanter subject is the rule of Julius Agricola, a Roman general who was sent to Britain about 80 A. D. He taught the natives to cultivate the ground, (the word Agricola means farmer), to build good houses, to make roads and bridges; he made the collection of taxes as easy as possible, and allowed no inferior officer to oppress the people. He defended them against their troublesome neighbors the Picts and Scots, who lived in the northern part of the island, then called Caledonia, the old name for Scotland. The Scots came from Ireland, but we know very little about the Picts except that they were probably a tribe of the ancient Britons. To keep them in their own country, Agricola built a line of forts stretching across Scotland, or rather Caledonia, from the Frith of Forth to the Clyde. In the next century, (the second after Christ), a stone wall sixteen feet high and twelve broad was built farther to the south, from the Solway Frith to the River Tyne. Traces of the latter, which was called "The Picts' Wall," may still be seen in Northumberland.

Britain had now settled down quietly into the condition of a Roman province. The conquerors, with that practical wisdom which marked everything they did, made the inhabitants as proud of being Roman citizens as they had been before of being independent Britons. Magnificent buildings were put up in various parts of the island; excellent roads were made, forts were built so strong that they were expected to last for thousands of years—they have all tumbled to pieces centuries ago—and all the evidences of what is called material civilization were abundant in the land. The most important town was York, (British, Caer-Ebroc; Latin, Eboracum), and very interesting remains of the Roman times have been discovered there. Among others is a heavy coil of auburn hair, found in the stone coffin of some British lady, with the jet pins still fastened in it just as she was buried with them perhaps fifteen hundred years ago.

We have seen that the Druid priests, as a body, were destroyed by the Roman general Suetonius. Their religion fell with them, and the Britons were obliged, in outward appearance at least, to adopt that of their conquerors, the old mythological system. It is not known at what time Christianity was introduced into the island. Tradition says it was at a very early period, and as the British church was represented by three bishops at the Council of Arles, in Gaul, in the year 314 A. D., we have proof that it was well established before that date. The first martyr to the Christian faith, St. Alban, is thought to have lived toward the end of the third century. The emperor Constantine made Christianity the religion of the whole Roman empire early in the fourth century, so we may look upon the inhabitants of Britain from that time as being wholly converted to the Christian faith. Constantine's father, Constantius Chlorus, an able general and most excellent man, lived in Britain for many years, and his wife, Helena, who was herself a Christian, is said to have been a British princess. The reign of Constantine was the happiest and most tranquil period of the Roman dominion in Britain. Dark times were to come, and the fair island was for centuries a scene of confusion and bloodshed.

CHAPTER II.

THE SAXONS AND THE HEPTARCHY.

MOST of the troubles of the Britons during the fourth century A. D. came from their unruly neighbors, the Picts and Scots. It also sometimes happened that they unluckily chose the wrong emperor when more than one laid claim to the Roman crown, and were severely punished when the next one set up his authority; but these were small evils compared to the torments they endured from the unconquered and unconquerable savages of the north. To add to their misery a new enemy appeared on the eastern coast, the Saxons, who were so destructive that a special officer was appointed to look after them, called "The Count of the Saxon Shore." For some years the great Roman general Theodosius, a worthy successor of Agricola and Constantius Chlorus, made Britain once more a land of happiness and peace. After his departure, they quite innocently took up the cause of a pretender. A large number of them followed him into Gaul; and when he was defeated and killed they passed into Armorica, that peninsula in the western part of France which separates the English Channel from the Bay of Biscay. They hoped to cross over from there to their own country, and try to hide away in Cornwall from the vengeance of the successful emperor, but being kindly received by the Armoricans they were induced to stay and settle among them. Here they were joined by so many of their countrymen that the peninsula received from them the name of Brittany, which it bears to this day.

The worst misfortune of all those which befel the unhappy country was yet to come. The Romans, themselves in terror of the wild nations who were ravaging their beautiful Italy, declared that they could no longer keep up an army in Britain. The Britons were in despair; they begged and prayed so piteously for help that skilful generals were several times sent to their relief; but the time came when prayers were of no avail, and about 420 A. D. the last Roman garrison set sail from Britain, to return no more.

Now was the chance for the Picts and Scots. They had already ravaged the country between the two Roman walls so many times that it had become a desert and they could not find there anything to steal or any people worth killing; so they came boldly over the southern wall, no longer guarded by Roman soldiers, and the Britons lost heart and hope. In the four hundred years during which Rome had been their mistress they had become tame and spiritless, having had but little use for their weapons, and now they were at the mercy of enemies as ferocious as they themselves had been when they fought against Cæsar. They sent to the Roman counsul Aëtius, governor of Gaul, a letter which they called "The Groans of the Britons." "The barbarians," they said, "drive us to the sea; the sea throws us back on the swords of the barbarians; we have nothing left us but the wretched choice of being either drowned or butchered." But Aëtius could not help them, and they had recourse to the Saxons, the general name given to the pirates who came over the North Sea.

Nobody knows exactly where these marauders came from, but probably it was from what is now Denmark, (then called Jutland), and the north-western part of Germany.

In an evil hour Vortigern, the chief man among the Britons, driven to despair by the constant inroads of the Picts and Scots, invited these Saxon pirates to come and help his countrymen against their northern foes. They came, they saw more than they had ever seen before of the beautiful and fertile island, and they made it their own. They fell on the land, as a modern writer expresses it, "like wolves on a sick deer." There were three of these heathen tribes, the Angles, the Saxons, and the Jutes; but in old times they were all lumped together as Saxons, while now it has become the fashion to speak of them all as English. The name is of no consequence, but the descendants of races thus mingled were destined to become the mightiest upon earth.

The Saxons, as we call them for convenience, landed at a place called the Isle of Thanet, in Kent. Since then the drifting sand has filled up the channel which separated it from the rest of Kent, so that it is a part of the main land; but we can still tell pretty nearly where our ancestors set foot, in England in the year 449 A. D., almost exactly five hundred years after the first visit of Julius Cæsar.

The Saxon leaders were two brothers, Henghist and Horsa, and it is said that the British King Vortigern married a blue-eyed daughter of Henghist, the pretty Rowena, so for a while all were good friends. But the Saxons, disregarding the fact that they had come to the island expressly as the allies and guests of the natives, made peace with the Scots and Picts, and then all together fell upon the cheated and betrayed Britons and plunged them again into the horrors of war. Horsa was killed in battle, King Vortigern was deposed by his own people, who thought he favored the Saxons too much, and fresh bands of pirates came over the ocean, at the invitation of their countrymen, who soon took possession of the whole island. Having a heathen religion of their own to which they were very much attached, they were particularly furious against everything that had to do with Christianity. They burned the churches, killed or drove away the priests and monks, and seized upon everything precious, such as the gold and silver vessels contained in the sacred buildings. It was not so much that they wanted these things as that they hated the people who had them. As soon as the dreaded name of "Saxon" was heard, the clergy gathered up such possessions as they could take with them and fled, leaving all the rest, including their few and precious manuscripts, to the mercy of the torch and axe. The wonder is that they were able to keep up as a church at all, in the midst of such frightful discouragements. The victory of the Saxons meant the triumph of heathendom over Christianity for the time being. As for the Britons in general, those who were not killed or made slaves were driven out of the country, most of them taking refuge among the mountains of Wales, where their descendants still live. Others went to Cornwall in the south-western part of England, a wild, rocky district where their enemies could not pursue them, while others again crossed over the channel to Brittany, which had already begun to be called by their name. They do not seem to have mingled very generally with the Saxons by marriage any more than they had done with the Romans. The truth is that the Saxons were by far the cleverer of the two races; and being absolutely without an idea of fair dealing or truth-telling, they had the simple-minded British Christians at a great disadvantage.

We must not close our account of the Britons without saying something about King Arthur, a person of whom so many wonderful stories are told that for a long time it was supposed that he was no more a real man than was Prince Bladud. But there seems no reason why there should not have been a heroic British prince of the name who fought bravely against the Saxons that were trying to destroy his country, and was finally killed in a battle with them. With him ends the story of the old Britons—a brave, simple-minded, unfortunate race. It is supposed that they were finally put down by the Saxons in the sixth century after Christ.

One curious story about King Arthur is that he had a large round table, made so that when he and his friends sat at dinner together there should be no head or foot to it, but all should be on an equality. The companions who used to feast with him there were called "Knights of the Round Table."

The Saxons did not form one undivided kingdom, any more than the Britons had done. Coming into the country at different times, as they did, each robber-chief ruled over as much land as he could seize and defend, and the island, or rather the southern part of it, (now called England), was divided, at some time, into seven small kingdoms. This arrangement was called the Heptarchy, the word meaning a government of seven, but there was nothing lasting about it. Sometimes there were more than seven, sometimes fewer, and there was never a time when there was not fighting going on among them.

The first of these kingdoms to be set up was Kent, in the south-eastern part of the island. This was settled by the Jutes, who are often spoken of as Saxons. Later arose the three kingdoms of the South Saxons, (Sussex), West Saxons, (Wessex), and East Saxons, (Essex). The part ruled over by the Angles was called Anglia, and was divided into the country of the North-folk, (Norfolk), and the South-folk, (Suffolk). The middle kingdom of the island was called Mercia, and the extreme northern one was formed of two provinces which together made Northumbria, this name meaning, "the land north of the Humber."

Now that the fierce Saxons are firmly established in Britain, the rightful owners of the land being driven away and the Picts and Scots shut up in their own country of Caledonia, we come to the most important thing that ever happened in their history after the migration.

In the course of the wars which everybody in that age of the world was always carrying on with everybody else, it chanced that some English children were carried to Rome to be sold for slaves. There they were seen by the good abbot Gregory, who was pleased with their fair hair and blue eyes, and asked who they were. "They are Angles," was the reply. "If they were Christians they would be not Angles, but angels,"* answered the

---

* "Non Angli, sed angeli."

abbot. From this time Gregory desired nothing so much as to go as a missionary to these fair-haired Angles who might so easily be made angels. After a while he was made Pope himself, and one of the first things he thought of was his old project for converting the English. He sent Augustine* with forty other monks, to the island, where they were kindly received by Ethelbert, king of Kent, who was also Bretwalda, (Britain-wielder), or head of all the tribes. Ethelbert had married a French Christian princess, named Bertha; and when St. Augustine asked leave to preach to the Saxons, Ethelbert consented, though he would not at first allow the monks to come under any roof for fear of evil spirits, but made them hold their meetings in the open air. After a while he became himself a convert, and as it was thought the proper thing in those days for the mass of the people to adopt the religion of their ruler, ten thousand of the warriors of Britain followed his example, and were baptized by St. Augustine, who was afterward made the first Archbishop of Canterbury. It would be too much to expect that all these converts became good and holy men; a part of them remained cruel, untruthful, and treacherous; but when the gentle and merciful religion of Christ had once found a footing among them it did produce some effect, and many of them left off their barbarous ways and set about tilling the ground and living peacefully. There were still doings horrible enough to make one's heart sick only to read about them; but, on the whole, the nation had taken a turn for the better. The other kingdoms, one by one, followed the example of Kent; churches

---

*Pronounced Augus'tine, accentuating the second syllable.

were built and monasteries founded;* and though the pagans at first attacked their Christian neighbors, they ended by believing in the god of the Christians and giving up those they had formerly worshipped. This was a good thing for them, too (though they did not know it), in their intercourse with other countries. During the fifth and sixth centuries, when the main part of Britain was heathen, it was scarcely mentioned by the writers of that time; but now it began again to take its place among nations and to be spoken of with respect. The world could not help knowing that a people who believed in Christianity were greater and nobler than those who had no better gods than Thor and Woden.

From the time of the first landing of the Saxons in 449 A. D., to the coming of St. Augustine in 597, about a hundred and fifty years had passed. Britain may now be said to have been completely conquered and settled by the tribes of Angles, Saxons, and Jutes. The British language was replaced by old English, (generally called Saxon) and the old Roman laws by those made by the Saxons for themselves. The next event of importance in connection with the Saxon Heptarchy is the bringing of all the kingdoms together under one government by Egbert, King of Wessex, in 827 A. D.

We owe a part of our knowledge of what I have been telling you to a monk named Gildas, who lived while Briton and Saxon were struggling together to see which

---

* A monastery or convent was a place where many men lived together in order to give up their whole time to religious duties. After a time women began to live together in the same way and for the same purpose; then, to distinguish the two kinds of institutions, those for women were called convents, and those for men, monasteries.

could keep possession of the beautiful country one owned and the other wanted; and another part to a monk named Bede, usually called "The Venerable," who came perhaps a hundred and fifty years later. Bede lived a beautiful life and died a beautiful death. He was probably the most learned man in England. The Pope wished to make him a bishop, but he chose to remain a simple monk and to spend his life in teaching. It is said that as many as six hundred young men came at one time to be instructed by him, for at that time there were no colleges or universities, and no schools except those in the monasteries. When Bede was a very old man, and near his death, he was busy in translating the Gospel of St. John into the Saxon language. The young monk who was writing it down for him said: "You must be very tired, master; will you not rest?" "No," said Bede; "there is but little more to do. Write quickly; I must finish my work." The last verse was written; he was laid, by his own desire, upon the floor, his head supported in his pupil's arms; and with the words "Glory to God!" on his lips, he passed quietly away.

You can see how strong an impression the Saxons left on the country they conquered if you notice the names of our days of the week. Every one is named after a Saxon heathen god or goddess; even Saturday, which most persons suppose to be named for the Roman Saturn, is from a Saxon god called Sæter. Sunday and Monday are from the sun and moon, Tuesday from Tuisco, Wednesday from Woden, Thursday from Thor, and Friday from Freya, the northern Venus. The names of the months, on the other hand, remain as the Romans left them.

CHAPTER III.

FROM EGBERT TO THE SIX BOY-KINGS.

BY the end of the eighth century the kingdoms of the Heptarchy, whether more or fewer than seven, were in a very unsettled state. There had been a great deal of annexing by strong monarchs and giving up by weak ones, which naturally takes place whenever it happens that one country contains several independent and rival states. Then there usually arises one person wiser and more able than the others, who gets hold of the possessions of the rest, one after another, and is finally acknowledged by all as their master. So it was with Egbert, who was at first only king of Wessex (that is, of the West Saxons). The whole country now began to be called England, (Angle-land), though the name did not come into general use until the tenth century.

'Egbert, before he became king of all England, spent some time at the court of Charlemagne, who ruled over France (the ancient Gaul). The latter, being a most enlightened man, encouraged learning in every way, and even had a school in his palace for his children and their companions. Egbert's own country had furnished one of the teachers in Charlemagne's "School of the Palace."

When Egbert returned to England, which he did on the death of a rival king of Wessex, his first work was to fall upon his neighbors, conquer them, and add their kingdoms to his own, until nearly all of what is now England submitted to him, though some kings were allowed to keep their empty titles. He was the last person to be elected Bretwalda, as he was the first king of all England; so the change from a Heptarchy to a monarchy was greater in name than in reality. Under his rule the country enjoyed more peace and prosperity than it had known for a long time, and the only serious trouble he had after uniting the seven kingdoms into one, was from a new enemy, the Danes, who had begun to make their appearance on the English coast.

The island of Britain, for the first thousand years of what we may call its civilized life, was always a mark for the ambition or the greed of other nations. First there were the Romans, then the Scots and Picts, then the Angles, Saxons, and Jutes, and now the Danes. The new pirates were as fierce, as strong, as cruel, as the English themselves had been when they swooped down upon the Britons, and at first one is inclined to say, "served them right!" But we must remember that these were not the same English as those earlier freebooters had been, but their descendants, grown comparatively peaceful, and willing to live quietly at home and mind their own business. The Danish flag became to them a sight of horror. It was of a blood-red color, with a black raven pictured on it; and when the wind waved the flag the Danes declared that the raven was flapping his wings in sign of victory. To the suffering English the emblem meant only misery and destruction.

On Egbert's death, (836), his son Ethelwolf became king. This prince had not the military spirit of his father, and the Danes began to come to England every year, landing sometimes in one place and sometimes in another, so that the unfortunate English never knew when to be ready for them. Fire, slaughter, and plunder, went with them everywhere, and they found a strange pleasure in destroying all that they could not use. They managed to make settlements, first on the Isle of Thanet, (where the Saxons landed in 449 and St. Augustine in 597), and then at a place nearer London called the Isle of Sheppey. Ethelwolf defeated them several times in battle, and then, though he knew that his country was bleeding from their cruel swords, went on a pilgrimage to Rome to see the Pope, taking with him his son Alfred, six years old.

Ethelwolf died not long after his return to England, (858), leaving four sons, each of whom became king in his turn. Of the first three, Ethelbald, Ethelbert, and Ethelred, ("Ethel" means "noble"), there is not much to be said. They all had to fight the Danes, but this, unhappily, is too old a story to be worth repeating; so we will pass on to the reign of Alfred, who was perhaps at once the greatest and the best man that ever sat on the throne of England. He became king by the death of his brother Ethelred in 872 A. D.

Noble, strong, wise, truth-telling Alfred! The smallest thing about him is interesting to us. In those days very few persons could read, and there were scarcely any books to be had for love or money; but Osburga, Alfred's mother, had been so fortunate as to get possession of a beautiful illuminated* book which she promised to the one of her sons who should first learn to read. Alfred at once set about studying, and was soon able to claim the book for his own. This was about six hundred years before printing was invented, so that each book had to be copied out by hand; and such work, taking much time, was very costly.

---

* A book having pictures on the margin of the page.

We do not hear anything more about Alfred until he was twenty-two years old, when his brother Ethelred, (a fine young man, much like Egbert), was killed in fighting against the Danes. It was a discouraging moment for the new king. Many of his towns and villages had been burned, the best and bravest of his subjects had been massacred, and much of the best land in his kingdom was left without ploughing or planting because the insolent Danes were settled in the very heart of the country, ready to snatch away everything as soon as it was grown and ready for use. Alfred had several fights with them, sometimes getting the better and sometimes the worse; but at length his followers became discouraged, his army melted away, and he wandered about alone dressed like a peasant and wondering what he should do next.

It is to this time of his life that the famous story of the cakes belongs. He had gone into the hut of a neatherd* to rest awhile, perhaps expecting to get a meal and a bed. The man's wife had some cakes baking over the fire and asked the stranger to turn them while she was busy elsewhere. As he had some other rather important things to think of, he let the cakes burn, for which she gave him a good scolding when she came back, saying that he would be ready enough to eat them, though he would not take the trouble to watch them.

Another story told of his wanderings is that he went in the disguise of a harper into the camp of Guthrum, the Danish chief, and, while amusing the Danes with music and good stories, gained important information about their camp. At length, thinking the time ripe for an attack, he got together as many men as he could at what

* Pronounced neat-herd.

was called "the island" of Athelney; the island being a piece of firm ground mostly surrounded by marshes, which strangers would find it hard to cross. From this place he marched forth with his army and defeated the Danes in a hard-fought battle. He made a treaty with them afterward, in which it was agreed that Guthrum and all his followers should become Christians, and that Alfred should give them a large tract of land in England, or rather, should allow them to keep what they had already taken for themselves.

Alfred now showed himself as good a ruler as he was a general. He seems not to have had one selfish thought, but to have lived entirely for the good of his people. When he was older he wrote, "So long as I have lived, I have tried to live worthily." And he did live worthily. His first care was to repair his ruined cities and forts, to organize companies of militia in places most likely to be attacked by the Danes, (for though Guthrum was put down, there were thousands more at home to come), and to provide a fleet or navy. As the people in England were not used to building war-ships, Alfred sent for men from other countries to teach them; and when the ships were built, his sailors had to learn how to manage them. And now, one thousand years after Alfred's time, the English is the ruling flag on all the seas.

Safety being provided for, Alfred's next thought was of improvement. He made excellent laws and had them carried out; he caused justice to be dealt to every man, rich or poor, and he rebuilt the ruined churches and provided for their being kept up. He had schools started where young people could learn at least to read and write, and said that every free-born youth who was able to afford it should "abide at his book till he could well understand English writing." This is somewhat like what is now called "compulsory education," except that we give it for nothing to people who can not afford to pay for it. He was ashamed of the ignorance of his countrymen. "When I began to reign," said he, "I can not remember one priest who could understand his service-book or explain it in English." All books used in the churches and most others were written in Latin, and Alfred was a writer of good Saxon prose. Some of his books were translations of useful works from Latin into English, and some were original.

A very interesting old book called the "Anglo-Saxon Chronicle" is supposed to have been begun in his time, perhaps by Alfred himself. It is an account of what took place in England during several hundred years, written by the monks at different monasteries, each set of them copying what the others had written and making additions of their own. It is from this that we get much of our knowledge of what was done in those far-off times.

King Alfred would not have been able to accomplish as much as he did if he had not been one of the most methodical as well as the most industrious of men. He divided his time into three parts; one-third of the twenty-four hours he gave to public business, one-third to study and religious duties, and the remaining third to sleep, eating and amusement. He had no clock, and as he wanted to know just how much time he spent at each occupation, he ordered candles to be made with notches so arranged that it took just an hour to burn from one notch to another. Then, because the houses, (even the king's palace) were so poorly built that draughts of wind made the candles flare, he invented lanterns in which thinly-shaved horn took the place of glass, a material still unknown in England.

Alfred had one more hard struggle with the Danes, about ten years after the defeat of Guthrum. A terrible pirate named Hastings ravaged the coasts, but he was driven away and then there was peace until the sorrowful hour of Alfred's death (901). He was worn out, doubtless with hard work, for he was only fifty-two, and ought to have lived still many useful years. But he had never spared himself, and probably thought that it was "better to wear out than rust out."

Alfred the Great left one son, Edward, afterward called "The Elder." The Danes took advantage of Alfred's death to invade England, and Edward drove them back just as Alfred had done. Then came his son Athelstan, another warlike king, who kept up the credit of the family and ruled England wisely and well. He hit upon a new idea for helping along commerce and increasing among his people the desire to visit distant countries. He declared that any merchant who had made three long sea-voyages on his own account, (that is, not being hired by anyone else), should be raised to the rank of *Thane*, or gentleman.

Athelstan had been a great favorite with his grandfather, Alfred, who gave him a little sword with a golden scabbard, and a warrior's belt set with precious stones. He was never married, and at his death his brother Edmund, a boy of eighteen, was made king. He was the first of a series called "The Six Boy-Kings."

In many ways, the Saxons laws and customs were different from those of other nations. First, there was their

Witanagemot, or Meeting of Wise Men, selected entirely from the higher classes. The king was expected to consult this assembly, and its consent was necessary to all laws. In those days no one had ever thought of representative government, so this senate consisted of such persons as the king chose to summon.

Some strange notions of justice existed. When a man was accused of a crime, the case was put into the hands of twelve men who heard what was to be said on both sides, and then decided on his guilt or innocence. This was all very well, but if there seemed to be any doubt about it, there were two ways in which one might clear himself. He might take a solemn oath that he was not guilty, if he could get other men, called compurgators, to swear to the same thing with him; or he might try what was called the *ordeal.* This obliged him to thrust his arm up to the elbow in boiling water, hold a piece of red-hot iron in his hand, or walk about blindfolded among burning ploughshares. If at the end of three days there was no sign of burning on his hands or feet, it was taken for granted that he was innocent.

The old English houses were what we should call very uncomfortable. There were no chimneys, a hole being made in the roof to let out the smoke; and we may be sure that a great deal of it stayed in. Our ancestors must have had strong eyes not to grow blind under such circumstances. There was no glass except in the windows of the very rich; some others used to tack up white linen to keep out the cold wind and the rain, but many did without any screen whatever. All the furniture was plain; no chairs except in palaces; only stools or settees without backs. At the same time, everything belonging to eating and drinking was as fine as they could get it. They had cups and dishes of silver and gold, (when they could afford it), and instead of glass goblets used curiously carved horns of cattle. The Saxons were great eaters and drinkers; they had few other pleasures except hunting and fighting; and it must have been a disgusting thing for a person of refinement to be present at one of their drunken revels.

CHAPTER IV.

FROM THE SIX BOY-KINGS TO THE NORMAN CONQUEST.

IT will be convenient to remember the boy-kings as three pairs of brothers: Edmund and Edred, brothers of Athelstan, and therefore sons of Edward the Elder; Edwy and Edgar, sons of Edmund; Edward the Martyr and Ethelred II., called the Unready, sons of Edgar. As some of these lived to be middle-aged men, the name "boy-king" applies only to the age at which they began to reign.

Edmund, the first of these, was called "The Magnificent," because he built fine houses. He had to fight the Danes, whether he liked it or not; and when he found that some remains of the old Britons, who lived in the mountainous country of Cumbria (now Cumberland), were secretly helping the Danes, he went against them with an army, conquered them, and made a present of them and their country to the king of Scotland, the former Caledonia. Edmund's early death at the age of twenty-four was owing to his own quick temper and lack of self-control. A robber named Leolf, who had been banished from the country, had the impudence to come in and seat himself at the king's table at dinner. Ordinarily there would have been nothing out of the way about this, for it was then the custom for anyone who wanted a meal to take a seat at any table. But Leolf, being a well-known criminal, was ordered away by the king's guards. He refused to go; and Edmund, being excited with wine, sprang from his seat and seized him by the hair. The ruffian drew a dagger and stabbed him to the heart.

Edmund's chief adviser had been a monk named Dunstan, who was a man of such great ability that it seemed natural for him to be at the head of affairs. This monk the king made Abbot of Glastonbury, and he soon gained with the common people a great reputation for holiness, and proved the most useful of ministers.* When Edmund was killed by the robber Leolf and his young brother Edred became king in his place, Dunstan took nearly the whole management of the kingdom into his own hands, and was as successful in putting down the Danes as if he had been a soldier instead of a priest.

There are some very curious stories told about St. Dunstan, as he was afterward called. He was of an excitable nature, and at one time in his life was a little crazy, owing to some previous ill-treatment. When he became a monk, being extremely active physically, he used to work at a forge in a little blacksmith-shop he made for himself. Here (he said) as he was working one day, the devil suddenly appeared to him and tried to tempt him to do wrong. He happened at the moment

---

* A minister, in England, means a person who helps and advises the king.

to have a pair of red-hot tongs in his hand, and with these he seized the devil by the nose and pinched him so hard that he roared horribly and broke away from him. This anecdote, devoutly believed at the time, shows the state of public intelligence in the tenth century.

Edred did not live long, and as he left no children, his nephew Edwy, a boy of sixteen, became king at his death. Edwy had married a beautiful girl who was related to him, and as the church which Dunstan represented did not allow such marriages, it made ill-feeling between him and the king. After the coronation the nobles sat down to a great feast, where they wanted to eat till they were stupid and drink till they were drunk, as was the custom of the Saxons. Edwy preferred to spend the evening with his wife and her mother, so he quietly left the table and joined the ladies in their apartment. This made Dunstan very angry, and he followed the king and dragged him back by force, abusing him roundly at the same time. Edwy naturally wished to get rid of such a minister, so he asked Dunstan what he had done with all the money he had used in King Edred's reign. Dunstan could not tell, for he had never kept any accounts; and Edwy made this an excuse for driving him out of the country. Dunstan, however, had plenty of friends among the clergy, and they took the beautiful Elgiva, Edwy's queen, branded her in the cheek with a red-hot iron and sold her for a slave. She was taken to Ireland, where the people took pity on her, cured her wounds and sent her back to her husband; but on her way Dunstan's friends, led on by Archbishop Odo, seized her and cut her with swords so cruelly that she died. When Edwy knew this he too died, of a broken heart, and his brother Edgar, a boy of fifteen, succeeded him.

It is pleasant, at last, to be able to make a break in this long story of cruelty and misery, and to say that Edgar's reign of seventeen years was a prosperous and peaceful one. With Dunstan's assistance he triumphed over all his enemies, and when he grew old enough to govern for himself, he ruled with so much firmness and good sense that it was said that gold bracelets might be hung up on every tree in the woods, and no one would dare to touch them.

He made friends of the Welsh (who were the descendants of the old Britons and paid tribute to England), by a very simple device. Both England and Wales were overrun with wolves, which were so ravenous that they would kill and carry off not only farm animals but little children, and sometimes even attack men. The Welsh were very poor and found it hard to raise money enough to pay their yearly tribute. Edgar allowed them to bring him every year three hundred wolves' heads instead of money, so that the country was soon cleared of these destructive animals.

Of a reign so prosperous there is little to tell. It is said that Edgar was once rowed in a boat on the River Dee (near Chester) by eight tributary kings, while he did the steering. This, if it ever happened, was probably done for a joke. Edgar's private character was not good. He carried off his first wife from a convent, and obtained the second, the beautiful Elfrida, by the murder of her husband. A few years after this second marriage, Edgar the Peaceable (so called because he was so ready for war that no one dared to attack him), died, leaving his kingdom to his oldest son, Edward, aged sixteen, the child of the nun whom Edgar had run away with. Elfrida, however, determined that her own son, Ethelred, should be king. On one occasion, Edward stopped at her castle to pay her a visit of politeness. As he was going away she handed him a cup of wine, as was the custom when a guest was leaving a house.* While he was drinking this, one of her servants stabbed him in the back. The poor boy put spurs to his horse and rode away; but he soon became faint from loss of blood, fell from his horse and was dragged along by the stirrup until he died. The murdered king has always had the surname of "The Martyr," not because religion had anything to do with the crime, but because he was killed unjustly.

Poor little Ethelred, the son of Edgar and Elfrida, might have been called "The Unlucky." He was only seven years old at the time of his half-brother's murder, and, it is said, wept bitterly at seeing the cowardly deed, whereupon his mother beat him so hard with a thick wax candle that he never after could endure the sight of a candle. When he grew older he was called "The Unready," which means without *rede* or counsel, and not, as many people think, that he was never ready for the Danes. Dunstan died soon after this child was made king; and from that time to the end of his life the Danes kept pouring in, plundering, killing and wasting wherever they went, while Ethelred knew no better plan for getting rid of them than that of giving them money to go. Of course they came back again for more, the bribe being made larger each time. To pay this heavy tribute a

---

* Wine offered at such times was called a "stirrup-cup."

regular tax was laid, called Dane-geld, or Dane-money, which pressed cruelly upon the people.

The country in France called Normandy, which had taken its name from the Northmen who conquered it, had now become very powerful, and Ethelred thought it would be a good thing to gain its friendship by marrying the beautiful Emma, called "The Flower of Normandy," sister to the reigning duke. Her beauty was but skin-deep, however; it did not go down to her heart, for she showed herself hard, grasping and selfish. Soon after his marriage, Ethelred ordered a general massacre of all the Danes in his kingdom, many of whom were peaceable settlers. Among those murdered was the sister of the Danish king Sweyn. She was married to an English nobleman, and saw him and her children butchered before her eyes. Sweyn took a frightful vengeance on the unhappy country, laying it waste year after year, until Ethelred succeeded in buying off the bloody foe once more with the hard earned gold of his people. At length the unequal contest ended; the English king fled to Normandy, and Sweyn became in fact king of England.

There were four of these Danish kings; Sweyn, who lived only six week after his victory, Canute (pronounced Knut, sounding the K), and Canute's two sons. The contemptible Ethelred, on hearing of Sweyn's death, went back to England with promises of amendment; but he was incurable. His brave son Edmund got together an army to fight Canute. Just at this time the weak and wicked Ethelred died, and Canute found his match in Edmund, whom the people called Ironside, on account of his strength and bravery. Battle after battle was fought, and rivers of English and Danish blood shed, until at last the chief men on both sides begged the two kings to stop fighting and come to some agreement. It was finally settled that Canute should take the northern part of the country and Ironside the southern. The latter was soon murdered, probably by Canute's orders, and the Danish king ruled over all England.

The reign of this remarkable man began by his putting to death in the most cold-blooded manner all the Saxons who stood in his way; but after he had had his fill of vengeance, and had cut off everybody whom he thought dangerous, he made the best king the English had had since the time of Edgar the Peaceable. Finding that the English were willing to submit to him, he sent away most of his Danish soldiers, and tried his best to gain the affections of the people. He made no difference between Dane and Englishman, but treated all alike, under just and equal laws. The two sons of Edmund Ironside he sent to the king of Sweden with a request that they might never trouble him again; but the Swedish king, being of a merciful disposition, sent the children to Hungary, where they were brought up under the care of his sister.

A story is told of Canute, which, whether true or not, shows what the English people thought of his good sense. It is said that when some courtiers had been telling him he was lord of the ocean, he ordered his throne to be carried down to the sea-shore when the tide was coming up. He then haughtily commanded the waves to retire, but seeing that they came on as usual, he turned to his abashed followers and bade them remark that there was something at their feet stronger than he.

Canute was a widower when he came to England, and while there married Emma of Normandy, widow of Ethelred the Unready. He died in 1035, after a reign of nearly twenty years. He was a convert from paganism, so that the persecution of the Christians ceased with the beginning of his reign. He made laws for putting down heathenism, and protected the interests of religion; he even tried to atone for his early crimes by building churches and monasteries. The English were satisfied with him, and had reason to be sorry for his death.

His son Harold (called Harefoot from his swiftness in running) succeeded him, though Canute had agreed with queen Emma that Hardicanute, her son, should be king at his death. But Hardicanute was away, and Harold, being in England, had himself proclaimed at once. He then sent for Ethelred's sons Alfred and Edward, and when they arrived in England killed all their attendants with circumstances of the greatest cruelty, and put out the eyes of Alfred, the elder of the two princes, who soon died from his wounds. On hearing of the horrid deed, Emma fled to Normandy with her remaining son, Edward, afterward called the Confessor.

Harold did not live many years, and at his death his half-brother Hardicanute lost no time in coming back to England. He caused the body of Harold to be taken out of its coffin and thrown into a marsh; he oppressed and misgoverned the people of England in every possible way; and there was great rejoicing when, in a year or two afterward, he died as he had lived, a miserable drunkard. And so ended the Danish rule in England.

The people of the country had had enough of Canute's family, and were glad to welcome back Edward, the youngest son of Ethelred the Unready and Queen Emma. This king, who proved to be the last of the royal line of

Saxons, passes over the pages of history like a shadow. His surname of "The Confessor"* grew out of the fact that he was more like a priest than a king. The real ruler of England during his reign was the Saxon Earl Godwin; a man of immense tact, energy and force of will, who managed everything in the king's name so well that nobody missed the royal figure-head. Edward was considered a saint even during his lifetime, and the singular practice was then begun of bringing children afflicted with scrofula or "King's Evil" to the monarch to be healed by his touch. The strange delusion on which this "touching" was based lasted for seven hundred years.

Edward married Edith Godwin, daughter of the great earl, who had, besides, half a dozen strong, fighting sons to help him keep the country in order. A pleasant story might be told of the gentle Confessor's life, but what we want to know is the history of the *people* of England—not merely biographies of their kings. So we must let Edward fade away out of sight, though his subjects did not soon let him go out of mind. For hundreds of years after his death the English looked back to his laws (which were really Godwin's) with regret, and longed for the good old times of Edward the Confessor. The one thing remaining to remind us of him is Westminster Abbey, which he began, though scarcely any of the present structure is his work. Edward died in 1066, and Harold Godwin, who since his father's death some years before, had been prime minister, caused himself to be proclaimed king. He had no right by birth to this title, but he had everything else that belongs to it; good sense and judg-

---

*A confessor is a priest to whom persons confess their sins.

ment, firmness, a clear head and a steady hand, and best of all, a real love for his country. The birthright king would have been Edgar the Atheling, or Prince, a grandson of Edmund Ironside; but there was no one to take his part, and William, Duke of Normandy, a relation of Edward the Confessor, was watching the progress of affairs, and getting ready to seize the coveted throne.

CHAPTER V.

THE NORMAN CONQUEST.

SOME years before the death of Edward the Confessor, Harold Godwin had visited Normandy, and while there had been induced by its duke, William, to take a solemn oath never to claim the crown of England for himself. It is said that when Harold had sworn to do this, the duke took off the cloth from the table on which the Englishman had laid his hand and showed him that it was a chest full of saints' bones, which were supposed to make the oath peculiarly binding. Harold was startled, but nevertheless had himself proclaimed king as soon as the breath was out of Edward's body. He had a quarrel with his brother Tostig, and the latter went to Norway and brought the king of that country back to England with him, together with a large army. Harold, unwilling to go to war with his brother, sent a messenger to him offering forgiveness and large possessions if he would lay down his arms. "And what will you give my ally, the king of Norway?" inquired

Tostig. "Seven feet of English earth for a grave," was the reply; "or perhaps a little more, as he is taller than most men." "Go back," replied Tostig to the herald, "and tell my brother to get ready to fight." The result was the battle of Stamford Bridge, in which Tostig and the Norwegian king were defeated and killed, and Harold marched in triumph to London.

Bad news met him on the way. William of Normandy with a large army had landed in England, near Hastings in Sussex. If Harold had listened to the advice of his friends, he would have put off meeting William until his own army was stronger, for he had lost many men at Stamford Bridge. But he was impatient and angry, and without waiting for reinforcements, set out for Hastings.

The battle that followed (October 14th, 1066), was a sharp and bloody one, and was decided, after a long day of fighting, in favor of the Normans. Harold was shot in the eye by an arrow, and after the moon rose that night, it looked on the dead bodies of the king, his two brothers, and many of the noblest men in England. It was a sad sight; and when Harold's corpse was dragged out the next day, from under a heap of the slain, the Conqueror, as we must now call William of Normandy, gave permission to his mother to take it away and bury it.

This is properly called the battle of Senlac, that being the name of the place where it was fought, about nine miles from the town of Hastings, though the latter has given its name to the battle. On the spot where Harold was killed, William built a magnificent church called Battle Abbey. The ruins of this are in excellent preservation, and many travelers turn aside from the more beaten tracks to visit the scene of the battle of Hastings.

England, though its king had fallen, was not yet conquered. In fact, William did not wish to reign as a conqueror, but as a lawful king. His ambition was to be chosen by the people themselves. The death of Harold left but one claimant of the crown, Edgar the Atheling, grandson of Edmund Ironside, and this young man, if he had been like his grandfather or like the Conqueror, no doubt would have fought for his rights—and been conquered, as Harold was. A few of the English leaders still stood up for him; but there was disunion among them, and when the decision took place, Edgar himself was among those who offered the throne to the Conqueror. On Christmas day, 1066, William I. was crowned in Westminster Abbey, both Normans and Saxons taking part in the ceremonies. The Archbishop of Canterbury made an address to the English in their own language, asking if they would have William for their king. They shouted out, "Yes! Yes!" A Norman archbishop whom William had brought over with him asked his Normans the same question in French, and they were equally vehement. The soldiers standing outside, hearing the noise, imagined that the English were doing some violence to their duke, and in their panic, set fire to the wooden houses near the Abbey, which burnt like tinder, and came near destroying the whole town. Such occurrences did not help to increase good feeling between the English and Normans.

William I. set out to be a sort of second Canute, and no doubt really meant to govern well, though strictly. But it was not long before the Saxons perceived that the best of everything was slipping out of their hands and falling into those of the conquerors. If an English gentleman had fought against William at Hastings, that was a reason for taking away all his property and giving it to some Norman favorite. Strong castles were built near the large towns (a part of the Tower of London dates from this time), and these were garrisoned by Normans, so that the English might be kept in order. The Norman barons who were set over the conquered people became tyrannical, and abused their power in such a way that the English, burning with indignation, only awaited a good opportunity to make themselves free again.

The year after he was crowned, William I. made a visit to Normandy. The ill-feeling existing between Saxon and Norman broke out more fiercely than ever when the master's hand was withdrawn, and many Englishmen of rank, unable longer to endure the insolence of their foreign lords, broke out into open rebellion. Plots were almost as plenty as towns, and William came back without delay. For some time he contented himself with moderate measures, inflicting punishment only in proportion to the wrong done; but losing patience at last, he took a cruel revenge. He sent a body of soldiers under a trained captain, to lay waste the country between the rivers Tees and Humber, a district sixty miles wide, and reaching as far inland as York. Over this whole extent nothing could be seen but burned towns, ruined fields, and desolate farm-houses. Most of the inhabitants fled to Scotland; those who could not get away were killed without mercy. It is said that a hundred thousand persons perished in the famine that followed the destruction of crops, animals and farm-implements, and wild beasts made their lairs in what had once been smiling homes. Fifty years afterward, a writer who traveled there, groans over the dismal sight, and says it is piteous to see the change.

After this there were no more attempts at rebellion on the part of the English, and no pretence of mildness and moderation on the side of William. The old inhabitants of the land were ruled with a rod of iron; their new masters grew daily more grasping and more arrogant. William could now go to Normandy and stay as long as it suited him, without fear that a hand would be raised against his authority. All offices were taken away from the unfortunate Saxons, and their finest estates were given to the king's Norman favorites, who built castles to protect their new property, while the original owners of the country sank almost to the condition of serfs.*

In Normandy, William's oldest son, Robert, rebelled against him, and in a battle between them the king was unhorsed and might have been killed but that Robert recognized his father's voice. The prince, struck with horror, threw himself on his knees and begged forgiveness; but William was too angry to be generous, and turned sullenly away.

Three things were done in England by William's orders which enraged the Anglo Saxons, though it seems to us now that one of them was a positive benefit to the country, while another was at least harmless. The first was causing a book to be prepared which contained a description of all the land owned by private persons in the kingdom, with an account of its products. This is called the Domesday book. It still exists, and has been translated into modern English. As there was no way of recording

---

*A serf is a kind of slave who may be sold by his master with the land he lives on, but can not be removed from it.

the ownership of property at that time, this was of real value; but the Saxons looked at it only as a means for getting more taxes out of them.

The second regulation which offended our ancestors was that at the ringing of a certain bell called the curfew,* at about nine o'clock in the evening, all lights and fires were to be put out. This was an old Norman custom, used as a protection against fire, and binding on Normans and Saxons alike; but the English hated it because they thought it a sign of slavery. The population of England at this time is supposed to have been a million.

The third cause of offence was a more serious one. William was extremely fond of hunting, and not finding any forest conveniently near to his own dwelling, he determined to make one for himself. He caused all the inhabitants in a tract of country in Hampshire, in the south of England, for the space of thirty miles, to be driven away from their homes so that the wild beasts might increase there. He tore down houses and churches, that the animals might not be frightened off, and paid nothing for what he thus took for his own pleasure. This hunting-ground was called the "New Forest," and a part of it is still an appanage of the crown of England. A writer of the time says of him, "He loved the wild deer as if he were their father;" better than he loved his subjects, for while the killing of a deer or even a hare was punished by putting out the eyes of the offender, the killing of a man could be atoned for by paying a small sum of money.

William's death took place in Normandy. The town of Mantes, in that country, had rebelled against him, and

---

*From the French *"couvre-feu,"* "cover-fire."

he had ordered it to be burned to the ground. In riding over it afterward to see whether his commands had been obeyed, his horse stepped on some hot embers and plunged so violently that the king was thrown on the pommel of his saddle, receiving injuries from which he died soon afterward. He was taken to a monastery near Rouen, and his two younger sons, William and Henry, came there to see him. Robert he did not wish to see, and his second son, Richard, had died by accident in the New Forest. As soon as the two brothers had found out what their father meant to leave them, they made haste to go to England and take possession, William of the crown, and Henry of five thousand pounds that had belonged to his mother, Matilda of Flanders; and the Conqueror was left to the care of his servants and the attendant priests. It is said that he regretted bitterly all his cruel deeds and needless bloodshed, and tried by gifts to the church and by releasing from prison some persons who had offended him, to pacify his conscience. The instant he died his servants took everything they could lay their hands on—even the ring from his finger and the sheets from his bed. Sheets were valuable things in those days, and the thieves were in such a hurry that the Conqueror's body rolled to the floor as they dragged the linen from under it. Some monks found it and laid it out decently; but it was not yet allowed to be carried to the grave in peace. William had built at Caen in Normandy two magnificent abbeys, one for himself and one for Queen Matilda, who died some years before him. When a grave had been prepared for him, and the coffin was about to be let down into it, a man suddenly appeared in the church and with a loud voice forbade the interment. "The land this church was built on," said he, "never belonged to the man you are going to bury here! It was my father's, and was taken from him by force; now it is mine, and I refuse my permission to the burial!" The priests were struck with shame at this rude interruption, and pacified the man by paying him sixty pence, after which he left them in peace.

William continued in England, with little change, the state of things called "The Feudal System." The main idea of this was that all land really belonged to the king, although those who occupied it were allowed to call themselves the feudal owners of it, and that in return for this privilege each land-holder must be ready to go with the king to battle whenever he was called upon. In other words, the land-holder must give military service instead of rent or purchase-money. The same system was kept up through the many grades of rank, down to the poorest farmer or owner of a little garden-plot; he must go to war whenever he was called upon, so there was a great body of fighting men always ready for action. But when there was trouble in the country itself, those masses of soldiers were as able to fight against the king as on his side; so that it was not always to his advantage.

After the first rising against William the Conqueror in England, Edgar Atheling, the grandson of Edmund Ironside, went with his two sisters to Scotland, where they were kindly received by its king, Malcolm, son of the Duncan who was murdered by Macbeth, as we read in Shakspeare's tragedy. Malcolm married the lovely Margaret, Edgar's elder sister, while the younger one, Christina, became a nun. Edgar returned to England and died at a good old age, nearly forgotten by everybody.

CHAPTER VI.

NORMAN ENGLAND. WILLIAM II. HENRY I.

THE feelings of the English toward their Norman conquerors may be best judged from their own writings. It should be borne in mind that every tax imposed by foreigners must have been odious to them, and that the king could not know all the details of what was done by his officers. Here is one account:

"The king sold out his lands as dear as dearest he might, and he cared not how iniquitously his sheriffs extorted money from the miserable people, nor how many unlawful things they did. They raised oppressive taxes, and so many were their unjust deeds it were hard to remember them."

The English opinion of the Domesday Book may be gathered from another chronicle. "He caused them to write down what property every inhabitant of all England possessed in land or in cattle, and how much money this was worth. So very narrowly did he cause the survey to be made that there was not a single hide nor a rood of land, nor—it is shameful to relate that which he thought no shame to do—was there an ox, or a cow, or a pig passed by that was not set down in the accounts, and then all these writings were brought to him."

There appears to have been no effort made by Robert, the Conqueror's oldest son, to take possession of the throne of England. His father had left it to his second son, William, commonly called Rufus on account of his red hair and beard, and Robert became Duke of Normandy. Most of the Normans in England would have preferred the rule of Robert, who was open-handed, (that is to say, careless), hot-headed and rash; but the Conqueror had not willed it so, knowing how unfit he was to govern a mixed people like the English. William Rufus easily persuaded the Saxons that he was going to be a very lamb in governing, so they made no objection to him; but it did not take them long to discover that he was more like a wolf. He made the taxes of the people almost intolerable, and cared nothing for the rights of any one. His character is summed up in one sentence by the historian: "he neither feared God nor regarded man." His temper was fierce and cruel; his character treacherous and grasping, and all his subjects, Norman as well as Saxon, were glad when death took him off after a reign of thirteen years. We read of him in the chronicle:

"Through his avarice, he was ever vexing the people with armies and cruel taxes; for in his days all justice sank and all unrighteousness arose. In fine, however long I may delay mention of it, all that was abominable to God and oppressive to man was common on this island in William's time and therefore he was hated by almost all his people."

It was not long after William II. was made king that he and his brothers fell out with one another. First he invaded Robert's country of Normandy; then these two made friends and both attacked Prince Henry, their younger brother, who had taken a castle belonging to Robert on St. Michael's Mount in Normandy. They besieged him there until he was so hard pressed that not only his army but he himself was suffering from want of food. On hearing this, Robert sent him supplies of meat and wine from his own table; and when William blamed him for this he answered, "Shall we let our brother die of hunger? Where shall we get another when he is gone?"

Prince Henry was soon obliged to give up, and wandered about for some years, very poor and disconsolate. William went back to England and was soon more hated than ever. One of his ways of getting money unlawfully was through the church. At the death of any person holding an ecclesiastical office, the income belonging to the place went by law to the king as long as it was vacant. On the death of Lanfranc, a learned and excellent man whom William I. had made Archbishop of Canterbury (in place of the Saxon prelate turned out for the purpose), William II. (Rufus) refused to appoint another, and so kept the English church without a head for five years. Then being taken ill and fearing that he should die, he sent in great haste for St. Anselm, (as he was afterward called on account of his holiness), and insisted on making him archbishop against his will. When the king recovered he went back to his old habits, indulging in every kind of vice and setting himself against everything that was good. Anselm bore the king's misconduct as long as he could and then left the country, and William had from that time no check on his wickedness. The spirit of his dealings may be judged from his answer when the archbishop remonstrated with him on his habitually breaking his word. The king asked in a rage: "Who can do all he promises?"

One good thing remains for which England is indebted to William II. The beautiful Westminster Hall in London, one of the grandest single rooms in the world, was built in his reign.

It was during this reign that the first crusade was undertaken.* Robert of Normandy wished to go on this crusade but had no money, and as William could always get money by force or fraud, he agreed to furnish Robert with what he needed. In return Robert mortgaged his duchy of Normandy to William; that is, allowed him to take possession of it, with the understanding that after five years it should belong to William, if Robert had not paid back the money. The king took possession accordingly, but before the five years were up he was dead, and had no more use for land or money.

William Rufus was extravagantly fond of hunting, like his father, and went out one morning with a party of his friends into the New Forest, to have a day's pleasure. During the day he became separated from most of his party, and that night a poor charcoal-burner, driving his cart slowly through the forest, found the body of the Red King with an arrow in the heart. Sir Walter Tyrrel, the friend who was last seen with him, ran away to France without waiting to tell what he knew about it; but afterward he said that he had shot an arrow at a deer, and that it struck a tree and then glanced off and killed the king. Many persons disbelieved this story, but there was no proof that Sir Walter had not told the truth.

Nobody pretended to be sorry for William's death. His life had been so mean, base, and selfish that it was a relief to know that he could tyrannize no more. He was never married, and the next king would naturally be one of his brothers.

---

*A crusade was a military expedition, the object of which was to take the city of Jerusalem, with the tomb of Christ, from the Mohammedans.

Robert, the older of these, of course had the best right; (that is, provided the English people wanted him, for they still went through the form of electing their kings) but Robert was on his way from the Holy Land, and Henry, the younger brother, was on the spot. Robert came back in a few weeks, to find his brother acknowledged as king beyond all question. He was angry at this; but they met together and were reconciled, the elder resigning all his right to the throne of England, and promising to be content with his own duchy of Normandy.

Henry was a wise and far-sighted man. He knew that the only way to keep his people in good humor was to govern them justly, so he gave them a charter, that is, a written paper declaring what their rights were, and promised to rule according to law. He showed his wisdom further by marrying Matilda, the niece of Edgar Atheling and daughter of that queen who was so good that she received after her death the title of St. Margaret of Scotland. The children of this marriage would thus be half Saxon and half Norman, and there could never be any more quarreling between the two races.

Henry I. was the first of the Norman kings who had much more education than enough to write their names. He had been fairly well instructed and was fond of study, so he went by the name of "Beauclerc," or "Fine-Scholar," by which he is called to this day.

Although the political rights of the English were in a manner assured to them by Henry I.'s charter, they were none the less heavily taxed. The Anglo-Saxon Chronicle says of one period, "Full heavy a year was this. He who had any property was bereaved of it by heavy taxes and assessments, and he who had none starved with hunger." The taxes, however, were no longer regarded as being imposed by the victors on the vanquished. Norman and Englishman came under the same law, and for all practical purposes the two nations were now fused into one. Socially, the Normans still despised the Saxons, and considered Henry's marriage with Matilda, (who, out of respect to their prejudices, took that name on her marriage in place of her own Saxon name of Edith), as beneath the dignity of a Norman king.

Henry treated his brother Robert very harshly. He was always jealous of him, and finding that the Norman barons, weary of Robert's misrule, were inclined to a change, he went to Normandy with a large army and fought the battle of Tinchebrai, where Robert was defeated and taken prisoner. Henry carried his brother to England and finally shut him up in Cardiff Castle in Wales, where he dragged out twenty-eight miserable years before death set him free. A story that Henry had his brother's eyes put out rests upon some authority; but we prefer to think it a fiction of the chroniclers.

It is toward the end of Henry's reign that we first read of Oxford as a place where regular instruction was given (1133). In early times it was called "Oxenford" (see Chaucer's Prologue to the Canterbury Tales). From the twelfth century onward, new halls for study were founded, and learned men were attracted to the town as to a literary centre. The tradition which connects the present university with King Alfred, rests only upon the fact that he founded schools somewhere, and that as early as the reign of Edward the Elder, (901–925), Oxford had become a place of importance.

CHAPTER VII.

THE WHITE SHIP. DEATH OF HENRY I. STEPHEN.

HENRY I. now had apparently all that this world could give him. His power was unquestioned, his country was rigorously kept quiet, and his domestic affairs were prosperous. The great misfortune of his life came upon him like a clap of thunder from a clear sky.

He had been in France with his only son, William, celebrating the prince's marriage to a daughter of the Count of Anjou. A splendid wedding party was in attendance, and all were in the highest spirits. It was found convenient, in going back from Normandy to England, for the royal party to sail in different vessels, as the ships of that time were small and ill-fitted to carry many people at once. The king sailed first, leaving the prince to follow in a beautiful new ship called the "Blanche Nef," or White Ship, offered by the owner for that purpose. "I had the honor of carrying over your father when he went to the conquest of England," said this man; "I pray you to use my new ship for your journey." The king answered that his own arrangements were made, but that his son would accept the offer with pleasure. The ship was crowded as full as it could hold. There were fifty "sailors of renown," as the captain called them, and a hundred and forty of the prince's company, including many high-born ladies, who had gone from England to the wedding. "Give the men three casks of wine," cried the prince, who had been drinking a great deal of wine himself; "let us all be merry together." Off they went; the sailors got drunk, and the ship had scarcely left the harbor when she struck on a rock with such force that it was seen instantly that she must sink. The captain hurried the prince with a few companions into a boat, ordering the men to row for their lives to the shore, which they could easily have reached. But among the ladies left on board to drown was the Countess Marie, a sister of Prince William; and he, hearing her piteous cries for help, insisted on going back to the ship to save her. Upon this, so many persons crowded into the boat that it sank, and the ship went down at the same moment. Of all that great company, but one escaped death; a poor butcher of Rouen who told the story. He was saved by clinging to a mast, and said that the captain might also have reached the shore but that on hearing of the prince's death he let go, and crying out, "Woe is me!" sank to the bottom like a stone.

For several days no one dared to carry the tidings to the king. At last a young boy was sent into his presence, and, falling at his feet in tears and trembling, told his story. The king fell down in a fainting-fit, and was never again seen to smile.

The little bride, who was only twelve years old, had come to England with her father-in-law, and was therefore safe. The Count of Anjou sent for his daughter and her dowry; the young girl was sent back, and afterward became a nun, but Henry took care to keep the dowry.

Henry now began to be anxious about an heir to the crown. He had several nephews, but was not very fond of them; and his oldest daughter, Matilda, married to the emperor Henry V. of Germany, had no children.

The emperor lived but a short time after the marriage, and Matilda was, with much difficulty, persuaded to marry Geoffrey Plantagenet, Count of Anjou. Two years before the death of Henry I. they had a son, named Henry after his grandfather, and called by the English Henry Fitz-Empress, as Matilda always kept the higher title of empress, even after marrying a count. The birth of this child delighted the old king, who felt that he in a manner took the place of the lost Prince William, and he caused his barons to swear fidelity to his daughter Maud, (a name for Matilda), hoping that she would be queen after his death. He might have lived longer but that he persisted in eating too largely of a dish of stewed lampreys, a kind of rich fish against which his physicians had warned him. He was not well at the time, and died from the effects of his imprudent meal.

Henry I. had great faults; he was self-willed, avaricious, deceitful, and, when it suited his purpose to be so, cruel, as was shown by his treatment of his brother Robert. He kept up the forest laws (game laws we should now call them) in their utmost severity, and was altogether a hard master. Yet, as he had undoubtedly great abilities, and was, according to the standard of the time, a just ruler, (for he allowed no crime to go unpunished in others), the English long clung to his memory with a certain fondness.

There were some things in Henry's time which showed that a gradual change was taking place in England. For instance, men were no longer obliged to undergo the "ordeal of battle," if they did not choose to do so. This was a Norman custom which was meant to take the place of the Saxon hot-iron trial. When two men had a quarrel either could insist on fighting it out with certain forms and ceremonies, and the victor was supposed to have right on his side.

We notice also the growing power of the Church in controlling men's actions. When Henry was about to fight his last battle with his brother Robert, in Normandy, a bishop, making an address to him in the presence of his soldiers, exhorted him not to follow the example of Robert, who was "abandoned to sloth and folly," but to testify against the abominations of the times, especially long hair and peaked-toed shoes. These latter were then made so absurdly long that the points were drawn up and fastened at the knee. As Henry professed his willingness to help along in the good work of reform, the zealous bishop seized a pair of shears and cut off the king's flowing locks. Then the greatest dandy of the court asked that his head might be operated upon; and after that the scissors were kept busy until all the fine gentlemen became a set of Roundheads. The efficacy of this sacrifice is proved by the fact that Henry won the battle.

Henry I. died in Normandy, and no sooner did the news of his death reach England than robbery and lawlessness ran riot through the country, and trade was brought to a stand-still. The Empress Maud, Henry's daughter, was away taking care of her husband, who was ill; so that the way was open for a usurpation. Just then Stephen, Earl of Blois, son of the Conqueror's daughter Adela and nephew to the late king, suddenly appeared in London with an army, and by promises and a liberal scattering about of Henry's money, of which he managed to get possession, induced the "Witan" to choose him king. Stephen was going to do great things. He would abolish the odious "Danegelt," which was still kept up; he would give up the new forests made by Henry I. and he would secure justice to every citizen. None of his promises were kept, but this was not altogether his fault. He was an amiable, well-meaning man, with pleasant manners and a ready smile, and would have been quite willing that every man in his dominions should have peace, prosperity and justice, if he could have bestowed these blessings; but he lacked force of character. Other men, stronger and fiercer than he, took things into their own hands, and poor England had not, since the time of the Danish invasions, had so bitter a period as his reign proved to be. To conciliate the favor of the Norman barons he allowed them to fortify their castles, which soon became mere dens of robbers; for it was not the habit of these "noblemen" to provide for themselves except by stealing from their neighbors. Here is a passage from the "Anglo-Saxon Chronicle," giving a Saxon account of what was endured in his reign by those suspected of owning anything that could be taken away from them:

When the traitors perceived that King Stephen was a mild man, and a soft and a good.... they no faith kept; every rich man kept his castles and defended them. They greatly oppressed the wretched people by making them work at these castles, and when the castles were finished they filled them with devils. They took those whom they suspected to have any goods and put them in prison, and tortured them with pains unspeakable. They hung some up by their feet and tortured them with foul smoke; some by the thumbs or by the head, and they hung burning things on their feet. They put a knotted string about their heads, and twisted it till it went into the brain. Some they put into a crucet-house, that is, into a chest that was short and narrow, and not deep, and they put sharp stones in it, and crushed the man therein so that they broke all his limbs.

Other "hateful and grim things" are described, all having for their object the same thing, namely, forcing people, by the infliction of bodily pain, to tell where they had hidden anything of value.

In the face of horrors like these we almost forget to be shocked at the commonplace fighting which went on, year after year, between Matilda's army and her cousin's. One great battle was fought in her behalf by King David of Scotland, who was her mother's brother. It was called "The Battle of the Standard" from the consecrated banners, taken from different monasteries, which floated from a tall pole carried in the midst of the English army instead of an ordinary flag. David was defeated, and came near being made prisoner. On the other hand, Stephen was captured in battle and loaded with chains; then Matilda's chief supporter, Robert of Gloucester, fell into the hands of the enemy and was exchanged by them for Stephen. Twice Matilda herself was taken prisoner. Once the king generously set her free and furnished her with an escort to her own party; the next time she was indebted to her own ingenuity or that of her friends for her escape. She was shut up by the besieging army in the castle of Oxford; and seeing no hope of relief she caused herself and three of her knights, all dressed in white, to be let down over the castle wall. It was in the depth of winter and the ground was covered with snow. The river Thames was frozen over, and the party crept along for six miles, strange to relate, without being discovered. They were almost frozen when they reached a place of safety. The castle and city surrendered to the king's forces the next day.

And so the wretched business went on. The land was

left untilled, the cattle died from lack of food, and a famine followed among the people. All over the land, no sight was more common than that of blazing villages and farm-houses; no sound more frequent than the despairing wail of people hunted from their homes. Young Prince Henry, Matilda's son, in the mean time, was growing up to be a man. When things got to their worst, and the people could bear no more, an agreement was made between him and Stephen that the latter should remain king as long as he lived, and that Henry should then peaceably take the throne. Stephen's son, Eustace, a young man of such violent passions that he seemed almost insane, was made so angry by the treaty that it brought on a brain fever of which he died, to the great relief of the English, who had foreseen in his father's death only an endless vista of civil war. Stephen did not live long after this, but died in 1154 after a disastrous reign of nineteen years.

The part of his conduct that it is least possible to defend was the fact that he had sworn to uphold the right of his cousin Matilda; and perjury was as much a sin in the twelfth century as it is in the nineteenth. His reign was a period of unspeakable misery to the English; but it is doubtful, under the circumstances, if there could have been anything but misfortune. It was not the time for the rule of a woman, even a judicious one; and the Empress Maud was haughty and revengeful, and never seems to have gained the love of the people.

Our old acquaintance, the Saxon Chronicle, comes to an abrupt end at Stephen's death. It had said its say; and there were others to take up the history of their country. The monk William of Malmesbury, who lived in this century, gives us some interesting accounts of things as he saw them, and Henry of Huntington, another monkish historian, flourished at about the same time. Geoffrey of Monmouth, who died in the same year with King Stephen, professed to write a history of Britain, but it is so full of absurd fables that we can not tell the false from the true. King Arthur, the last Briton who stood out against the Saxons, is his favorite hero.

And now we have done with the Norman kings; men of great talents, and, with the exception of Stephen, of strong characters. They came as usurpers, but the benefits they conferred upon England by introducing there a higher form of civilization than was known among the Saxons, can hardly be overrated.

We have had, also, the last invasion of England. Romans, Saxons, Danes, Normans, in turn conquered and occupied the land, and we have the best of what each nation left. Norman, Dane and Saxon, together with a little addition of British blood, have combined to form the modern Englishman, and we are English, with some admixture from every civilized nation upon earth.

CHAPTER VIII.

THE FIRST PLANTAGENET.

IN the days when men went to battle with the visors of their helmets down, so that no one could see their faces, it was convenient to have some special mark about them which should distinguish one from another. Geoffrey of Anjou, who married the Empress Maud, daughter of Henry I. of England, chose to wear a sprig of broom-plant (*planta genista*) in his hat, so he was known as Geoffrey Plantagenet. His son, Henry II. of England, kept the name, and for more than three hundred years Plantagenet kings sat on the throne of England.

There was no need of an election by the Witan (which we must now call the Parliament) to enthrone Henry Plantagenet. He was welcomed by every one. Being half Saxon and half Norman, the quarrels of a hundred years were ended in him. Normandy, Anjou, and several other countries were his by inheritance, and he married Eleanor of Aquitaine, the divorced wife of Louis VII. of France, who brought him the rich countries of Guienne and Poitou, besides some smaller ones. Seldom has a young man of twenty-one stepped at once into such possessions. Henry was a very different person, in appearance, from the smooth, courteous, handsome Stephen. He was rough-looking, red-faced, bull-necked, and very strong and determined. He found in England much to do and much to undo. He began by sending away the foreign soldiers brought over by Stephen, and who had been living on the fat of the land while Englishmen were starving; he pulled down the castles which had sheltered licensed thieves and murderers, and he took back, from those to whom both Matilda and Stephen had given it unlawfully, much public property. He caused the laws to be respected, and justice done to everyone, rich or poor. A writer of his time says, "He did not sit still in his palace, as most kings do; he went about and saw things for himself." He knew, also, how to choose fit helpers; and this brings us to the name of one of the most remarkable men of any age—Thomas à Becket.

Before we go farther into sober history you ought to hear a pretty story about the mother of Becket. It may not be true, but even if it is not, it is a charming little romance.*

Gilbert à Becket, the father of Thomas, was an Englishman who went to the Holy Land either on a crusade or a pilgrimage, and was taken prisoner by a Saracen. His master treated him kindly, and even allowed him some intercourse with his family. The Saracen had a young daughter who was much interested in the English captive, and they grew very fond of one another. After a while, Becket had a chance to escape, and did so, with his servant, Richard, without any further thought of the Saracen maiden. He went back to England, and became a prosperous London merchant.

But the young girl was not so easily satisfied. She had learned from Becket just two words of English— "London" and "Gilbert." Being determined to find her lover, she stole away secretly from her father's house; and with these two words, and some jewels to pay her passage, she made her way to London. On arriving there she wandered about the streets calling out in her soft, sweet voice, "Gilbert!" "Gilbert!" London was not so large then as it is now, and it happened that Richard, who was still Becket's servant, saw her and took her to his master. Fortunately, Gilbert was not married; and as soon as the faithful Saracen could be baptized she received the Christian name of Matilda instead of the

---

* Pronounce this word ro*mance*, with the accent on the second syllable.

heathen one she had borne before, and he made her his wife. Such is the story, told by a writer living in England at that time.

Thomas à Becket, the son of Gilbert, after receiving a good English education, studied law at the great university of Paris, and there, it is said, got rid of the Saxon accent which had clung to him until then and prevented his being quite the fine gentleman. When he went home to England he took his place at once as a thorough man of the world; for, though belonging to the clergy, it was not necessary for him on that account to devote himself especially to religion. He was gay, brilliant and popular, and a brave soldier. The king, who was very fond of him, promoted him from one position to another until he reached the highest—that of chancellor. He was considerably older than Henry, but the king treated him as a companion, sometimes indulging in what we should call pretty rough jokes. One day they were riding along together when they met a miserable beggar, scantily clothed. "Look at that poor wretch," said the king. "Don't you think it would be a good idea to give him a warm cloak?" "Certainly," said the dignified chancellor; "it is a kind thought, and I hope you will carry it out." "Well," answered the king, "suppose we give him yours;" so he seized Becket's rich scarlet cloak, trimmed with ermine, and tried to drag it off. The chancellor held fast to it, until at last the clasp snapped and Henry flung the cloak to the beggar, who was probably the most surprised man of the company.

Thomas à Becket had inherited a great deal of money from his father, and he spent it in a princely manner. His table was spread every day for as many guests as could sit at it, and when there were more than could find places there, they sat on the floor, which was covered thickly with rushes in summer and straw in winter. It was thought a proof of the unbounded luxury in which the chancellor lived that the rushes and straw on his floor were laid down fresh every day, (this was out of respect to the courtiers' fine clothes) while common people did not have their rushes changed more than once a week. At all houses, rich or poor, the bones and other remnants of food were thrown on the floor, during the meal or after it, to be scrambled for by the dogs.

It will help to give us an idea of these feasts, where wine was served in golden goblets and meat on silver dishes, to know that forks were not in use at table, nor were knives a part of the table furniture. Each person carried his own pocket-knife, and cut from the main dishes such pieces as he desired, and instead of forks they used their fingers.

On some occasion King Henry wished to send an ambassador to France, and Becket, being the most splendid person in the kingdom, was naturally chosen to go. He thought he would do honor to the situation, and traveled, if we may believe Fitz Stephen, his admiring friend and biographer, with a retinue of nearly a thousand persons. When he went into a town, two hundred and fifty singing boys heralded his approach; a long train of wagons followed, each drawn by five horses, with a driver to each horse. After these came twelve horses carrying smaller articles, each with a monkey on his back. Two of the wagons carried ale, to be given out to the people as they passed along; others contained the gold and silver vessels used at the chancellor's table, and the rest bore the various garments in which his servants were to appear. After these came a train of ladies and gentlemen, soldiers and attendants, all splendidly dressed and equipped, and finally Becket himself, in superb array. After making all due allowance for exaggeration, it must have been a magnificent procession.

A great change was now to take place. The king had certain plans which he wished Becket's help in carrying out; and he thought the best way to do this would be to make him Archbishop of Canterbury. Becket was strongly opposed to this; he shrank from the responsibility, and said plainly to the king, in effect, "You will be disappointed in me. We shall certainly quarrel, for you claim rights as king which I, as archbishop, can not allow." But Henry was not used to being disappointed, and insisted on having his own way. Becket immediately laid down all his splendors, wore sack-cloth and a hair-shirt, scourged himself, lived on bread and water, and practised every form of self-denial which is supposed to elevate the soul by mortifying the body. He daily washed the feet of thirteen beggars to prove his humility, and wept over and lamented his sins like any common penitent. So far his conduct concerned only himself and the friends who had assembled round his table in the days of his magnificence; but when he resigned the chancellorship in order to devote himself to his spiritual duties, the king was seriously offended. There was never any real cordiality between them afterward.

During the hundreds of years in which the clergy (which included all monks, as well as priests and bishops) had been increasing in power and importance, many of them had become exceedingly corrupt, and led very bad lives. It had grown to be a practice in the church that when one of these persons committed a crime he should be judged only by the clergy themselves, (who might let him off with some slight punishment) and not by the law of the land. Henry saw that this was not right, and declared that all persons should be treated alike and tried in the regular courts. After a great deal of angry disputing, a council was called at Clarendon at which both sides were represented, and a paper called the "Constitutions of Clarendon" was drawn up accepting the king's decision, which most of the clergy, the archbishop among the rest, swore to observe.

Becket, who had consented to the Constitutions sorely against his will, soon obtained permission from the Pope to break his oath. He did not think it prudent to remain in England, but went to France, where he was received with great kindness by the king of that country. After six years of self-imposed banishment, some friends made peace between him and Henry, and he returned home, Henry asking him the first time they met, whether he had gone away because he thought England was too small to contain them both.

The archbishop, however, was not altered by absence. He was an old man now, but his spirit was unbroken, and he showed the same determination as ever. He had made up his mind that the Church should be the greatest power in England, and the king was equally resolved that the Law should rule. Enraged by the archbishop's continued encroachments, Henry once exclaimed, "Is there no one who will rid me of this insolent priest?" Four Norman knights who heard the angry words spoken left the king's presence without telling him of their intention, crossed the sea (for Henry was then in Normandy), and rode with all speed to Canterbury. There they had a stormy interview with the archbishop, desiring him to take off the excommunication from one of their own friends, who had plundered the church in Becket's absence, but this he steadily refused. At the usual hour he went into the cathedral to perform the vesper service. He had been warned that the knights meant to kill him, but he scorned to take any measures for his own defence. The ruffians then came into the church and struck at him and hacked him with their swords, until they left him dead on the cathedral floor. In Canterbury Cathedral is still shown the place where the cowardly act was done.

Henry was horror-struck at hearing of the foul deed, for, angry as he was, he had not expected to be taken at his word. His first care was to be reconciled with the Pope, and to give up everything that he had been fighting for. He actually annulled the "Constitutions of Clarendon" and thus undid a measure that it had been the object of his life to accomplish—a proceeding which necessarily diminishes our respect for him.

The next event of importance in English history is the conquest of Ireland. This country had before been independent, ruled over by five so-called "kings" who were always at war with one another, and did not mind slicing off noses, digging out eyes or tearing out tongues any more than we mind killing vermin. Ireland was nominally Christian, having been converted by St. Patrick in the fifth and St. Columba in the sixth century; and for a long time the Irish monasteries were the centres of learning and piety. Ireland was called "The Isle of Saints and Scholars." But the people had gradually fallen back into a state of barbarism, and their continual quarreling among themselves prevented them from making any improvement.

Henry had received, some years before, permission from the Pope to conquer this island, for the pontiffs in those days assumed the right to dispose of all the countries of the earth; but hitherto there had been no convenient time for it. Now the old story of history repeated itself. One of the kings asked for help against another, and Richard de Clare (called Strongbow) went over with a band of soldiers, conquered the opposing army, married the king's daughter Eva, and made himself master of the king's dominions. These he was not allowed to keep, but Henry, having subdued the rest of the country, granted Strongbow a large estate there, while retaining for himself the title of king. Since that time (1172) Ireland has belonged to England, and a very troublesome piece of property it has proved to the English, who have not yet seen the last of the perplexities brought on them by the ambition of Henry II.

Henry's declining years were far from peaceful. His sons all rebelled against him, with the connivance of their mother, Eleanor of Aquitaine, who seems to have had a genius for making mischief. The king of France, Louis VII. also took part with the sons. Prince Henry died of a fever and Geoffrey had his brains dashed out at a tournament, leaving only Richard and John to continue the war against their father. Some of Henry's subjects joined the rebels, and William the Lion, king of Scotland, entered into the alliance against him. As these things were considered a judgment on the king for Becket's murder, he resolved do public penance for it. With his usual quickness, (respecting which Louis VII. of France said, "The King of England does not sail nor ride; he flies, like a bird!"), Henry went quickly to Canterbury and, dismounting as soon as he came in sight of the old towers, walked barefoot to the cathedral. There he remained all night in prayer, causing himself to be scourged by eighty monks, each of whom gave him a blow as he passed. When he returned to London the first news that met him was that William the Lion, king of Scotland, had been taken prisoner in battle, with a large part of his army. The archbishop had already been made a saint by the Pope, and for hundreds of years his tomb at Canterbury was the resort of pilgrims, while his shrine vied with the most famous in Europe in regard to the miracles said to be wrought there.

By the time King Henry was fifty-six years old he was quite worn out with anxiety and unhappiness. His remaining sons were again in rebellion, helped by Philip Augustus of France, who had succeeded the weak Louis VII.; and Henry, in desperation, signed a treaty granting whatever was asked of him. So much agitation brought on a fever, and in the midst of it a paper was brought to him to sign, by which he agreed to pardon all those of his own subjects who had been in rebellion. He commanded that the list of names should be read aloud to him, and the first one that he heard was that of his youngest and favorite son, "John, Duke of Mortagne."

It was the last drop of bitterness in the king's cup, and it filled it over-full. He would hear no more; he cursed the day of his birth, he cursed his rebellious sons with a fury that nothing could induce him to alter, and then he turned his face to the wall muttering, "Let things go as they will;" and so died—a disappointed, heart-broken man. In spite of great faults and weaknesses, Henry had been a good king for England. He was in advance of his age in his ideas about the rights of kings (of the rights of "the people" nobody had then any notion), but his doctrine that the rulers of a country should manage its affairs without interference from foreigners, is one which has since become a part of the law of nations.

The main writers in Henry II.'s time were Fitz Stephen, who wrote the life of Thomas à Becket, the historians Gerald of Cambridge, Roger of Hoveden and Walter Map; and Wace, a Norman poet who wrote histories in verse.

CHAPTER IX.

RICHARD I. AND THE THIRD CRUSADE.

THERE has been a great deal of sentimental nonsense talked and written about Richard Cœur de Lion (in English, Richard the Lion-hearted) but the plain truth is that he was, in the general plan of his life, as selfish a man as ever misruled the English people. He was brave in battle; so were thousands of others; he could be generous when it would make a show and gain him credit; but he began his career by an unnatural rebellion against his father, without a shadow of excuse for it, and he continued through most of his life to do the things which were for his own pleasure and glory, and to neglect his plain duty, which was to take care of his kingdom of England.

One person, at least, had reason to be glad of Richard's accession — his mother, Queen Eleanor, whom Henry had kept shut up in her palace for sixteen years, on account of her encouraging the rebellion of her sons and trying to escape with them to France. We can scarcely blame him for wishing to put her where she could do no more harm, but she had her own wrongs to complain of. He openly showed that he preferred another woman, Rosamond Clifford, called Fair Rosamond, to the queen; so they were a very unhappy couple. A romantic story is told about this Rosamond, to the effect that the queen suddenly appeared before her with a dagger in one hand and a cup of poison in the other, and asked her which she would choose. According to the story, Rosamond chose the poison, and drank it then and there, under the queen's eyes; but the real Rosamond in real history became a nun, and spent her life after the king left her, in the convent of Godston, where the sisters were very fond of her.

To return to King Richard. No sooner was he in his father's place than he discovered that rebellion was a very wicked thing, and immediately punished the persons who had taken his part against his father. Then he was crowned with great splendor; for Henry had left an immense sum of money in the royal treasury, and Richard could indulge his taste for display. A horrible incident attended his coronation at Westminster. Certain Jews, who as a nation had been forbidden to come to it, ventured in, bearing large gifts, which they thought would make them welcome. Richard received the gifts willingly enough, but some of the people, to show their hatred and spite against all Jews, drove them out with abusive language and pelted them with sticks and stones. Upon seeing this, others spread the report that the king had ordered the Jews to be killed, and a general massacre of those unfortunate people took place. The frantic multitude not only attacked those they met out of doors, but burst into their houses, stabbing men, women, and children, or throwing them out of the windows into the street, where they were soon dispatched by the infuriated crowd. Only three men concerned in these brutal outrages were punished, and these, not for what they had done to the Jews, but because in the confusion they had set fire to the houses of some Christians.

The contagion of lawlessness soon spread to other cities, where the wretched Israelites were murdered by hundreds. At York, after terrible cruelties had been committed against them, some five hundred of them took possession of the castle in the absence of the governor, and tried to defend themselves there. A mob of citizens battered at the gates for two or three days, and at last the Jews found it useless to keep up the attempt. After destroying, as far as they could, their jewels and other valuables, the greater part of them agreed to die by their own hands. They killed their wives and children, and then, having set fire everywhere to the castle, stabbed themselves. A few cowering wretches, hiding away as well as they could from the flames, were found by the assailants when they succeeded in breaking down the gates, and on these they wreaked their vengeance; but the greater part of their victims were already blackened corpses.

None of these things moved Richard, nor did he make any effort toward checking the hideous deeds of his subjects. He was busy preparing for a crusade. The Holy

Sepulchre (and of course the city of Jerusalem) had been conquered again by the Mohammedans after the Christians had held it for eighty-seven years, and the warriors of Europe were going to the Holy Land to try to get it back again. This was the third crusade, a second one having been undertaken about forty years before, for the purpose of taking some Turkish cities in Palestine. All these undertakings required enormous sums of money; and Richard, besides using up the vast treasure left by his father, obtained much more, some of it by dishonorable means, some by merciless extortion. "I would sell London," he exclaimed, "if I could find a bidder."

Philip Augustus of France joined him at Messina, in Sicily, and here Richard was also met by his promised wife, Berengaria of Navarre, who presented herself under his mother's escort. As it was then the season of Lent, the Catholic church would not allow of their marrying, and the fleets set off for Palestine. When they drew earn the island of Cyprus, a violent storm obliged some of the English vessels to seek for shelter in one of its harbors. This was rudely refused by Isaac Comnenus, the king of the island; so Richard must stop to fight him before going on with his crusading business, and had the satisfaction of making him prisoner and taking possession of the island, which he left some of his soldiers to guard. The foolish old king was put in silver chains, and kept in them until he died, some four years afterward; while his daughter was compelled to become a waiting-maid to Berengaria, whom Richard married before leaving Cyprus.

When he at last arrived in Syria, after waiting the greater part of a year in Sicily and Cyprus, he found Philip's army so much weakened by disease and battle that the men had begun to lose heart. They were besieging the town of Acre, a strong fortress, guarded by the magnificent sultan Saladin, who was at least a match for his Christian foes in soldiership, and superior to both the leaders in nobility of character. The arrival of Richard put new spirit into the crusading army, and after some terrible fighting, Acre was taken. A treaty was made in which Saladin promised to give up the true cross (which was supposed to be still preserved at Jerusalem) to pay an enormous ransom in gold for such of his soldiers as were in the Crusader's hands, and to restore without ransom all his Christian captives. Part of the treaty he said he could not carry out within the forty days agreed upon, and asked for an extension of time; which the Christian king answered by bringing out three thousand Saracen prisoners and having them hanged in sight of their own people.

Philip of France had no share in this murderous deed; he had already left the Holy Land, disgusted at Richard's arrogance and vain-glory, jealous of his superior fame as a fighter, and ill from the effects of the sultry climate. He left ten thousand men under Richard's command and then returned to France, having first taken an oath to do nothing in England contrary to Richard's interests.

On his way back he stopped in Rome, where the Pope absolved him from his oath, and when he reached home he and John lost no time in conspiring against Richard. The latter was now left to conduct the war alone. His example inspired his soldiers, and they fought on for a year and a half, not hindered by heat or disease or loss. Richard took the city of Ascalon, and several others, but when the army arrived in sight of Jerusalem there was so much opposition from his officers to spilling more Christian blood and spending more Christian time and money on the almost hopeless work, that he was obliged to give up. He returned to Ascalon, where he found that the fortress needed repairing, and as it suited him to help the laborers by working at this with his own hands, he insisted that all the other commanders should do the same. When the Duke of Austria, saying that he was not a mason, refused to join in the work, it is said that Richard struck him.

It was at last decided by all the Crusaders that they might better go back. They were wasting precious human lives as well as money to no purpose; and there were those among them who had business at home, even if the king of England had none. So Richard, as representing the whole body of the Crusaders, made a truce with Saladin which was to last three years, three months, three days, and three hours. This being done, the wasted army set sail from the shores of Palestine, which most of them never saw again.

Richard's ship was wrecked on the way home, and he was cast ashore in the dominions of the Duke of Austria, the very one whom he had insulted at Ascalon. He tried to disguise himself, but his kingly ways betrayed him, and the Duke sent him on to the Emperor of Germany, by whom he was kept in prison for more than a year. A pretty story is told as to how his friends at home found out where he was. Richard was a fine musician, and had himself composed songs which he and his favorite page, Blondel de Nesle, used to sing together. Blondel was determined to find out where his master was, so he strolled about to the different castles in Germany singing a song composed by Richard himself; "O, Richard! o mon roy!" When he reached the right castle, a well-known voice from the tower above joined in, and Blondel carried the good news to England.

This would be a beautiful story if it were true. The only trouble about it is that it was invented by some poet who wrote long after both king and minstrel had been laid in their graves. It illustrates, however, the strong personal feeling which subsided between master and man in the age of chivalry.*

After some bargaining Richard was permitted to ransom himself; and the English, proud of their warlike king, who had brought them so much glory and so little good, soon raised the money needed. Ladies gave their jewels, the people submitted willingly to extra taxes, and at length Richard stood once more upon the shores of his own country.

His brother John and Philip of France had done what they could toward unsettling the government, but the people were too much in favor of law and order to venture on any great change; and Eleanor, the mother of Richard and John, who was as true to Richard as she had been false to her husband, used her great influence in her elder son's favor. When Philip heard of Richard's being set at liberty he wrote to John, "Take care of yourself, for the devil has broken loose." But John did not need to "take care" of himself in this sense. Richard generously forgave all his misdeeds, and remarked as he did so, "I wish I could forget his injuries as easily as he will forget my pardon!"

---

*For a description of chivalry see "A Short History of France," p. 114.

Against Philip his feelings were very bitter, and as soon as he had raised money enough he invaded his dominions. To obtain money for his wars, the king no longer depended upon taxes, but resorted to the most unscrupulous measures. Among others, he ordered the great seal to be broken, and then announced that no grants made under that seal were legal, unless the fees belonging to the grant were paid a second time, under a new seal which he caused to be made for the purpose. In short, he was what in our day would be called a swindler; but no one thought of applying an equivalent word to him because he was—the king.

In the course of the war Richard heard that one of his Norman vassals had found a treasure hidden in his land. Richard demanded this, and on the owner's declining to give him more than half of it, immediately besieged him in his castle of Chaluz. The garrison defended themselves bravely, but the castle was taken, and Richard, wounded in the fight, ordered every man to be hanged with the exception of Bertrand de Gourdon, who had shot him with an arrow. "What harm had I done you," he asked, "that you should wish to kill me?" "You slew my father and my two brothers with your own hands," answered Bertrand, "and you would have slain me if you could. Do your worst; I am content to die, since I have rid the world of a tyrant." Richard, who by this time knew that his wound was mortal, ordered that the young man should be set free; but as soon as he was dead, his officers put Bertrand to most horrible torture and then hanged him.

Richard's character was a strange mixture of a certain kind of loftiness, with intense selfishness and absolute disregard of his plainest duty. He was a fine soldier, but much more than that is needed to make a good king or a good man. With his abilities, for he had plenty of brains, he might have ruled well and made his people happy; but his one desire was for personal glory, and the rights of others were but as dust in the balance.

In Sir Walter Scott's novels of "Ivanhoe" and "The Talisman" the romantic side of Richard's life is portrayed. It is not necessary for a novelist to say all the ill that he knows of his hero. We can enjoy the heroic part of the story, but it is only right that we should hear the other side too. Of his ten years' reign, Richard spent in all only six months in England; four in preparation for the crusade, and two on his return from that expedition, and in both these cases his only object was to force money from his subjects. Justice, law, and order were apparently no concern of his. If he could obtain the means for his personal gratification, the interest of a million or two of people could take care of itself.

One of the best-known names in England during Richard's reign was that of Robin Hood, a famous outlaw* who lived, with a band of men like himself, in Sherwood Forest. Their sole business was highway robbery, and they made a great merit of occasionally giving to the poor what they stole from the rich. The clergy were the objects of their special dislike, and they delighted in taking property belonging to the Church.

---

*A person who has committed certain crimes which put him out of the protection of the law, so that any one is allowed to kill him at sight.

CHAPTER X.

JOHN LACKLAND AND THE MAGNA CHARTA.

ENGLAND had good reason to be sorry for the death of Richard I.; for, bad as his rule had been, it was not so utterly disgraceful as that of his worthless brother John, and the people could then take pride in their king's great schemes, though the money for carrying them out had been wrung from their own life-blood. But there was nothing to admire in John. From his boyhood he had been base, mean, and treacherous, and it is probable that the dread of these qualities accounted for much of the grief shown at Richard's death. Henry II. had jokingly given his youngest son the nickname of "Lackland," because he did not inherit any special province, as the others did, though he was to be amply provided for; and the name has stuck to him ever since, made doubly appropriate by his loss of the rich Continental possessions which had for so long been the glory of the English nation.

Arthur of Brittany, son of John's older brother Geoffrey, had been put forward by his friends as the rightful heir to the throne, and his claim had been at first supported by Philip Augustus of France; but upon the marriage of Philip's son Louis with Blanche of Castile, John's niece, the French king abandoned the claim of Arthur, whom John kept in confinement.

An impenetrable cloud of mystery hangs over the fate of this unfortunate prince. When he was sixteen years old he escaped from the custody of his uncle and raised a force in Brittany to go against him, but was defeated and again made prisoner. After this all is deep darkness; the most apparently trustworthy account of his death states that John, taking him out in a boat to the middle of the Seine, stabbed him with his own hand and threw his body into the river.

In Shakspeare's tragedy of "King John" we have the main facts in the life both of the king and of his unhappy nephew, though the poet has taken some liberties with the less important details. When the facts became known, the barons of Brittany appealed to Philip to make war on the murderer of their young duke. Philip was the over-lord (suzerain) of both Brittany and Normandy as well as of all the other countries within the limits of France, and was therefore bound to protect any one of them against the encroachments of another. He lost no time in invading Normandy,- which one would have expected John to defend with all his might. But his mind was occupied with something else. Having fallen in love with a beautiful girl, Isabella of Angoulême, who was betrothed to Hugh de la Marche, he divorced his own wife, and having obtained the consent of Isabella's parents, married her without regard to her previous engagement. At the time of Philip's invasion of Normandy, John was idling away his time at Rouen with his new queen, feasting and dancing, seeing tournaments and listening to minstrels, while Philip was taking city after city and castle after castle, almost without resistance. At last the French army approached Rouen, and John fled hastily across the Channel. Philip took possession of Rouen, and Normandy was reunited to France after having belonged to English kings for nearly a hundred and forty years.

It was the best thing that could have happened to England. Humiliating though it was to the Englishmen of that time to see one of their fairest possessions slip away from them through no fault of their own, it really secured the independence of their country. Up to this time the kings of England had passed more time in France than in their adopted country; their main interest had lain in their Continental possessions, and it was well that English kings should have English hearts, and not owe a divided allegiance. From the time of John, England was a country by itself.

Philip's conquests did not stop with Normandy. All the earldoms in France which had come to England with the "Angevins,"* Anjou, Maine, Touraine, etc., were taken by him, leaving only a remnant in the hands of the unworthy John.

The old question of authority had never been quite settled between the king and the church. Henry II., as we have seen, had annulled the Constitutions of Clarendon, the safeguard against ecclesiastical tyranny, and since then the clergy had been allowed to have their own way in everything, provided they were ready with their angels† to fill the king's purse when he needed money. Just at this time, however, the Archbishop of Canterbury died, and the vacancy was filled by Pope Innocent III., without referring to the king. The person chosen was Stephen Langton, an excellent and very able man, against

---

*Belonging to the Anjou family.
†A gold coin, so called from its being stamped with the figure of an angel.

whom there could be no personal objection; but John stood out bravely for his right as king and against foreign interference in English affairs. The Pope at once laid the whole kingdom under an "interdict." By this all public religious services were forbidden; the churches were closed, the bells stopped ringing, no marriages or burial services could be performed, no masses said for living or dead. The baptism of new-born infants and extreme unction for the dying were alone permitted. The people trembled for fear worse things should come upon them, and began, rather under their breath, to murmur against the king, who cared nothing for their displeasure. Then the Pope excommunicated King John, and wound up by pronouncing a sentence of deposition against him; that is, declaring that he was no longer king, and that his subjects were excused from any further obedience to him. Of course he was furiously angry at all this, and began to prepare for war. As he had already taken all he could get by ordinary means, he had to look about for something extraordinary, and remembered the Jews, whom it was always in order to rob and oppress. One instance will show his methods: Having demanded an enormous gift from a rich Jew who refused to make it, he had him shut up, and caused a tooth to be pulled each day out of the poor man's head, beginning with the double ones. The Jew bore it until seven teeth were gone, and on the eighth day he paid the money. We may imagine how such people loved King John.

But all his tricks (and there were many of them) could not ward off his misfortunes. The Pope having told the king of France that if he would invade England all his sins would be forgiven, Philip got an army together for that purpose. Just as he was ready to set out, the English barons, who had no mind to see a French army land upon their shores, made ready for defence. At the same time, the Pope sent a legate or messenger, named Pandulf, to persuade the king that the best thing he could do would be to submit. So John, deserted by everyone, and with Philip's army standing ready to cross the Channel, appointed a public meeting between Pandulf and himself, at which he gravely took off his crown and laid it at the legate's feet, to be put on again by him as a subject of the Pope; he consented to Langton's being archbishop, and promised to pay the Pope an annual tribute of money (1213). The next day, Archbishop Langton took off all the Pope's sentences, and John, having fallen as low as he could in his own estimation and other people's, set about planning fresh wickedness.

As soon as this ceremony was over and the king was sufficiently humbled, the Pope sent word to Philip that as John was now a faithful and obedient son of the Church, any one opposing him would be considered an enemy to true religion, and would be dealt with accordingly. Philip's anger at this change of face knew no bounds, and he pressed on his preparations for the grand invasion more vigorously than ever. Then the English people, who were not wanting to themselves in times of emergency, fitted out a fleet which fell upon that of Philip in the harbor of Damme, in Flanders, and utterly destroyed it. This was the first of the many struggles that have taken place at sea between the French and English. It was soon followed by the battle of Bouvines, in Flanders. John had turned the tables on Philip by invading Poitou, which was in Philip's dominions. The English king was helped by his nephew, the Emperor Otho of Germany; yet Philip won a splendid victory, and John made the best of his way back to his own country.

His subjects were now thoroughly tired of a man whose tyranny, cruelty, meanness, and lawlessness left no one safe, and determined to force him into an agreement by which they hoped to be able to bind him. At their head was Stephen Langton, a thoroughly patriotic man, who by the way, brought on himself the displeasure of the Pope by his efforts to reform the newly-reconciled son of the Church; but Langton saw so clearly what was right that not even the Pope's censure made him hesitate. There was much discussion between the king and the barons, who really represented the people of England, though they had not been chosen by them; and at last, both parties met at Runnymede, a pleasant place on the banks of the Thames near where Windsor Castle now stands. Here we approach one of the greatest events in English history, over-topping both foreign war and domestic rebellion. John angrily declared that he would never grant such liberties to his people as would make himself a slave; but the barons were too strong for him, and sorely against his will he signed "The Great Charter"* on the fifteenth of June, 1215. This repeated some of the declarations of Henry I.'s charter, which had always been so dear to the people; but contained besides these many new provisions, among which stands the famous sentence, "No free-man shall be imprisoned, outlawed, or exiled, or dispossessed of his lands, but by the lawful judgment of his peers,† or by the law of the land."‡ Many

---

* Magna Charta; (pronounced *Carta*).
† Equals.   ‡ A translation, as the Charter was written in Latin.

kings afterward swore to observe this charter; many of them broke their oaths; but the great principle laid down in it has remained from that day to this the safeguard of English liberty, and we have inherited its protecting influence. *

By signing an agreement like this, King John felt that he had thrown away his own privileges, and his first effort was to find out how he could avoid keeping it. He sent at once for assistance to his friend the Pope, who obligingly annulled the Great Charter, and declared it not at all binding on the king who had sworn to it. The foreign mercenaries† which John had sent for, arrived at the same time with the Pope's bull, and John let them loose on the English people, to carry fire and sword through the whole extent of England. There had not been such merciless destruction since the time of the Conqueror. John himself accompanied the army, and, as a sign of his displeasure, set fire each morning to the village where he had spent the night.‡

The barons seem to have thought when the charter was signed that they had nothing more to do; and they were unprepared for such an attack. In despair of securing their rights by their own efforts, they sent word to Prince Louis, oldest son of Philip Augustus, that if he would come to England with an army and fight for their rights, he should be their king. John they could endure no longer.

---

* "From her worst king and meanest reign,
   How sprang old England's greatest gain!"—Old rhyme.

† Soldiers hired to fight for some other country than their own.

‡ At an earlier period in his career he had caused twenty-two prisoners of war to be starved to death at once in Corfe Castle.

Louis spent a long time in making preparations, and at last arrived, nearly a year after the signing of the charter. For some time the English were enthusiastic about him, but after a while they began to see that they had made a mistake. He was a Frenchman, and by this time England had become thoroughly English. There was fighting between him and John; castles were besieged and taken, and the desolating civil war might have continued as long as it did in the time of King Stephen, but that the death of John, most welcome to the perplexed and harassed nation, brought it to an unexpected end.

The broad, shallow bay called The Wash, on the coast of Norfolk and Lincolnshire, has a road along the shore which can be traveled only when the tide is low. In passing over this with the rising tide, King John lost not only some of his soldiers, but the treasure chests which carried his money and the crown-jewels. The distress of mind caused by this accident threw him into a fever, which soon ended his miserable life. He traveled on as far as Swinstead Abbey, near Newark, where the monks took as good care of him as they knew how; but as they gave him fresh peaches to eat and new cider to drink—probably not the best food for a man in a high fever—he did not last long, and relieved England of his presence by dying, after a reign of seventeen years, in 1216.

It is a singular proof of the detestation in which this king's name was held by the English people, that nearly two hundred years afterward, in the insurrection of Wat Tyler, the rebels made it one of their conditions that no king of the name of John should ever be permitted again to reign in England.

CHAPTER IX.

HENRY III. SIMON DE MONTFORT. FIRST HOUSE OF COMMONS.

THE English began to show the French prince the cold shoulder as soon as they knew of John's death. The king had left a son, nine years old, and the barons (who stood for England) said, "This child has done no harm; why should we deprive him of his birthright on account of his father's sins?" So Louis took himself and his soldiers home again. The little Prince, John's son, was crowned without delay as Henry III. The real crown had been lost with King John's other valuables in the Wash, so a jeweler hastily made a plain gold band which was placed on his head by the Pope's legate, and he was made to say that he held his crown as a subject of the Pope. A better part of the little king's entrance into public life was that he promised to observe his father's charter — the Magna Charta. He never thought of keeping this promise, when he grew to be a man, but it was good for the people to be thus reminded of their rights. The Earl of Pembroke, a wise and upright man who had married Henry's sister, was appointed Protector of the kingdom until the king should be of age. The Earl lived only three years after this; but his place was taken by another equally admirable man, Hubert de Burgh, who governed well in Henry's name until the latter, grown to manhood, took things into his own hands, and poor, weak, unsteady, helpless hands they were. The whole of de Burgh's after life shows that any charge of baseness against him, such as appears in Shakspeare's "King John," must rest upon a mistake. It was to his promptness and energy that Prince Louis owed the naval defeat which took away the last hope of establishing a French king in England. De Burgh, who was governor of Dover Castle, gathered a band of resolute men together and drove away the ships sent to Louis's assistance.

As the young king grew to manhood he showed himself frivolous, unstable, and self-willed, having neither the dignity of a man nor the docility of a child. The flatterers about him persuaded him that de Burgh was the evil genius of the country, and Henry turned like a viper which the fire has warmed into life, to sting his benefactor. The king himself had made some inglorious campaigns in France, the failure of which was laid at de Burgh's door, and the faithful minister was dragged from a chapel where he had taken refuge, and carried to the shop of a smith who was ordered to rivet shackles on his legs. "Never!" cried the smith. "You shall kill me before I will put iron on the man who freed my country from the Frenchman and saved Dover!" Finding that the smith would not be bullied, the ruffians tied de Burgh to a horse, and thus strongly guarded, he was taken to London and thrown into the Tower. After some time he escaped, but did not appear again in public life.

At the age of twenty, Henry made an imprudent marriage with Eleanor, daughter of the Count of Provence, in France. Her friends and relations fastened themselves upon the English like leeches. Four of her uncles came with her, and were sumptuously supported at the public expense; and the court was filled with foreigners who were lodged, fed, and entertained by King Henry as if he had possessed the purse of Fortunatus.

There is a story about him which would be incredible but that it rests on good authority. One day some one was admiring the beauty of his little children, and he was so much pleased with the compliment that he ordered them to be weighed, using silver coins instead of ordinary weights, and then scattered the money among the crowd. And this was when the whole country was so poor that the government officers scarcely knew how to find the wherewithal to meet the common expenses.

In addition to such follies, Henry made costly expeditions into France, from which he was obliged to retreat with loss and disgrace; and but for the forbearance of Louis IX. (called St. Louis), he would have lost the little French territory which still belonged to the English. As there was no longer any hope of getting money legally, the king tried a new plan. He "took the cross;" that is, he made a vow to go on a crusade; and for this purpose extorted gifts from everybody, especially from the Jews, whom he plundered without mercy; and when he had collected the money he said nothing about the crusade, but spent it as before. When his first son was born he sent out messengers to ask for gifts, in city and country. "God gives us the child," said some one, "but the king sells him to us." A dozen years afterward the king himself went out on a visiting tour and begged everywhere for money from the people who entertained him. When these methods failed, he would take by force such provisions and other things as he needed for the royal household, without paying for them; and his judges sat in the courts, not to punish crime, but to raise money.

Any offender could buy himself off, the fine being in proportion, not to the offence, but to the amount the accused was able to pay. All this was in direct violation of the Great Charter, in which the king was made to say, "We will not deny, nor delay, nor *sell* justice to any man." But the Charter had long been a dead letter.

It was not only the king who was thus robbing the people with both hands, but the Pope. The latter, taking advantage of Henry's weakness, demanded constantly more and more tribute; and all the chief offices in the Church were filled with Italians. The pontiff also offered a tempting bait to Henry in the shape of the crown of Sicily, which he gave him—on condition of his winning it for himself. The king's vanity was excited by the offer, and the Pope spent millions of money on his account; but the crown of Sicily was as far off as ever. The king found himself saddled with an immense debt, and as every other means of raising money had been exhausted, he was obliged once more to have recourse to a Parliament.

The Parliament of that day must not be confused with such as make the laws for England now. It was a continuation of the Saxon "Witan," and was composed only of nobles, who came when they were summoned by the king and were dismissed at his pleasure. The word is a French one, and means "talking."

In the Parliament now called by Henry, Simon de Montfort, Earl of Leicester (son to that other Simon whose crusade against the Albigenses had been such a scandal to Christendom*), proposed a new government, having nothing to do with the king, which should reform

---

* See "A Short History of France," p. 77.

all abuses and restore law and order to their afflicted country. The assembly intended to carry out these plans met at Oxford, and was called in derision of its excited and stormy sessions "The Mad Parliament." De Montfort, supported by a body of knights in full armor, was the moving spirit, and a set of laws proposed, called "The Provisions of Oxford," which the king, as well as the barons, swore to observe. Henry did not observe them, and things went on from bad to worse, until at last the two parties found themselves in open opposition. The struggle which ensued is called "The Barons' War."

Prince Edward, Henry's oldest son (afterward King Edward I.), was for some time on de Montfort's side; but some unreasonable demands of the barons made a coolness between them, and in the battle which followed they were on opposite sides. This battle was fought near Lewes* in Sussex, and resulted in a victory for the insurgents. The king, Richard Earl of Cornwall, his brother, and Prince Edward, were all taken prisoners. Henry was slightly wounded in the battle, but crying out, "I am Harry of Winchester, your king; don't kill me!" was spared and led to a place of safety.

An agreement was entered into between de Montfort and the king's party, by which the whole matter was referred to arbitration. No arbitration was attempted, however, for the common people were perfectly satisfied with the government of "Sir Simon the Righteous," as they fondly called de Montfort. But the earl's supporters among the nobility grew fewer and fewer. They were jealous of his abilities and of his high position, and when he summoned a parliament in 1265, the year after the

---

* Pronounced Lew-es.

battle of Lewes, only twenty-three barons came at his call, though the clergy were there in large numbers. De Montfort then conceived the brilliant idea of appealing to the people, as it would be called now-a-days, and sent out writs* in the king's name, commanding the sheriffs to hold an election at which two knights from each county, two citizens from each city, and two burgesses from each borough, should be chosen to represent the people of England. Here we have the first meeting of the House of Commons. Since that time the Lords and the Commons together have made laws for England under the name of Parliament, as our own Senate and House of Representatives make laws for us under the name of Congress. Thus the first truly representative body of men in England was called together by Simon de Montfort, Earl of Leicester, in the year 1265, half a century after the signing of the Great Charter.

But the great leader was approaching his fall. The nobles dropped away from him and ranged themselves on the side of the king's party, until at last a clever stratagem set Prince Edward free. The Earl of Gloucester had sent him a present of a fine horse, which, as he was carefully guarded, no one objected to his receiving. He went out for a little airing on his new horse, and asked the soldiers who were with him to run races to see who was the best mounted, offering to bet on their success. When all their horses were thoroughly tired, he put spurs to his own and galloped away over the crest of a hill to where a small body of his friends were awaiting him, while the guard stood stupidly looking on, their horses

---

*The writ here spoken of was a summons to attend a meeting of Parliament.

unable to follow the fresh, fleet one which Edward's friends had provided for him.

It did not take the prince long to gather an army which met that of de Montfort at Evesham in Worcestershire. When the latter saw in what good order his enemies advanced, he remarked, "They come on in wise fashion, but it was from me they learned it."* After another look he exclaimed, "Now God have mercy on our souls, for our bodies are the prince's!" The battle was short and sharp. De Montfort and his son Henry were killed, and "The Barons' War" was over.

But little remains to be told of the reign of Henry III. His son Edward, having established order in the country, went to work off his superfluous energy in a crusade, the seventh, and, as it proved, the last, of these ill-fated and life-wasting expeditions. He was to meet Louis IX. of France at Tunis, in Africa, and go with him to Jerusalem, as his own great-uncle, Richard Cœur de Lion, had gone with Philip Augustus, Saint Louis's grandfather; but on arriving at Tunis he found that the good king had died some time before, and he proceeded on his journey alone (1270). Henry died (1272), at the age of sixty-five. His is next to the longest reign in English history, having lasted from the death of King John, fifty-six years.

Though the years since Henry had grown to manhood had been marked by wretched misrule, yet they were years in which the English, as a people, were making great progress. They were learning the value of self-government and of resistance to tyranny, and no future king would have found it possible to resort to the degrad-

---

* So Napoleon remarked, toward the end of his career, that he had taught other generals to beat him.

ing expedients used by Henry for getting money. With the admission of the Commons to Parliament came an era of self-respect.

To do King Henry justice; with all his weakness and meanness he was neither cruel nor treacherous, as his father, King John, had been. He was not without a spice of humor, as he showed when several archbishops and bishops came to remonstrate with him against unlawfully raising people to high positions in the Church. "It is true," said he, "I have been faulty in that respect. I obtruded you, my lord of Canterbury, upon your see; I was obliged to employ both threats and entreaties, my lord of Winchester, to get you elected, when you should have been sent to school: my proceedings were very irregular and violent, my lords of Salisbury and Carlisle, when I raised you from the lowest stations to your present dignities. It will become you, therefore, to set an example of reformation by resigning your present places and trying to get advancement in a more regular manner." This anecdote rests on the authorship of Matthew Paris, who has been called "The last, as he was the greatest," of the monkish historians. Several others flourished during this century, but there are getting to be too many of them for separate mention.

One thing we have to remember in Henry's favor; it was he who began the beautiful Westminster Abbey which we now see. The Confessor's church had mostly tumbled to pieces by that time; but Henry had unbounded veneration for the original builder, whom he adopted as his patron saint, and for whose mouldering relics he wished to provide a suitable shrine. The Abbey was not finished in his day nor for many years afterward;

but it must have afforded him great satisfaction to see its graceful proportions beginning to take shape in solid stone.

Although it is impossible to give the names of many writers within the narrow limits of our history, we must find room for that of Roger Bacon, who was in some respects the most wonderful man of his age. He was the first man of science that England produced, and his discoveries, without the means of knowledge which now can be had by any school-boy, show how genius, aided by industry and perseverance, can make its way in spite of hindrance. Do not confound this Bacon, who was a humble monk, with the brilliant philosopher of Queen Elizabeth's day. They lived three hundred years apart; but any century and any country might be proud of a man like either of the renowned Bacons.

CHAPTER XII.

EDWARD I. CONQUEROR OF WALES.

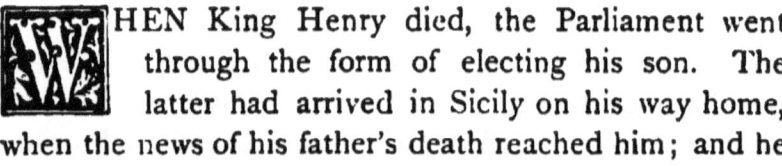HEN King Henry died, the Parliament went through the form of electing his son. The latter had arrived in Sicily on his way home, when the news of his father's death reached him; and he was in so little haste to take possession of his inheritance that he spent more than a year traveling in Italy and France before again setting foot on his native land.

His crusade had not been a successful one. Landing at the city of Acre, the only one that remained of all the

Christian possessions in Palestine, he fought some battles, took Nazareth, and performed wonders in the way of personal prowess; but beyond that, there was nothing to be done. He was accompanied by his devoted queen, Eleanor of Castile, to whom he had been married for many years. He had one adventure, according to the old chronicles, almost worth going to Syria for. While reclining one day in his tent just recovering from a fit of illness, a messenger came with a letter from the Sultan Saladin, his foe; a descendant, probably, of the chivalrous adversary of Richard I. As Edward took the letter the man stabbed him with a dagger, meaning to pierce his heart, but only wounding him in the arm. Edward was not so ill but that he sprang from his couch, seized the three-legged stool on which his tumbler of cooling drink was standing, and with it beat out the brains of the cowardly assassin. Fearing that the dagger had been poisoned, Queen Eleanor dropped on her knees at the bedside and sucked the blood from the wound. No evil effects followed, and the memory of Edward's *"chère regne"** as he called her, has always since been loved and honored by the English people.

Edward was thirty-four years old and in the prime of manly vigor when he arrived in England. He was tall and slender, but very strong, and received the nickname of Longshanks, from the length of his legs. A more honorable addition to his name was that of "The English Justinian."† After his coronation he spent some time in establishing law and order throughout his domin-

---

* Beloved queen.

† In allusion to a Roman emperor who prepared and enacted a grand code of laws.

ions, and then his active mind began to seek for some more exciting occupation. This was furnished him by events which occurred in Wales.

Wales, as you remember, is the country where the Britons took refuge when the devouring Saxons descended upon them. King Arthur is the last of their princes to appear on the page of history until the time of Edward I. of England, when Llewellyn, at that time Prince of Wales, refused to come before the English king and pay the customary homage. Having repeatedly summoned him to do so, Edward marched into his country, and after several years of fighting, Llewellyn, who had in him all the proud spirit of the ancient Britons, his ancestors, was killed in battle. Edward then declared the country to be part of England, and when David, Llewellyn's brother, continued the war and was betrayed into the hands of the English, he was hanged as a traitor. With him perished the last spark of Welsh independence.

Edward showed a haughty and vindictive spirit by causing the head of the unfortunate Llewellyn to be cut off and placed on the Tower of London with an ivy-wreath on it, in allusion to an old Welsh prophecy which said that Wales should never be conquered until a prince of that country should be crowned in London. However strongly we may condemn Edward's action, we can not deny that the conquest was of great benefit to the Welsh, who were still a semi-barbarous nation, and who by being gradually assimilated to the English, made great strides in prosperity and civilization.

A horrible story to the effect that Edward ordered a general massacre of the bards, or poets, of Wales, because he thought that they encouraged their countrymen to rebellion, was long believed in England, and has only lately been received as what it is, a tale of romance. The poet Gray, however, who lived in the eighteenth century, has made the old tradition the foundation for his grandest poem, "The Bard."

Some time after the close of the war, the Welsh urgently demanded of Edward a prince of their own nation. They were not satisfied to be a part of England, and thought that if they had another prince, who would pay the desired homage, all might go on as before. Edward never had the least idea of gratifying them in this, but he put them off by promising them a prince born in their own country, who could speak no English. They were much pleased with this, and when the king soon afterward appeared on a balcony of Caernarvon Castle in Wales, holding his new-born son in his arms, and told them here was a prince for them born in their own country who could speak no English (and he might have added "nor any other language") they could only laugh and make the best of it. From that day to this the oldest son of the English sovereign has borne the title of Prince of Wales.

A cruel persecution of the Jews stains the annals of Edward I.'s reign. They were accused, truly or falsely, of clipping the coin;* this was made a capital offence, and as the mere possession of a clipped coin was considered a proof of guilt, 280 Jews were hanged in one year in London alone, as being guilty of that crime. Some years after this, the whole Jewish population was thrown

---

* It was the custom, for convenience, to cut silver coins into halves and quarters, there being no small silver currency; it was therefore easy for evil-disposed persons to clip a fragment from each piece.

into prison, under pretext of a crime said to have been committed by one of their nation, and were only released on payment of a fine of £12,000. At last, after another interval, the whole race was banished from the kingdom (1290). Their lands and houses were forfeited to the crown, but they were allowed to carry away their money and jewels, which proved so great a temptation to the sailors that many Jews were murdered for these before reaching a foreign shore. Jews were not permitted to live again in England for nearly three hundred years.

We come now to what occupied the last fifteen years of Edward's reign, his quarrel with Scotland; but before beginning on this, we must go back to an earlier period to explain the state of affairs there.

Alexander III., king of Scotland, a descendant of Malcolm and the Saxon princess Margaret, had seen all his children die before him. There was not even a grandchild living except one little girl named Margaret, the child of his daughter Margaret, who had married the Prince of Norway. This child was called "The Maid of Norway;" and at the death of her grandfather Alexander, she was sent for to be queen of Scotland. Edward I. had a plan for marrying her to his son, the Prince of Wales, but before the poor little thing could reach Scotland she was taken ill, and died on one of the Orkney Islands. If the marriage had taken place it would have prevented a long and bloody war, and hundreds of years of ill-feeling between the two nations; but things turned out otherwise.

The Scottish people were in great perplexity. A king they must have, for nobody thought of doing without one in those days; and the only persons available for the office were those who were descended from the three daughters of David, Earl of Huntington, brother of William the Lion. Lord Hastings, who was son of the youngest sister, saw that he had no chance, and withdrew from the competition, leaving two candidates, John Baliol and Robert Bruce,* between whom it was necessary to make a choice. Each side had sturdy partisans, and rather than go to war about it, both parties agreed to leave the matter to Edward and abide by his decision. Edward willingly accepted the office of arbiter, but hampered his acceptance with a condition very different from what the Scots expected. He demanded to be received as over-lord (lord paramount) of Scotland; in other words, whoever was chosen king must do homage to him for the *whole* of Scotland. It had for a long time been recognized that the king of England had rights over certain districts there — Strathclyde, for instance, in the southwestern part, which was granted to them by Edward the Elder; but this demand was unprecedented. They saw that they were in Edward's power. To refuse to accept his arbitration on his own terms would be to make an enemy of him, which they could ill afford to do, and would also be likely to plunge them into civil war. The Scottish council consented to his condition and Baliol and Bruce each solemnly swore that if he should be the chosen one it should be as Edward's "man," bound to do homage to him for the kingdom of Scotland.

Edward, acting on a principle of hereditary right now universally agreed to, decided that Baliol, being in direct descent from David of Huntington's oldest daughter, was the rightful heir to the crown. The Scottish people

---

* Not the Robert Bruce about whom so many romantic stories are told, but his grandfather.

accepted his decision without question, and Baliol was crowned at Scone, on the old stone always used for the coronation of Scottish kings, and which, afterward carried to England by Edward, still forms part of the English throne in Westminster Abbey.*

When Edward went to Scotland the first time after this matter was settled, he arranged that his queen should follow him there. She set out to do so, but died on the way; and Edward, in the deepest grief, at once moved southward to accompany her body to its tomb in Westminster Abbey. At each place where the funeral procession rested for a night on the way, he caused a beautiful stone cross to be erected in memory of her. The one in London was at the place now called Charing Cross, (though the cross itself was long ago pulled down), and the word Charing is said to be a corruption of the French word "Chère regne"—Edward's dear queen.

There are but two of the thirteen crosses left now, those at Wolverhampton and Waltham; but no stone monument is needed to keep fresh in English hearts the memory of the beloved Eleanor of Castile.

While the negotiations were still going on with Scotland, Edward became involved, quite unexpectedly, in a war with France (1293) which had in the end some bearing on the relations with the northern country. The original cause of quarrel was slight—only a fight between an English and a Norman crew who came to fill their water casks at the same well near Bayonne in France.

---

*An old legend claimed it as the stone which formed Jacob's pillow at Bethel. A modern saying is, that wherever that stone lies, there Scotland rules; apropose to which it is remarked that many English ministers are of Scottish blood, Gladstone among the rest.

A Norman was killed in the scuffle; and, the incident being noised abroad, other sailors took up the quarrel, and English and Norman vessels could not meet at sea without doing some mischief to one another. The Channel became the scene of continual acts of piracy; and at last a Norman fleet of two hundred vessels was attacked by an English fleet of eighty, or, as some writers say, only sixty ships (it is the English who are telling the story!), and almost entirely destroyed. In consequence of this, Philip IV., the king of France, summoned Edward (who as Duke of Guienne was Philip's vassal), to answer for the misdeeds of his sailors. Edward declined to go, but sent his brother as deputy. To him Philip proposed that he should give up Guienne for forty days, merely as a matter of form, and let him put French soldiers into the garrisons during that time. The simple-minded deputy readily agreed to this, but he trusted to Philip's honor, a quality unknown to the French king. Guienne was not restored; Edward invaded it, and there was some fierce fighting done. For a long time victory was doubtful; the province was taken and retaken, and at last, many years after the two parties of sailors had quarrelled as to which should drink first at the crystal spring, Guienne was formally restored to England.

The most important result of this war was the alliance formed between France and Scotland, secret at first, but openly acknowledged at a later time. For centuries afterward, a common hatred of England joined in close friendship two nations entirely unlike in position, language, and modes of feeling, against another which should have been the natural ally of its nearest neighbor.

CHAPTER XIII.

THE WAR WITH SCOTLAND.

IT might be thought that with the recognition of John Baliol as king of Scotland, all trouble would have been at an end; but such was not the case. Edward repeatedly summoned Baliol to London to answer for certain legal decisions with which England had nothing to do, and which it was within the province of the Scots to settle as they pleased. He refused to permit Baliol to appear by deputy, as he himself had done when summoned in a similar case to Guienne; and when the Scottish king obeyed the call, treated him with such insolence that Baliol, though a mild-tempered man and not very tenacious of his dignity, could endure it no longer. He refused to attend an English Parliament to which Edward summoned him, and the English king instantly marched upon the Scottish town of Berwick * and took it with brutal cruelty. The inhabitants, to the number of eight thousand, were massacred in the streets; and a few Flemish merchants, who were bravely defending themselves in the Town Hall, were burned alive in it. Here Edward received a message from Baliol renouncing his allegiance to him, upon which he exclaimed: "The felon fool! If he will not come to us we will go to him!" and immediately marched northward through Scotland, taking the principal cities on the way. Dunbar and Edinburgh made a brave stand, but at Stirling Edward found that

---
* Pronounced "Berrick."

"the garrison had run away, leaving none but the porter, which did render the keys." He was determined to make thorough work of it, and, the chronicler says, "went himself into desolate places where there was no more than three houses in a row between two mountains." He returned to Berwick, "having conquered and searched the kingdom of Scotland, as is aforesaid, in twenty-one weeks without any more." Baliol gave himself up and was taken prisoner to England. Here he was kept for two years, and was then allowed to go to France, where he ended his life in peaceful obscurity.

It has been commonly said that Scotland has never been conquered. Permanently, it never has been so; but, for the time, it was as much a possession of the English crown as Normandy was a possession of the king of France. The country was in Edward's hands; an English governor and his council took the place of the Scottish king and his nobles, and every fortress had an English garrison. But this did not last long. In the breasts of the Scottish people still burned the fire of national freedom, and an army of husbandmen, under the leadership of William Wallace, gave a check to English dominion from which it never fully recovered.

In Wallace himself we have again the right man for the right time. Very little is known of him personally, though we feel so well acquainted with him as the hero of Miss Porter's novel, "The Scottish Chiefs," that we may be excused for sometimes confusing romance and history. But it is certain that his great heart beat only for his country; and that he looked for his supporters, not among nobles and men of renown, who fought for glory and the love of adventure, but among the Scottish peasants, who had little to lose but liberty. Wallace sought nothing for himself; he had not, as far as we can see, any special interest in Bruce, who, after Baliol's death, was recognized by the Scottish party as king; he was only determined that his country should be free. He was cruel in war, as were all the military captains of that day. None of them, except perhaps Saint Louis, had learned that, though war may be necessary to enforce the right, revenge is always barbarous. All we can say of him is that in this respect he did not rise above the spirit of the time.

The first great battle between the two nations was fought near Stirling. The English governor of Scotland, Earl Warrenne, who was in command, sent to offer terms of peace; but Wallace uttered the feeling of his whole army when he answered: "We have not come here for peace, but to free our country." By choosing his ground skilfully, he defeated the enemy with great slaughter, and the spirits of his party rose accordingly. Among the slain was Cressingham, the treasurer of England, to whom the Scots bore such hatred that they cut his skin into strips and made bridles of it. It was the ferocity of a barbarous age, and in French history, as late as the following century, we find a similar incident.*

Edward now concentrated his forces at Falkirk. His sixty years had not taken away his strength nor dulled his vigor; and though he broke two of his ribs the night before the battle, he fought on just the same. Wallace, on his part, was prepared for a desperate struggle. He said to his men: "I have brought you to the ring; now hop (dance) if you can!" They could not hop to the

---

* See "A Short History of France," p. 130.

same tune that the English did; they were defeated, with the loss of fifteen thousand men, and Wallace, after fighting until most of his friends had fallen, fled for his life.

For several years we hear but little more of him. He kept up a straggling partisan warfare, much like that in the Carolinas during our Revolution, doing what harm he could without bringing his little band into danger of capture; but at last he was basely betrayed into Edward's hands, taken to London, and there executed for treason, according to the barbarous provisions of English law (1305).* When charged with the crime, he answered: "Traitor I can not be, for I was never a subject to the king of England;" but he was too dangerous an enemy to be spared when he was once in Edward's power. The king has been severely blamed for his execution; but we must remember that, to Edward, Wallace was like any other rebel, an enemy to be got rid of at any cost; and that the halo of patriotism which centuries have thrown so brightly around his head was not visible to his foe, who saw in him only a mischievous disturber of the peace.

The Scottish and French wars could, of course, be carried on only at an enormous expense, and with money England was poorly provided. The king, who was too proud to appeal to Parliament, tried in all sorts of ways

---

* The prisoner was hanged enough to choke, but not to kill him; then his heart was cut out of his body and thrown on a fire already kindled for the purpose. The head was set up where it could be seen by as many persons as possible, and the rest of the body, cut into quarters, was shown in different places. This continued to be done in cases of treason down to the middle of the 18th century.

to get what he needed. He asked the clergy for contributions; they resisted. He levied taxes by his own authority, on wool and hides. That on wool was known as "The Evil Toll." Some of his principal nobles warned the sheriffs to collect no more taxes until the charters had been confirmed by Edward. So, after struggling for a while to get his own way, and finding that though he was resolute, the people were so also, he gave up gracefully, called a Parliament, saying that "what concerns all should be approved by all," and thus established the great principle that the people of England can not be taxed except by their own consent (1297). We applied the same principle to ourselves in our Revolution; it cost ns a bloody struggle, but we won in the end. Thus out of evil came good, for Edward would never have consented so to limit his own power if he had not been hard pressed by Scotland on one side and France on the other.

It is amusing to be told, in connection with the new Parliament formed of Lords and Commons together, that serving in it was expensive and unpopular; and that it was often the custom of the Commons, when they had voted the money required, to break up their part of the assembly and go home, leaving the laws to be made by the lords. It took a long time to educate the people up to their privileges.

Edward never gave up trying to conquer Scotland. The first Robert Bruce had been dead for some years; his son, the second Robert, died in the same year with Wallace, and we now come to the well-known Robert Bruce, who began his public career by an act of murder and sacrilege. At twenty-three years old he was a soldier in Edward's army, and was undecided, when his father died, whether it would be best for him to continue a peaceful subject of England or to renew the old claim of his family to the Scottish throne. The latter meant war to the knife with Edward, for the Baliol family were under his protection. Just at this time Bruce met John Comyn, Baliol's nephew (called "The Red Comyn"), in a church, and while disputing with him about their respective claims, drew his dagger and plunged it into Comyn's body. It was a wicked deed, but it was done, and nothing was left for Bruce but to brave it out as best he could. Gathering together as many of his friends as he could muster at short notice, he went secretly to Scone to receive his title of king in due form. It had always been the privilege of the Earls of Fife to place the crown upon their sovereign's head. It was fortunate for Bruce that the earl of his time was absent, for he was a friend of the English; so the ceremony was performed by Fife's sister, the Countess of Buchan. Edward had carried off to England not only the coronation stone, but the royal robes and crown jewels. Friends, however, supplied what was needed, and Robert I. was declared king of Scotland. "Now you are queen and I am king," he said proudly to his wife after their coronation. "I'm afraid we are only playing at being king and queen, like children," answered the more prudent Mary. It was not long before they were separated. The wife was taken prisoner, and eight long years passed before they met again.

Edward's anger at this act may be imagined. Every one who had had anything to do with crowning Bruce was punished if it was possible to get at him; even the Countess of Buchan was captured and exhibited in a cage at Berwick, while Bruce's sister suffered the same indignity at Roxburgh. After a battle, in which Bruce was defeated, he fled to the mountains, and as many of his followers as were taken suffered death.*

Once more Edward set out for Scotland, determined this time to put an end to Bruce and his pretensions, but his strength was not equal to the effort, and he died at Burgh-on-the-Sands, within sight of the Scottish shore. He was in the sixty-eighth year of his age, and had reigned thirty-five years.

Edward I. was unquestionably a great man. His worst fault was ambition, which, in the matter of the Scottish war, turned to absolute hatred of those who opposed him. In Westminster Abbey you can still read the inscription placed there by his order: "Edward I. The Hammer of the Scots. Keep Covenant."†

In enforcing law and order his course recalled the days of Henry Plantagenet. Like him, he came after a time of fearful misrule, when neither life nor property was safe, and he established such order, and was so well known for his stern justice, that the thieves and highwaymen who had been in the habit of going about in armed bands, found it best to follow some other kind of business. One

---

*The famous story of Bruce and the spider belongs to this period. It is said that Bruce, disheartened by a long succession of misfortunes, was lying in a wretched hut and wondering whether it was worth while to keep up his efforts, when he saw a spider who was trying to fasten the first thread of her web to a beam in the ceiling. Six times she failed and fell back again, Bruce watching her, meanwhile, with intense interest. The seventh time she succeeded in fastening the thread; and the weary king, determined not to be outdone by a poor insect, decided to make one more trial. After this he was successful.

† Edwardus Primus. Malleus Scotorum. Pactum Serva.

of the laws passed during this reign throws a strong light on some dangers of the time. No hedges, woods, or shrubbery, nothing, in short, except large trees, was to be allowed within two hundred feet of a public highway, on either side of the road. If the owner of the property, (a "lord" of it as he is called in the Act), does not clear away the shelter for thieves thus described, he is to be made answerable for any robbery committed there.

The strength of Edward I.'s character is all the more noticeable because he comes between a weak father and an indolent, pleasure-loving son. The contrast is sharp and painful.

It was in Edward's reign that the celebrated statute of "Mortmain" was enacted. The practice of leaving property by will to the church had become a source of loss to the king because property so left fell into an ownership which could not die, which therefore might hold it forever, while in all other cases it must fall into new hands at the end of each owner's life if not oftener; and if there were no other claimant, it fell to the crown. The unbroken grasp of the church was likened to that of a dead hand—"morte-main."

CHAPTER XIV.

EDWARD II. BANNOCKBURN.

THE last instructions of Edward I. to his son the Prince of Wales, then twenty-three years old, were that he should not recall Piers Gaveston, a young Frenchman from Gascony who had already brought the prince more than once into trouble, and that he should, on peril of his father's curse, carry his bones (*i. e.*, his body) with him into Scotland, and never bring them back until that country was conquered. Edward II., as disobedient to his father after his death as he had been during his life, instantly recalled the unworthy favorite, sent his father's corpse back to Westminster to be buried, and having marched the army laboriously collected by Edward I., a few miles into Scotland, disbanded it and returned to England. Gaveston soon became his only companion and counsellor, all Edward I.'s ministers being dismissed with scorn. Edward disgusted his father's friends still more by giving his own niece in marriage to Gaveston, and by making him guardian of the kingdom when he himself went to France to celebrate his marriage with Isabella, daughter of Philip the Fair. There was no end to the favorite's insolence and the king's folly. Gaveston thought it very witty to call the haughty English gentlemen by absurd names. The Earl of Lancaster, the king's cousin, was, in his elegant language, "the old hog,"* or sometimes, "the play-actor." Aymar de Valence, Earl of Pembroke, who had a dark complexion, was nicknamed "Joseph the Jew;" and the Earl of Warwick became "the black dog of Ardennes." Warwick said he would teach him that the dog could show his teeth; and every one of these men was resolved upon his ruin.

By the time the king returned from France after his marriage the discontent had grown to fury. There is an old proverb which says, "Whom the gods would destroy, they first make mad;" and the two young men were ex-

---

* In allusion to the boar's head which appeared on the earl's escutcheon.

amples of it. When King Edward first met his favorite, in the presence of a crowd of high-born guests come together to pay their respects to the young queen, he and Gaveston flew into one another's arms and embraced like school-girls, forgetful of the presence of any one else. As soon as possible Edward made a present to Gaveston of a hundred thousand pounds in money, besides all the rich gifts bestowed on him by his father-in-law, Philip the Fair, which was looked upon by the queen and the uncles who came with her, as an insult. The queen's own outfit was furnished from the spoils of the Knights Templars whom Philip had, with cruel treachery, lately destroyed in France.* She was a girl of only thirteen years old, and no one who saw her handsome face could have guessed what misery and disgrace were to spring from this seemingly promising union. When the barons insisted that the king should banish Gaveston from the country, Edward did it by making him Lord Lieutenant of Ireland. He next induced the Pope to absolve his favorite from the oath he had been forced to take never to return to England; back he came, more insolent and reckless than ever, and again the king's imprudent affection displayed itself. Edward's misgovernment increased year by year; the public money was wasted and the public welfare disregarded while he and Gaveston feasted and revelled as if the one object of life had been frolicking together. The barons managed to get hold of the favorite, and after a mock trial, he was beheaded near Warwick Castle. When Edward heard this he was filled with grief and rage. He tried to raise an army to fight the rebellious barons, but his subjects were more in sym-

---

* See "A Short History of France," Chapter XI.

pathy with them than with him. In the meantime, the rebels were coming against him with a much larger force than he could bring together; and some friends, in pity for his forlorn condition, and desiring to ward off a civil war, made peace between them.

Robert I. of Scotland (Bruce) was by this time pretty firmly seated upon his throne, but the English felt that their national honor called for a renewal of the war; and now that Gaveston was out of the way, they raised such a splendid army as had never before marched out of England. The king, as a matter of course, took command of it. Nothing was spared, and the king started at the head of his troops for Stirling Castle, which Bruce was besieging. But he never reached the castle, for at Bannockburn, two miles distant, was fought the battle which decided the fate of Scotland.

Robert Bruce the king was a very different person now from the vacillating, self-seeking youth who plunged his dagger into the breast of the Red Comyn eight years before. He had had long years of hiding and poverty before he could feel secure of even his life; and had learned those lessons of self-control and patient endurance of hardship which adversity can best teach. Since he had been king in reality as well as in name, he had governed his country admirably; and though the people in some parts of it were still exposed to sudden attacks from the English, in the cruel spirit of the time, when burning and ravaging seemed to be the natural order of things, the country in general enjoyed a season of peace.

Bruce's army of 30,000 men was not in number more than a third as large as Edward's, but all were animated by one spirit, the love of country; while on the English side was sullen dislike of the king among the common people and open unwillingness to help him on the part of the nobles, many of the latter having refused to join him at all.

Bruce chose his position with great judgment. There was a mountain on one side, a swamp on the other, and the little brook Bannock in front. Along the bank of this stream he had caused pits to be dug, covered with turf and bushes, and into these were driven stakes, with sharpened points sticking upward. Tradition tells us that the day and night before the battle were spent by the Scotts in fasting:

"They dynit none of them that day,"

says the poet who celebrates the battle.

On the day itself the English came prancing along in their shining armor, full of pride in themselves and contempt for their enemies, the latter, being poorly provided with horses, fighting mainly on foot. The pits which had been dug threw Edward's horsemen into confusion; and taking advantage of this, Bruce sent Sir James Douglas to charge upon them, and they were utterly routed. The English infantry seeing them fly, were thrown into consternation. One and all they broke their ranks and fled, their officers finding it impossible to rally them. As there was no place where the great host could take shelter within eighty miles, they might almost all have been made prisoners, but that the Scots preferred plundering the English camp, where they found a vast amount of booty. Edward and the remains of his army hastened on to Dunbar and from there took ship for Berwick, leaving ten thousand dead and wounded on the field; and the attempts to conquer Scotland were brought, for the time at least, to a close (1314).

The adventures and exploits of Bruce were long the subjects of Scottish song and story. Toward the end of the same century, John Barbour's poem of "The Bruce" woke again the echoes of national pride; and in the century following a minstrel called "Blind Harry" celebrated with no less ardor the brave deeds of Sir William Wallace. We are all familiar with the noble song of Burns beginning:

> "Scots, wha ha'e wi' Wallace bled;
> Scots, wham Bruce has aften led!"

It is supposed to be addressed by Bruce to his army before the battle of Bannockburn.

The misery caused in England by the Scottish war was increased by misfortune at home. In the year of Bannockburn there was a poor harvest; and the government, disregarding the natural law which we know as that of "supply and demand," undertook to regulate the price of provisions. This only made matters worse. The next season, in addition to famine, there was a disease among the cattle which carried off many thousands of them. The great barons, who had been accustomed to feeding and caring for hundreds of retainers whose services they claimed in war, being no longer able to support them, turned them out to beg, steal, or starve, and the country was again filled with bands of plunderers. In the midst of all this distress, the king was occupied with two new favorites, the Despensers, father and son, less mischievous than Gaveston but hated on account of the favors bestowed on them. The earl of Lancaster, always in the opposition, headed those who were against the Despensers. A chance turn of affairs in the king's favor enabled him to defeat the earl and take him prisoner; and the old man was beheaded before his own castle gate. He was mounted on a poor starved pony without saddle or bridle, pelted with stones, and thus led out to execution. Twenty-eight knights taken with him were hanged, drawn, and quartered. Such was the idea of war in those dreadful times.

Queen Isabella, who had long despised her husband, now formed a plan to separate herself from him. Making a frivolous excuse, she took her oldest son to Paris, where she was soon followed by a favorite of her own, Roger Mortimer, and no persuasions could induce her to return. It brings tears to one's eyes even now to read Edward's pathetic letters to her and his son; but it was of no use. She went to Flanders, and there performed the one good action of her life by betrothing her son to the count's daughter, Philippa of Hainault.

Many of the discontented nobles, with their followers, had joined Isabella and Mortimer in Flanders, and there they contrived dark plots against the unfortunate king. Having collected a sufficient number of men to carry out their purposes they sailed for England, where Isabella so gained over the Parliament that Edward II. was deposed and the young Prince Edward crowned in his place. In the meantime the king was hurrying from place to place, trying to hide from his enemies, who by this time included almost all his subjects. At last, abandoned and deserted by all, he was seized, and after being passed along from one hard-hearted keeper to another, came to his end in Berkeley Castle. He had before this been shamefully insulted; a crown of hay was placed on his head, and the soldiers brought him ditch-water to shave with. At this the tears ran down his cheeks, and he said to his tormentors, "I have some clean warm water here [his tears] in spite of you!" Finally the queen and Mortimer began to see signs of a change of feeling among the people; and, to prevent any possible reaction of feeling, the king was barbarously murdered (1327).

The poet Gray has put into the mouth of his "Bard" a prophecy of this event:

> "Mark the year and mark the night,
> When Severn shall re-echo with affright
> The shrieks of death through Berkeley's roof that ring,
> Shrieks of an agonizing king!"

Poor Edward! His life was all wrong from the beginning. He made the mistake of preferring pleasure to duty; he was a disobedient son, and he had no sense of responsibility. His whole life was one of shifts and evasions. But he suffered fearfully for his faults and follies; and the memory of his misfortunes softens somewhat our indignation at his misdoings. He was at the time of his death only forty-three years old, and had been king for nearly twenty years.

CHAPTER XV.

EDWARD III. THE HUNDRED YEARS' WAR.

EDWARD III. was a boy of fourteen when the crown was placed on his head in 1327. His father was still living, but the government was carried on entirely by the queen and Roger Mortimer.

While he was away from London on an expedition against the Scots, his promised bride, Philippa of Hainault, came from Flanders escorted by her uncle; and not finding the bridegroom they followed him to York, when he and Philippa were married in the grand old minster.

Mortimer, who had now become Earl of March, made, in the king's name, what was thought a disgraceful peace with Scotland. The independence of that country was fully acknowledged, all claim to homage being given up. Robert Bruce was recognized as king, and his only son David, was betrothed to Edward the Third's sister, Joan.* The English were enraged at what seems to us a very sensible agreement; the ill-will toward Mortimer grew stronger than ever, and a plot was formed against his life. The king himself, now seventeen years old, was the leader in this. It was difficult to secure Mortimer, who lived with Isabella at Nottingham Castle, as the keys were brought every night to the queen, who slept with them under her pillow. But the governor told the conspirators of a secret underground passage by which they could enter the castle.† Through this they went, after dark, the king meeting them at the end of the passage. In silence and darkness they crept up stairs, till they heard Mortimer's voice. They then rushed in and took him prisoner, in spite of the entreaties of Queen Isabella, who called out from the next room, "Oh, my sweet son, spare my gentle Mortimer!" A parliament was called expressly to judge him. He was

---

* Pronounced "Jone"; not "Jo-an."

† The entrance to this is still visible at Nottingham, and is called "Mortimer's Hole."

declared guilty of treason, and condemned to be hanged at Tyburn. This was the first execution at that famous place, which was, until recent times, still used for the same purpose.

Though there can be no doubt that Mortimer deserved to suffer death (for he confessed that he had directed King Edward's murder), the hasty action in some measure defeated its own object, since at a later time the sentence was reversed on account of its being illegal, and through a royal marriage with one of his descendants, the blood of this very Roger Mortimer flows in the veins of Queen Victoria.

After Mortimer's death, Edward III. took the government into his own hands, and confined his mother to her house of Castle Rising, making her an occasional formal visit, but not allowing her to have any share in public affairs. At the age of eighteen, he already showed so much sense and discretion that the turbulent barons ceased to oppose him, and the country put on an appearance of peace and prosperity.

Robert Bruce died about a year after the battle of Bannockburn, leaving a son of only eight years old (the little David, already betrothed to Edward's sister, Joan) to be king after him. This gave a new impulse to the war which was always going on between England and Scotland. Edward Baliol, the son of John the former king, raised an army with which he defeated the friends of King David at Perth with great loss. The Scots were by no means united in support of their young king, and Baliol was crowned at Scone, David and his betrothed wife, called by the Scotch "Joan Makepeace," being sent to France for safety.

Edward III. of England, now joining his forces with those of Baliol, fought a great battle at Halidown Hill, near Berwick, completely defeating the Scots, and securing the town of Berwick as a possession to England. Baliol, however, was not allowed to remain in Scotland, and David Bruce returned to his kingdom.

Meantime, Edward III.'s ambition was taking a new turn. The affairs of France were in a disturbed state, as no one of Philip's IV.'s three sons (the last of whom, Charles IV., was now dead) had left any male heirs, and what was called the Salic law in France did not permit a woman to reign there (on account, an old writer says, of the imbecility of the sex). This traditional law had never been formally enacted by statute; but as it had prevailed in France for nine hundred years, the French people had no mind to do away with it. Edward laid claim to the throne through his mother, Philip's sister. There were two reasons against this: one being that it was for the French people, and not for the king of England, to decide what the Salic law meant; and the other, that two of Isabella's older brothers had left daughters, each of whom had a son. Notwithstanding this, Philip of Valois, nephew of Philip IV., was proclaimed at once by the council, so entirely was the Salic law understood to provide for unbroken male succession.

Edward's ambition, however, took no account of any objections, so he plunged his country into a war that lasted, off and on, for more than a hundred years, wasting millions of English money and tens of thousands of English lives, and leaving at last the English possessions in France far smaller than when the war began.

The first struggle between the two nations took place

on the water. Having obtained as many foreign allies* as he could, Edward set sail with a fine fleet and army for Flanders, where he met the French fleet, and won a complete victory in the harbor of Sluys.

His great trouble in all these wars was, of course, the want of money. At first the parliament granted it very willingly, but after a while they grew tired of the continual demands for it, and protested that they could raise no more. The clergy were very generous to him, and gave him, voluntarily, one tenth of their incomes; he borrowed from the merchants of Florence and other foreign cities all the gold they would lend; he pawned the crown-jewels, both his own and Philippa's; and finally, he sent word to all the gentlemen in England who had an income of £40 ($200) or over to come at once to London and receive the honor of knighthood, or else pay a fine. This kind of "Stand-and-deliver" practice was not uncommon in those days. Of course each knight paid a fee to the king when he received the title of "Sir," and a blow on the shoulder from his Majesty's sword; but many of them would rather have been excused from accepting the honor. With Edward it was always "Heads, I win; tails, you lose." They paid a fine if they stayed away; a fee if they came.

We come now to the battle of Cressy—the first great English battle on French ground. Edward had a comparatively small army—less than 30,000 men, all told,—while Philip VI. had, the English historians say, from eight to ten times that number; but they had no such general as Edward. He drew up his army on the gentle slope of a hill, with a windmill at the top from which he

---

* Pronounced al-*lies*, with accent on the second syllable.

could watch its operations (the windmill is there yet), and a small ditch in front. There were first used "bombards, which, with fire, threw little balls of iron to frighten the horses!" This is the first time the use of cannon is mentioned. Roger Bacon had invented or discovered gunpowder, but he did not make any practical use of it, and would probably have been shocked to learn that his new mixture would ever be employed for killing men. The cannon at Cressy did not do much harm to the enemy, and had a bad habit of exploding after a few balls had been fired, which caused them to be looked on with small favor until stronger castings came into use.

The prince of Wales, named Edward, like his father, was at this time sixteen years old, and was fighting in the field like anybody else, when some one brought word to the king that his son was hard pressed by the enemy, and asked for help. "Is my son dead, or unhorsed, or badly wounded?" inquired Edward. "No, Sire, but he is fighting hard, and needs your aid." "Let the boy win his spurs,"* answered Edward, "for I wish, if God so wills it, that the day may be his." The French were tired with marching when they began the battle; their officers were not equal to handling so great a host; and though they fought fiercely, the English bowmen won the day.

Never before had such a victory been gained by any English army. Thirty-five thousand of the enemy lay

---

* In allusion to the honor of knighthood, by which gilt spurs were given to a young squire who had fought bravely, instead of the iron ones worn by all common horsemen. For a detailed account of the usages of Chivalry, see "A Short History of France," p. 115.

dead upon the field, including many of their highest nobility and eleven princes of the blood. The blind old King of Bohemia, determined to have his share of the glory, rode into battle between two knights, their horses tied to his, that he might not be lost in the crowd. All were slain, and the Prince of Wales adopted the three ostrich feathers which formed the Bohemian king's crest and his beautiful motto, "Ich dien"—"I serve"—as his own, and they have been borne by every Prince of Wales from that day to this. It is said that the French gave the young Edward the name of "The Black Prince," from the color of the armor he wore on that day.

From Cressy, King Edward marched with his army to Calais, not very far off, which he besieged for nearly a year before he could make it surrender. During this time a battle was fought at Neville's Cross, in the northern part of England, with poor unlucky King David, son of Robert Bruce, who always seemed to be on the losing side. This time he was taken prisoner and carried to London. Philippa, who had been left regent of England while Edward was in France, was present at this battle. She rode through the ranks encouraging the troops, and then retired to her tent to pray for their success.

The Parliament were so delighted with the victories of Cressy and Neville's Cross that they gave Edward all the money he wanted. The tax on the exportation of wool was one of those given at this time to the king, which caused Philip of Valois to speak contemptuously of him as "The English Wool Merchant." Edward had his jest in return, for on learning of an oppressive tax on salt raised by Philip for his expenses (every person, even the poorest, being obliged to buy a certain quantity of salt each year for the king's benefit), he remarked that his French rival truly reigned by the *Salic* law.*

But we have left Edward too long besieging Calais. (No doubt the hungry sufferers there thought the same). When the town was first invested by his army, the garrison turned out seventeen hundred useless people, women, children, and old men, who could not fight and only helped to eat up the provisions, and Edward kindly gave them each a good meal and two small pieces of money, letting them go where they pleased. Later in the siege, when he had become very angry at being kept there so long, they sent out five hundred more starving wretches; but the king would do nothing for them, and most of them died miserably in sight of his soldiers.

When the siege had lasted nearly a year, the garrison could hold out no longer. Edward at first threatened to kill them all, but finally agreed that if six of the principal citizens were sent to him, barefooted, with ropes around their necks, he would let the rest go free. Wild was the grief in Calais when the hard terms were made known. The burghers met in the town-hall to consider the matter, and for a long time a dead silence prevailed. At last the richest and most honored man in the town, Eustace de St. Pierre, arose and said he would be the first. One by one, five others followed him. Then the governor, Sir John de Vienne, was mounted on a little pony, for he was too weak to walk, and amid the loud weeping and wailing of their fellow-townsmen, he led the six men to the gate of the city, and delivered them, with the keys, to Sir Walter Manny, whom Edward had sent to receive

---

* "Sal" was the old French word for salt.

them (1347). When they were taken to the king, their cheeks wasted by hunger and their tottering legs scarcely able to support them, every heart was moved by pity—every heart except the king's. He had made up his mind, and he was not going to alter it for the entreaties of any number of his own brave soldiers. "Strike off their heads!" said he fiercely. But now good Queen Phillippa came up to him, and falling on her knees, begged him for her sake to grant their lives.

The king at first made no answer; he was struggling with his anger, but at last he said, "Dame, I wish you had been anywhere else; but as you want them, I give them to you. Do with them as you please!" Philippa soon signified her pleasure in the matter. She ordered that the six citizens should each have a good dinner, a suit of handsome clothes, and a present in money. Her victory at Neville's Cross was outdone by the one she gained at Calais.

King Edward tried his best to make Calais an English town. He turned out the French inhabitants and invited his own people to come in and settle it; but even the offer of houses rent-free did not bring very desirable tenants, and after a while he was glad to let some of the rich burghers come back to give respectability to the place. Still, it remained largely English, and that may have been the reason why the English were able to keep it for more than two hundred years.

CHAPTER XVI.

THE BLACK PRINCE.

FOLLOWING closely upon the success at Calais came that terrible pestilence known in Europe as the "Black Death" (1348–49). In London alone, 50,000 persons are said to have died of it, and France was in so terrible a condition that both armies stopped fighting and waited for better times.

We have now another curious instance of the effort to interfere, by legislation, with the natural laws which govern supply and demand. As the number of laborers in England became fewer, by reason of the plague, those who were able to work demanded higher wages; upon which laws were made fixing the rate of wages at a certain sum per day, and threatening severe punishments to those who refused to work at that price. This, of course, produced great irritation, and was soon abandoned.

Philip of Valois, king of France, died in 1350, and was followed by his son John, called, with very little reason, "The Good." For several years unhappy France was the scene of continual ravaging by two English armies, King Edward's in the north and the Black Prince's in the west. The Prince, sailing up the river Garonne, carried his army into the richest part of France, "one of the fat countries of the world, the people good and simple, who knew not before what war was;" and there they broke into private houses like an army of locusts in a rice field, devastating all they found before them. The same old writer before quoted says: "They carried off everything. The country was very full and gay, the rooms adorned with carpets and draperies, the caskets and chests full of fair jewels. But nothing was safe from these robbers." All this made the English dreaded and detested, and the inhabitants would not tell them anything about King John's movements, so that the Black Prince suddenly found himself within fighting distance of the French army near Poitiers, in the very neighborhood where great battles had taken place centuries before.* The French had a very large army, and the Prince a very small one, but he was a consummate general, and it is harder to manage a great number of men than a smaller one. To avoid the battle, the Prince offered to restore all his conquests, provided he and his soldiers might retire unharmed to Bordeaux; but John the Foolish, in the pride of numbers and vainglory, would accept nothing less than the unconditional surrender of the entire army. "I will never be taken prisoner but with sword in hand!" was the answer. "God defend the right!"

 The Prince chose his ground, as his father had done at Cressy, with great skill, and his superior tactics won the day. King John, fighting bravely to the last, was taken prisoner with his youngest son. The number of Frenchmen killed and wounded did not fall short of 10,000 men. This was in 1356, just ten years after the battle of Cressy.

 The Black Prince treated his royal captive with great respect, waiting upon him at table with the utmost

---

* One between Clovis and the Visigoths, 507, and another between Charles Martel and the Saracens, 732. The latter is commonly called the battle of Tours.

humility, and saying that it did not become him, as a subject, to sit at table with a king. When they arrived in London, and the brilliant procession passed through the streets, the king of France was mounted on a superb white horse, while the prince, his conqueror, rode by his side on a little black pony; all which must have been vastly consoling to King John. The monarch did not show much spirit after his capture, though he had fought well in the field. He made a treaty with the Black Prince so dishonorable to France that his son the Dauphin refused to agree to it, and several years were taken up in talking over the matter. At length an arrangement was proposed by which the king was set at liberty, leaving two of his sons as hostages for the ransom. This is called the Treaty of Bretigny (1360).

France was in no condition to raise the immense ransom demanded, for the whole country was a prey to quarrels among the nobles and insurrections among the peasants. King John's sons found it dull in England, and one of them ran away; all of which decided the king to return to that country as a prisoner, remarking that though honor was banished from the rest of the world, it should be found in the breast of kings. And when honor and comfort coincided so completely as they did on this occasion, we can not wonder that the palace of the Savoy (his London dwelling-place) again received its royal inmate, who was entertained there in luxury, without a care or any necessity for exertion. He did not live long after his return, and was royally buried by King Edward.

David Bruce, who had been a captive since the battle of Neville's Cross, was also permitted to go home to raise a ransom, and also returned to captivity when he failed to secure it. After eleven years the payment was arranged for, and King David went back to his own country to finish a weak and discreditable reign.

The Black Prince was now established at Bordeaux in France with a regular court of his own. He married his cousin, the "Fair Maid of Kent," with whom he had been in love since they were children, though both had been married in the interval. And here he might have spent a happy, peaceful life, and been king after his father's death, but that the passion for military glory led him into an expedition which ruined his health, wasted his money, and finally sent him home to die in the prime of life, to the unspeakable injury of his country.

There was reigning at this time in Castile (a country in Spain) a certain King Pedro, who had deserved and obtained the title of "The Cruel." Being opposed by his half-brother, Henry of Trastamare (which means "from across the sea") he fled to Bordeaux, where he was kindly received by the Prince of Wales, who thought that a legitimate king, no matter how wicked, should be supported against a usurper, no matter how good. He promised to go himself into Spain with an army to help the cruel Pedro, and as he could not spare enough of his own soldiers, he took into his pay some of the "Free Companies," bodies of troops who fought only for plunder, owing allegiance to no country in particular, but as ready to fight for one as another. They had just been serving against this very Pedro, on behalf of Charles the Wise of France, son of King John. Pedro promised the Prince of Wales to reimburse whatever money he should spend for him; and the prince, too honorable himself to suspect fraud in another person, set out in high spirits for Spain.

He received the treatment he might have expected from the wicked brute for whose benefit he had undertaken the war. After fighting the battle of Navarete, and putting Pedro on his throne again, he asked the latter to pay him the money he owed. Pedro kept putting him off with excuses, and the prince was forced at last to return without getting any satisfaction.* But the evil did not end here. Thousands of his men died from the excessive heat, and he himself went back to France broken in health, deeply mortified at the result of his campaign, and loaded with an enormous debt which he had no means of paying. The Free Companies, on his failure to keep his promises to them, fell to plundering the people again. The prince needed, besides, money for his own soldiers, and to supply this he imposed the always unpopular "hearth-tax"—a certain sum of money to be paid by each family, of which his French subjects complained bitterly. Every tax is odious which takes as much from the poor man as from the rich. The people of Guienne brought the matter before Charles V., who summoned Prince Edward to come to Paris and answer for his conduct. "Yes, I will come," he replied, "but it will be with helmet on head and with sixty thousand men at my back!" He did not go, however, for his summer in Spain had so broken him down that he could not even mount his horse; and both parties, by way of getting

---

* It is gratifying to know that this villain of a king at last got what he deserved. He was killed in battle by Henry of Trastamare, who became king of Castile, was much beloved by his subjects, and was the ancestor of Queen Isabella, the friend of Columbus.

even with one another, went on inflicting suffering on the poor and helpless.

The prince did not keep up his character for humanity and gentleness when he came back from his unfortunate expedition. Illness and disappointment had soured his temper, and when the town of Limoges, which had rebelled against him, was taken by his soldiers, he ordered a general massacre of all the inhabitants, including women and children, in which three thousand persons were killed in cold blood.

The prince's failing health now obliged him to return to England, and he had the mortification of seeing the country he had conquered recovered piecemeal by the king of France, until at last nothing was left of all that had been taken by his father and himself except the cities of Bayonne and Bordeaux in Guienne, and the town of Calais. Nothing to show for all the misery, the broken hearts, the ruined homes, wealth squandered, fair provinces destroyed, valuable lives lost,—but some useless possessions; and all this the consequence of one man's ambition!

Besides losses abroad, there was trouble at home. The barons, taking advantage of the king's increasing age and weakness, tried to regain their old power, and to disregard the will of the people as expressed in Parliament. The prince took the people's part, but at his death (1376) the nobility, headed by John of Gaunt, his brother, again interfered, and all was undone. The Black Prince was buried in the great cathedral at Canterbury, where his gauntlets and helmet and leather surcoat, all worn and dusty, can still be seen, suspended over the tomb.

Queen Philippa was now dead, and the king abandoned himself to the society of a low woman named Alice Perrers, who robbed him of everything she could lay hands on, and scandalized the whole country by her shameless conduct. A year later he died (1377) in the sixty-fifth year of his age, having just completed a reign of fifty years.

We must not, however, let the sad ending of this great reign blind us to the glory of its better days—not only military glory, though there was enough of that; but

> "Peace hath her victories,
> No less renowned than War."

The grand fourteenth century, of which Edward's reign just covered the middle part, saw civilization advancing with such strides as it had never yet taken in the nation's history. The military achievements of this period have been told in a connected series, because they have fixed dates, and are in some degree dependent on one another; but they are the least important of the events in that splendid half-century.

To Queen Philippa is due the honor of giving an impulse to English manufactures. Up to this time England had exported her wool and received it back in the shape of cloth from the looms of the Continent; Philippa encouraged her countrymen, the weavers of Flanders, to settle in her adopted country, and thus laid the foundation of the great manufacturing system which still continues a chief source of England's wealth. Manufactures lead to commerce, and on this Edward's great mind was brought to bear. He is called "The Father of English Commerce." The arts, too, flourished. The beautiful Windsor Castle rose in its stately magnificence, and New

College at Oxford still keeps green the memory of William of Wykeham, its architect-bishop.

Edward III.'s reign may be especially marked as one of law. He obeyed the laws himself and taught others to respect them; while he never decided anything of importance without consulting Parliament, which he called together no fewer than seventy times. One of the most important acts passed by this assembly ordained that cases in the law-courts should thenceforth "be pleaded in the English tongue;" a proof that the Norman element was losing its last hold on England.

But to the reading world the true glory of Edward's reign lies in the fact that England now possessed for the first time a national literature. The semi-Saxon dialect which until then had formed, with French and Latin, the only medium for writing, gave way to something enough like modern English for us to understand it. Many of its words are now out of date, but we can still read the works of Chaucer and of Wycliffe in the language they themselves used, without needing to have it translated. Chaucer is our first great poet; to Wycliffe we owe the first steps in that Reformation carried out a hundred and fifty years later by Martin Luther. The names of Langland, Gower, and Mandeville belong also to this reign, but they find a place more properly in the history of literature.

One institution of Edward's is perhaps more widely known than others of greater significance; the establishment of the "Order of the Garter." The story is that the Countess of Salisbury, a beautiful woman much admired at court, happened to drop her garter at a ball; whereupon the king, to check or prevent rude levity, picked it up and bound it round his own knee, saying, "Honi soit qui mal y pense."* And he took occasion from the incident to found a society to which kings and emperors are proud to be admitted.

From the time of King John, who had at first stood out so boldly against the Pope and then given in so weakly, England had paid a yearly tribute to Rome. This went on as long as Edward was still a minor; but when he became king he ceased to send it. When the Pope threatened him with the terrors of the Church, Edward did what he always did when an important matter came up—consulted the Parliament about it. They soon decided that the Pope had no authority in England, and that the tax must never be paid again. The seat of the papacy had been changed from Rome to Avignon, and the popes for the greater part of that century were mere tools of the kings of France, so that the English king had a double reason for withholding his tribute.

One of the acts passed by Edward's Parliaments strikes us as rather amusing. So much jealousy of the legal profession had arisen that practising lawyers were declared incapable of being chosen members of Parliament.

CHAPTER XVII.

RICHARD II. WAT TYLER. BOLINGBROKE.

RICHARD of Bordeaux, son of the Black Prince, became king when Edward III. died. He was only eleven years old, and the government naturally fell under the control of his uncles. Several of

---

*"Evil to him who evil thinks."

these sons of Edward III. play parts so important in history that one can not understand it fully without knowing their names. They are given in Shakspeare's play of Henry VI. for the same purpose. They were: 1, Edward, Prince of Wales, father of Richard II.; 2, William, who died young; 3, Lionel, Duke of Clarence; 4, John of Gaunt, Duke of Lancaster; 5, Edmund, Duke of York; 6, another William, who also died young; 7, Thomas, Duke of Gloucester.*

A Council of Regency was appointed to carry on the government while Richard was under age, with the three sons of Edward III. who were still living (Nos. 4, 5, and 7) as its leaders; but the eldest of these, John of Gaunt,† soon managed to become the real head.

The war with France went on, without glory but with the usual waste of life and money. War must be paid for, and the Parliament laid a new tax which, being demanded from rich and poor alike, bore most heavily on those who had but little to pay with. This was a poll-tax of three groats‡ on each person over fifteen years of age. The tax-gatherers were rude and brutal, as might have been expected; and when one of them insulted the daughter of a laborer, the father struck him dead on the spot with the hammer he was using at work. This man

---

* Edward III. was the first to introduce into England the title of Duke, conferring it upon his own sons. Before that time the highest English dignity was that of Earl.

† So called because he was born at Ghent in Flanders. The English made as bad work with Continental names as the Romans did with British ones.

‡ Equal to about 25 cents of our money, but meaning far more than that to the poor workman.

whose name was Walter, was called Wat the Tiler,* commonly shortened to Wat Tyler. His friends and neighbors applauded what he had done, and very soon a general rising among the peasants threatened the country with a new danger. Up to this time all civil wars had been between the king and the nobles, or among the nobles themselves; but here was something the upper classes were quite unprepared for—a rebellion of their inferiors. These peasants still held their land partly under the old feudal system, which required personal service in the place of rent. This placed the tenant at the mercy of his landlord, and great dissatisfaction was the result. A priest named John Ball, a follower of Wycliffe (Froissart calls him "a mad priest," but he had a great deal of method in his madness) went about stirring up the people to assert their rights as *men*. "By what right," he said, "do these lords and ladies flaunt in their velvet and ermine while we are clothed in rags? They have wine and rich food and fine wheat bread; we have oatmeal and straw to eat and water to drink. They have fine houses, and can stay in them; we have wretched huts, and must labor in the wind and the rain. And yet it is our work that gives them all these good things.

"When Adam delved and Eve span,
Where was then the gentleman?"

It was a kind of socialism not well organized nor wise in its methods, yet feeling after its natural rights. The killing of the tax-gatherer by Wat Tyler was the spark

---

* A man who laid tile roofs. In these disturbances the leaders took names from their trades; "Hob Miller" and "Jack Carter" for instance.

that set the country in a blaze. Everywhere men stopped their work and hurried to join the insurgents, who soon formed a body a hundred thousand strong and marched to London. The great Duke of Lancaster (John of Gaunt), who was hated as the representative of aristocracy, ran away and took refuge in Scotland. The young king, now sixteen years old, showed good sense and spirit. The rioters attacked and burned the palace called the Savoy, then belonging to John of Gaunt, and the new buildings of the lawyers at the Temple. At a personal meeting with the boy-king, he asked what they wanted. "We want our freedom!" they shouted. "We will that there shall be no more serfs!" "You shall have it," answered the king; "I promise it." Satisfied with this, a large proportion of the mob dispersed and went quietly home, carrying with them copies of a precious "emancipation paper" which thirty clerks had been busy all day in writing out. About thirty thousand of them, however, remained in the city with Wat Tyler, to make sure that the king's promises were fulfilled. The next day, as Richard was riding through the town, he met the chief himself, with whom he had a parley. The Mayor of London, fearing that the king was in danger, struck Wat down with his dagger, and a servant killed him. The mob broke out into wild cries for revenge. "What would you have, my masters?" asked the young king. "Have you lost your leader? I am your king and I will be your leader. Follow me." And riding bravely at their head, he led them into the open country, where he promised to grant their wishes and a full pardon for all offences, upon which they dispersed.

When the king's uncles returned, however, they

refused to abide by what he had done. It was, indeed, illegal, for only the land-owners had the right to free their bondmen. Still, the promise was made to get them to lay down their arms, and should have been kept when they had done so. When the question was brought before the Parliament, they pronounced the king's grants null and void, saying that their serfs were their goods, and that no one could take away their goods without their consent. "And this consent," they remarked, "we have never given and never will give, were we all to die in one day." Legally they were perhaps right, morally they were wrong, and politically they were unwise, because the lower classes would have been worth more to their masters as well as to themselves as freemen. The "villains"* did not directly gain their object; but the expression of their determination drew attention to the subject, and serfdom gradually melted away.

The Council of Regency also came back, and then began the work of punishment. It is said that fifteen hundred persons were hanged for this outbreak, in spite of the king's pardon; a sad example of bad faith in these "noble" fugitives! As the friends of these victims sometimes cut down the bodies so as to bury them decently, the order was given to chain the bodies to the gallows, which was the origin of "hanging in chains," so long practised in England.

The king's uncles were restless, intriguing men, who allowed him no voice in the government; and he one

---

* This name was first given to persons bound to feudal service because their dwellings were built round the *villa* or castle of their lord.

day surprised the Duke of Gloucester, whom he especially disliked, by asking him in Council, "Uncle, how old am I?" "Your Highness is in your twenty-third year," answered the Duke. "Then I am able to manage my own affairs," replied the king. "Gentlemen, I am very much obliged to you for the care you have given to public duties up to this time, but I shall not need your services any longer." From that time Richard took the government on himself.

At first everything went well. The king had some years before this married Anne* of Bohemia, called "The Good Queen Anne," on account of her kind and charitable disposition. At her death, wishing to preserve peace with France, he married a child of eight years old, Isabella, the daughter of Charles VI., called "the Little Queen."

One of the frequent invasions of England by Scotland at this time resulted in the battle of Otterburn, which forms the subject of Chevy Chase, one of the best-known of the old English ballads. Both sides claimed the victory, the English because the bravest Scot, Lord Douglas, was killed, the Scotch because they took prisoner Henry Percy (surnamed Hotspur from his fiery temper), son of the Earl of Northumberland. On the whole, the Scots had rather the best of it.

It was not until the last two years of Richard's reign that the faults lying concealed in his character began to show themselves. He is accused of causing the death of the Duke of Gloucester, whom he had always disliked; but a more serious offence was his dispensing with a Parliament and replacing it by a committee dependent on

---

* Pronounced "Ann," not "An-ne."

himself. Forced loans, the sale of pardons, refusing justice except on payment of bribes, all followed; but nothing could supply his boundless extravagance. He is said to have employed ten thousand persons in his household, three hundred of them being in the royal kitchen. We read also of gorgeous apparel, of superb furniture, of costly jewels. To crown all, he estranged from himself, by caprice and injustice, the most powerful subject in the kingdom.

His cousin, Henry Bolingbroke, son of John of Gaunt, had a quarrel with the Duke of Norfolk, and the king allowed them to try the "wager of battle." The champions are mounted, ready to begin the fight; the king and queen, with as many lords and ladies as can gain admittance to the raised seats around the lists, are in place, the challenge is given and returned, when suddenly, just as the spears are in rest and the impatient horses ready to start, the king throws his "warder," or sceptre, on the ground and the heralds cry "Stop!" This means that there will be no fight that day. Then the capricious Richard, without any decision as to which is right in the quarrel, banishes his cousin Bolingbroke for ten years and the Duke of Norfolk for life.*

The people had despised the king before; now they hated him, for Bolingbroke was their idol. The bitter feeling was increased when at John of Gaunt's death, three month's after his son's exile began, Richard seized all his vast possessions. Having suddenly determined to go to Ireland to put down a rebellion there, he heard mass with his little queen, and then, lifting her up in his arms, he kissed her, saying, "Adieu, madam, till we meet

---

*See Shakspeare's play of "Richard II."

again." The people of London said: "Now goeth Richard of Bordeaux to his destruction. He will never return again with joy, no more than did Edward the Second, his great-grandfather, who was foolishly governed by too much believing of the Despensers." The parallel was remarkably just. Richard had bad luck in Ireland; he did not succeed in his expedition, and he was detained for several weeks by contrary winds. In the meantime, Bolingbroke had arrived on the coast of Yorkshire, in England, with an army. Although he declared that he came only to demand his father's estates, he marched through the land like a conqueror. Towns and castles everywhere opened their gates to him. Even the Duke of York, the Regent in Richard's absence, went over to him with his soldiers. Richard wandered about helplessly from place to place, losing strength as his adversary was gaining it, and the army which a faithful friend had gathered together to help him dispersed because "they could hear no tidings of the king." The net was closing around him. Betrayed by false information, he rode directly into an ambush of his enemies, and the Earl of Northumberland took him prisoner and lodged him in Flint Castle.

Bolingbroke was soon on the ground. He met Richard with an appearance of respect, but carried him to London and shut him up in the Tower, where he was compelled to sign his abdication. Then a Parliament was summoned to meet at Westminster Hall for his deposition—that very Westminster Hall which he had remodelled and beautified, making it very much what we see it now. He was accused of the murder of his uncle, the Duke of Gloucester, of the execution of several of his own subjects, and of answering when asked to do justice according to the law, "The laws are in my mouth; I alone can make and change them; the life of every one of my subjects and his lands and goods are at my will and pleasure." It was also charged against him that he was "so variable and dissembling that no man living, who knew him, could or would trust him." Richard was then formally deposed by the parliament; Henry of Lancaster came forward and took the usual oaths, after which the archbishops of Canterbury and York led him up to the throne, "all the people wonderfully shouting for joy" (1399).

During the latter half of the fourteenth century, many new ideas had been stirring in the minds of the people. It often happens that political and religious reforms go hand in hand. The desire for freedom of thought belongs naturally with the demand for other kinds of freedom, and the age which produced Wat Tyler's rebellion was also the age of John Wycliffe. This earliest reformer not only fearlessly exposed the corruptions of the Church and the avarice and tyranny of the Pope, but uttered doctrines declared to be heretical —that is, not such as the Church believed. His followers received the name of Lollards, for some reason not now understood, and soon became so numerous as to form a very important sect. John of Gaunt openly sympathized with them, as did the Princess of Wales (widow of the Black Prince) and Richard's queen, Anne of Bohemia. The poet Chaucer is also supposed to have belonged among them. Wycliffe was tried for heresy, but received no further harm than being turned out of the University of Oxford. His great work lay not only in preaching new doctrines and stirring people up to purer lives, but in making the first complete translation of the Bible into English. The clergy in general frowned upon this because it led people to the adoption of the Bible, instead of the authority of the Church, as a rule of faith; but to the masses it was like cold water to a thirsty soul, and it was received with thrilling eagerness and read from one end of the land to the other. There were no printed books then, but copies made by hand were multiplied through the industry of willing transcribers until there were few persons in England able to read who could not in some way find the means of getting at the translation.

The aristocrats of learning were by no means pleased with the new order of things. "Scripture is become a vulgar thing," wrote a priest of the day, "more open now to men and women who know how to read than it was wont to be to clerks themselves."* But in spite of all opposition the doctrines of Wycliffe grew and prevailed.

---

* "Vulgar" means common to all; thus the translation of the Bible into Latin was called the "Vulgate" because it was in the common tongue. "Clerks" (clerics) means here the clergy, who had been until this century almost the only persons who had any knowledge of books. A learned man of any profession was called a clerk.

CHAPTER XVIII.

HENRY IV. SHREWSBURY. HENRY V.

HENRY IV. was a usurper in a double sense; for not only had he supplanted Richard, the reigning king, but he had taken the place of the heir presumptive.* This was a grandson of Lionel, Duke of Clarence, third son of Edward III. Lionel's daughter, Philippa, had married the Earl of March, a descendant of Roger Mortimer, and their son, Edmund Mortimer, was the lineal successor to Richard II. But he was a child only seven years old, and the English Parliament exercised its right in passing him over and bestowing the crown on his cousin, the Duke of Lancaster.

But little is known of the fate of the unfortunate Richard II. It is certain that he was kept a prisoner for several months, being removed from the Tower in London to Pontefract (Pomfret) Castle. A conspiracy being formed to replace him on the throne, Henry IV. settled the matter by causing him to be murdered, and then exhibiting his body in London so that there could be no question as to the fact of his death. As has often happened in such cases, a report arose that Richard had escaped, some other dead body being shown as his; but there is no doubt that his life, as well as his crown, was sacrificed to Henry's ambition (1400).

---

* A person who will succeed to the crown if no one shall be born having a better right. "Heir-apparent" is the person who will succeed unless he dies before the reigning sovereign.

The poor little widow-queen was sent home to France (without her jewels and her dower), and for seven years refused all offers of marriage; but was at last induced to wed the Duke of Orleans, brother of the king of France, and the finest French poet of his time, who has left some charming verses about her, entitled (in the English translation), "The Fairest Thing in Mortal Eyes."

The early years of Henry's reign were stained by a persecution of the Lollards, who had now become a numerous and powerful sect. William Sawtry, a clergyman, was burnt alive for heresy, being the first person to suffer death in England for this cause. Other forms of punishment were used, such as imprisonment, branding on the cheek, and whatever tortures might be supposed to lead men to repent of thinking differently from those around them; and for a time the so-called "heresy" apparently died out, to reappear in the next century as the doctrine of the English church and the law of the land.

The most notable feature of Henry IV.'s reign was a series of conspiracies against him, which seemed to those about him a judgment on his unjust dealings with his predecessor, Richard. The first one, already mentioned, was put down with great severity, all the persons concerned in it being executed for treason; but the subsequent plots were more wide-spread, and ended in an appeal to arms.

The conspirators represented the three countries which make up the island of Great Britain. The Earl of Northumberland and his son Harry Percy (the "Hotspur" of Otterburn), headed the disaffected English; the Earl of Douglas brought an army of Scots, and a Welshman named Owen Glendower, who was trying to make his country once more independent of England, had raised a large force in Wales. There had lately been a battle with the Scots at Homildon Hall, where the Earl of Douglas had been made prisoner by Hotspur, and the latter gave him his liberty that they might together make common cause against the enemy.

The three armies were to meet at Shrewsbury, but Henry was too quick for them. He attacked the forces before Glendower came up, and while Northumberland with a part of his command was still on the way, and gained a complete victory. He and his son Henry, Prince of Wales, fought desperately; the brave Hotspur was killed, and Douglas taken prisoner. Henry did not show a revengeful spirit after his victory. Some of the principal offenders were beheaded, but the Earl of Northumberland was pardoned, and a general amnesty was issued to the common soldiers.

In Shakspeare's two plays of Henry IV., we find all these circumstances treated in the most picturesque manner. He is not always correct as to details, but he gives the spirit of the age, and we remember the facts better if we read the plays after studying the history.

It was not long before Northumberland was again engaged in a plot against the king, this time in the company of Scroop, Archbishop of York, who had been a party to the previous rebellion. This time the rebels were put down without a battle, and the king, determined to make an enduring example, had the archbishop executed. Northumberland escaped, and was afterward killed in battle. Henry sent to the Pope the armor worn by Archbishop Scroop, with the scriptural message. "'This have we found; know whether it be thy son's coat or no."

The lawless character of the time is shown in the capture of a Scottish ship (in time of peace) having on board the young Prince James of Scotland (afterward James I.), whom his father was sending to France to keep him out of the way of enemies at home. Henry took possession of this boy of eleven years old, who was kept for nineteen years a prisoner in England. He received an education suitable to his high position, and was kindly treated, according to the ideas of the time; but he would have preferred his liberty.

Henry IV. was not an old man when he died, but since he became king he had led a hard life. Shakspeare makes him say:

"Uneasy lies the head that wears a crown."

Plots and surprises and disappointments at home had been his food for the first nine years of his reign, while the wars with France and Scotland were a continual tainted seasoning for the rest of it. He had lost the popularity which he enjoyed while his people were yet groaning under the oppression of Richard II., and stood in a manner alone. England prospered under his government, and, as is the case with many kings whose title is questionable, the knowledge that the hereditary claimant was still living and might at any time succeed in overturning his precarious seat, made him careful to keep strictly within the laws and on good terms with Parliament —a circumstance favorable to the belief that those governments are best which depend entirely on the consent of the governed; that is, are elective and not hereditary.

Henry IV.'s relations with his oldest son, the "Prince Hal" of Shakspeare, have been the subject of much discussion. The poet, following some of the chronicles, makes the prince wild and dissipated, but this is by no means proved. It is possible, however, that his father's jealousy may have shut him out from any active share in the government.

Henry IV. had long cherished a desire to visit Jerusalem and see for himself the holy sepulchre, a journey to which was supposed to do so much toward atoning for the sins of a life-time; but the cares of state did not permit it. In the last years of his life he was subject to epileptic fits, and one of them came on while he was at his devotions in the chapel of Edward the Confessor, at Westminster. He was carried into a room in the abbot's house near by, and on coming to himself asked where he was. "In the Jerusalem Chamber," was the answer. "I always wanted to die in Jerusalem; now I shall have my wish," said the king, and soon afterward passed away, in the forty-sixth year of his age and the fourteenth of his reign (1413).

Henry IV. had some fine qualities; he was prudent, energetic, and just in the administration of the laws, and if he had acquired the crown in the regular course of things, he might have been one of the favorites among English kings.

Henry V., called from the place of his birth, Henry of Monmouth, came to the throne in the flush of youthful vigor and national popularity. If any unworthy actions or qualities had ever been attributed to him, they had long been forgotten. He was now twenty-five years old, handsome, courteous, good-humored, well educated, and trained in all soldierly exercises.* His first acts showed a generous spirit. The Earl of March (the true heir to the throne in the eyes of many of the people) was set free from imprisonment and treated with the greatest kindness. Henry obtained the release of young Percy, Hotspur's son, who had long been a prisoner in Scotland; and he had the body of Richard II. removed from its unhonored grave and interred with royal state in Westminster Abbey. The horrid persecution of the Lollards, shame to say, went on under his sanction.

In spite of burnings and brandings, the Lollards increased in number and boldly defied the laws which sought to silence them. For some years an irregular warfare was kept up against them on the ground of their being dangerous to the State as well as to the Church, and many of them suffered death. Their leader, Sir John Oldcastle (Lord Cobham) after escapes, reprieves, and many adventures, finally suffered a horrible death,† being suspended by an iron belt over a slow fire, and thus roasted to death (1418).

---

* There is a statement that when one of his boon companions was brought before Chief-Justice Gascoigne for some offence, the prince went with him, and on the judge's refusal to release the prisoner struck him in the face. Upon this Gascoigne committed the prince for contempt of court, and sent word to his father that he had done so. The young man went to prison with a good grace, and Henry's only comment on the circumstance was, " Happy is the king who has a judge so firm in the performance of duty, and a son so willing to submit to the law." It is a good story, whether true or not.

It may interest our young readers to know that Richard Whittington, famous for the clever story that some one invented about his cat, was Lord Mayor of London in Henry IV's time.

† The official record says that he was "sweetly and modestly" condemned to be burnt alive.

A grim corner in the Archbishop of Canterbury's palace at Lambeth is still called "The Lollards' Tower," and in the centre of one of its rooms may be seen a round post to which, it is said, the prisoners were bound while suffering torture.

We turn from these horrors to the other events of Henry's short reign. He was as ambitious as his great grandfather, Edward III., and like him found a promising field in the fair provinces of France, now distracted by a civil war, and always tempting to the invader. His reasoning was, "If my ancestors had a right to France, so have I." (He ignored the other alternative: "If my ancestors had not, so have not I.") Perhaps he really persuaded himself that France would be a great deal better off under his rule than torn by factions, the poor crazy king and wicked queen and selfish nobles quarreling among themselves for the government. The Archbishop of Canterbury encouraged him, in order, it is said, to keep him from inquiring into the abuses of the Church; while Henry himself is charged with wishing to distract his people's attention from his own doubtful title. He found little difficulty in procuring supplies for his invasion, for the whole English nation was wild with enthusiasm at the idea of a war of conquest; and his preparations were made with great energy. Fifteen hundred o. the ships of that day were required to transport an army that could now be carried by thirty large steamships; and when all was ready, Henry proceeded on his way to Harfleur in Normandy.

CHAPTER XIX.

AGINCOURT. TREATY OF TROYES. DEATH OF HENRY V.

IT required a siege of five weeks to take the town of Harfleur, in France, and when it was taken Henry had serious thoughts of abandoning it and going home again. His army was wasted by disease, and the French, as he heard, were collecting in great numbers to oppose him, but he determined to march to his own town of Calais and then decide what it would be best to do.

The French did not get their army together very quickly, for they were divided among themselves, and the different parties hated each other quite as much as they hated the English; perhaps more. When they were ready, they sent to ask Henry by what road he intended to march. "By the one that will take me straight to Calais!" he answered, and sent the messengers away with a present of a hundred crowns. He was not going out of his way to find the French, nor did he mean to refuse to fight if he met them. As they neared the little village of Azincourt (which the English have changed to Agincourt) they saw the splendid French army waiting for them to come up. Henry sent his Welsh squire, Davy Gam, to reconnoitre, and asked him how many French he saw. "Enough to be killed, enough to be made prisoners, and enough to run away," said Davy.

The English army was in poor condition. Of the 30,000 men who had sailed from England not more than 6,000 were now in fighting order, and these were half starved, and tired with marching. (We have to take the English story for these statements of inferior numbers in the winning of great victories). The French are said to have had 60,000 men. This time the enemy had the choice of a position, but they chose their ground badly, and thus neutralized the effect of their greater numbers. King Henry heard some one saying that he wished ten thousand of the stout, idle men in England might be with them that day. "Not so, friend," said the king; "The fewer we are, the greater glory we shall win. For my part, I would not have a single man more." The French were in high spirits, and, the chroniclers tell us, spent the night before the battle in carousing and playing at cards for the prisoners they expected to take. No quarter was to be given to the common soldiers; but persons of rank were to be held for ransom. The English, on the contrary, had a refreshing sleep, except those who, expecting this to be their last night on earth, spent it in devotion.

When the day of battle came, Henry V., whose necessity seems to have sharpened his ingenuity, directed that each one of the archers should carry, besides his bow and arrows, a battle-axe and sword, and a stake pointed at both ends. After having discharged their arrows they were to drive the stakes into the soft, damp ground with their battle-axes, and then fall back and shoot again. The stratagem answered its purpose; the French, advancing as the English retired, came unexpectedly upon the sharp points of the stakes and fell into confusion. The fighting was desperate for three hours, both sides doing wonders of personal bravery. At the end of that time the unmanageable French army was routed and fled from the field. Their heavy armor was their destruction, while the English archers, who had thrown off a great part of their clothing, moved about so easily from place to place that they did frightful execution in the crowded ranks of their enemies.

The French lost in this action, it is computed, not less than 11,000 killed, among whom were the flower of their nobility. These last are reported to have despised the common soldiers, saying, "*This* battle must be won by *gentlemen!*" On the English side the loss was comparatively small—some writers saying forty men and some 1600; so we may take our choice. The Duke of Orleans, husband of England's "Little Queen," was one of the 14,000 prisoners taken on this occasion, so the English had two captive poets at once, Prince James of Scotland (afterward James I.) being the best English poet of his day, as the Duke of Orleans was the finest French one.

Henry was in no condition to follow up his victory. After making a truce with his enemies, he returned to England, where he was received with such demonstrations of joy as had never before been made for any victory. The people could not wait for him to land; they rushed into the water and themselves dragged the ship to shore; the bells rang like mad; triumphal arches were built across the roads, and showers of roses and laurel were strewn under the horses' feet; grand lords and ladies, splendidly dressed, filled the windows and balconies, and from the highest to the lowest each strove with the other which should be most extravagant in expressions of praise. In the midst of all this the king rode quietly along, not looking at all elated, but taking everything soberly, and, as an old writer says, "with reverent demeanor." Perhaps he was thinking of the heaps of dead he had left behind him; perhaps the groans of the dying still filled his ears; possibly he was wondering how the people would like the burdensome taxation necessary for carrying on the war. At all events, he won "golden opinions" for his humility and modesty.

Two years after this, Henry was ready for another invasion. He was determined to conquer Normandy, the old possession of his ancestors, and the English nation again willingly contributed the means. In France itself, the civil war had reached a pitch of horror probably without its equal in the history of any civilized country.* The Duke of Orleans (son of the "Little Queen" whose husband was taken at Agincourt) headed one party and the Duke of Burgundy another, and as each in succession got the upper hand, the lawlessness and butchery seemed to increase. Henry at once laid siege to Rouen, the capital of Normandy, which was defended by its citizens until they were starved out. "War has three handmaidens ever waiting on her," said he, "Fire, Blood, and Famine; and I have chosen the meekest maiden of the three." During the siege, fourteen thousand country people who had taken refuge in the city were thrust out to die between the walls and Henry's camp; he would do nothing for them. The city at last surrendered, and his army was set free for further conquest.

While the siege of Rouen was yet in progress, the treacherous murder of the Duke of Burgundy by a follower of the Dauphin Charles (son of the insane king)

---

* For a detailed account of these doings, see "A Short History of France," Chapter XIV.

as they met for a peaceful conference, threw oil on the flame of civil strife. The son of the murdered duke, wild for revenge, made an alliance with England, promising Henry the sovereignty of France if he would help him against the Dauphin. The queen, who hated her son, took part with them, and a treaty was concluded at Troyes (1420), perhaps the most extraordinary ever made by any set of people in their senses. It was agreed that Henry V., king of England, should be Regent of France as long as Charles VI. lived, and king of it at his death, to the exclusion of "Charles, calling himself Dauphin," and that he should marry the Princess Katherine, the French king's youngest daughter, "without expense to the said king of France;" that is, he took her without a dowry. No wonder that the fair kingdom was considered a sufficient *dot!* The fact that this astounding treaty was hailed with joy by the French people shows to what misery they had been reduced by civil war. They knew Henry to be strong and just, and, when not opposed, kind; and they looked for a breathing-time of peace. The marriage was celebrated at once,* and the company hoped for some festivities in the way of tournaments; but the king had other work on hand, and the next morning set out at his usual business of besieging cities just as if he had not been married at all. He was not, however, entirely indifferent to his wife's amusement, for he sent to England for two harps, that they might make music together. When all the towns in Normandy had opened their gates to him,

---

* For an amusing (imaginary) account of the princess and of Henry's courtship, see Shakspeare's "Henry V.," Act. III., Sc. 4, and Act. V., Sc. 2.

he went back to Paris to take formal possession of his new kingdom. He assured the people (or rather the nobles, for "the people" were not to be seen, any more than the cart-horses) that he would love and honor the king of France, and that the ocean should cease to flow and the sun no more give light before he should forget the duty a monarch owed to his subjects. There was a splendid feast held. To be sure, the same accounts tell us that the poor were dying of starvation by hundreds and the streets were full of little children crying aloud for bread; but perhaps some crumbs of the feast may have fallen to them. As the fountains "ran wine," we may hope that more important needs were satisfied at the same time.

And how fared England all this while? It was gradually becoming drained, not only of its money, but of its men, a more precious possession than money. Those of note and ability were crowding into Normandy, to settle on the confiscated estates liberally bestowed by Henry on his favorites, and there was such great danger that England would in time sink into a mere dependency of France that it was thought necessary to make special laws against this possibility. It was a reversal of the situation which existed under William the Conqueror. Then the Normans forsook their pleasant land to receive as gifts the estates of conquered Saxons; now the descendants of both deserted their homes in England to enrich themselves on the spoils of France. It was fortunate for the island country that the conquest was not a permanent one.

Henry now went back to England to obtain a supply of money from Parliament. This the Commons granted without hesitation, in order that, as they said, "the cities and provinces now in arms against the king being subdued, France might be entirely annexed to the English crown." They also made some provisions to avoid the possibility that, on the other hand, England might be annexed to the French crown; but they showed their confidence in him by giving him all that he desired.

An anecdote is told of this time which shows that "the wager of battle" was not favored by the king. Two men having applied to him for permission to fight in single combat, their neighbors begged that the request might be denied. "No!" said Henry, "they are welcome to fight it out; but if one is killed I shall hang the other for murder." It was surely not during this reign that duelling became again popular.

Once more did Henry set out for France, with an army superbly appointed and in the highest spirits. After some months of hard fighting, during which he succeeded in driving the Dauphin's army into the South, he was cheered by the arrival of Queen Katherine with an infant son, born at Windsor Castle. But his career was almost over. In the midst of a triumphant campaign he was attacked by a mortal disease, and after a short illness died at Vincennes, in the thirty-fifth year of his age and the tenth of his reign (1422).

His dying commands were characteristic. He desired his brothers on no account to release the Duke of Orleans (taken at Agincourt and still a prisoner in England) until his own son Henry should be of age, and not to make peace with France without obtaining at least Normandy for England; and he solemnly declared that it had been his intention, as soon as the "troubles" in France were over, to undertake a crusade for the recovery of Jerusalem. So hard was it even at that late day, to let go of the old idea.

There are few characters in history which stand in as strong a light as does that of Henry V., and yet it is difficult to form an entirely just idea of him. He was the idol of his own people, who could not find a fault in him; and in France he was in many parts of the country welcomed as a deliverer. Individual instances of cruelty must without doubt be charged against him, but it is not fair to judge the actions of almost five hundred years ago by the standard of today. It seemed, not only to Henry but to most of the thinking men in his own country, that his claim on France was a just one; and, this being allowed, all else followed as a matter of course. In his private character he had his full share of virtues; he was kind, generous, faithful, considerate of others, and of refined tastes. In his public acts he was upright and reasonable, and had the strong intellect and clear judgment which enabled him to form wise plans and to carry them out effectually. Shakspeare's play, "Henry V." although eulogy from beginning to end, only faithfully reflects the feelings universal in Henry's own time.

CHAPTER XX.

HENRY VI. WAR IN FRANCE. JACK CADE.

BABY of nine months old was now, according to the language of the world, king of two mighty countries. He received the homage of Parliament sitting on his mother's lap; and was formally turned over to the care of a governess, Dame Alice Boteler, with orders, issued in his own name, "from time to time reasonably to chastise us, as the case may require." Queen Katherine, a frivolous and cold-hearted woman, married secretly, soon after her husband's death, a Welsh gentleman named Owen Tudor,* and, as far as appears, cared nothing more for her son.

Henry V.'s next younger brother, John, Duke of Bedford, a man of great ability and of unblemished character, was made regent of France; the second brother, Humphrey of Gloucester, a rash and hot-tempered person, became Protector of England, and Cardinal Beaufort, a half-brother of Henry IV., was appointed personal guardian of the boy-king. All this was not accomplished without much wrangling, which was typical of Henry VI.'s whole reign; and the gentlest and most peaceful of men, as he turned out to be, grew up amid scenes of continual quarreling and bloodshed.

Charles VI. of France, whose life had been only one long scene of misery, survived his great son-in-law but two months. He missed the unvarying kindness and

---

* The son of Owen Tudor and Katherine was father of Henry VII. the first Tudor king of England.

consideration which Henry was almost alone in showing him, and dropped into the grave unnoticed except for the tears and lamentations of the poor, and the respectful attendance of the Duke of Bedford. His worthless queen soon sank into the neglect she merited, and died at last, unhonored by rich or poor.

Among the chief mourners at Henry V.'s funeral was one whose fate has been the subject of many a romance —King James I. of Scotland.* Two years after this he was set free on payment of a large ransom, though the word "ransom" was not used in the treaty, for fear it should raise a question as to his illegal capture. The sum demanded was stated to be for his "maintenance"— that is, his board, lodging, and education. While in England, he had fallen in love with Jane Beaufort, niece of the Cardinal, whom he had first seen when he was a captive in Windsor Castle; and his poem called "The King's Quair" records the story of his love for her. When he went back to Scotland he took her with him as his queen, and the first year's instalment of the sum to be paid for his "maintenance" was remitted as her wedding portion.

Although the persecution of the Lollards had nearly died out by this time, owing to the pressure of other matters, one effort of parting rage deserves to be mentioned. At a council held thirteen years before, it had been decreed that the body of John Wycliffe should be "taken from the ground and thrown far away from the burial of any church;" and in 1328 this sentence was carried into effect. His body was dragged out from its grave in Lutterworth church-yard, burnt to ashes and the ashes thrown into a brook. "So," says Fuller, writing

---

* See especially Miss Yonge's story of "The Caged Lion."

two hundred years later, "they did convey his ashes into Avon; Avon into Severn; Severn into the narrow seas [*i. e.* Bristol Channel]; they into the main ocean. And thus the ashes of Wycliffe are the emblem of his doctrine, which is now dispersed all the world over."

All this time the war was going on in France. In a general way, the Duke of Bedford was master of northern France, and the Dauphin (for so Charles VII. continued to be called for many years), of southern France; and in order to conquer the latter, it was necessary for the English to obtain possession of the town of Orleans. It was while they were besieging this that the famous "Battle of the Herrings" took place. Bedford had sent down a quantity of salted herrings, the season being Lent, for the soldiers around Orleans. This convoy was met by a detachment of the enemy, and, the herring-barrels being broken up by the cannon, the fish were scattered over the field. The assailants were finally driven away, and as many fish as could be collected were shovelled into wagons and conveyed to the English camp.

Meantime the defenders of the city were in danger of famine. They were already put on short allowance, and had begun to discuss the question of a surrender, when deliverance came to them in an unexpected manner.

In the village of Domrémy on the borders of Lorraine, in France, lived a young peasant girl named Jeanne Darc, who had been accustomed to spend much time alone in the fields, and who fancied that she heard there supernatural voices commanding her to free her country from the English. Having with great difficulty obtained the consent of the Dauphin to take command of a troop of soldiers, she dressed herself in shining white armor and set out on her mission, carrying in her hand a consecrated banner and wearing (never using) a curious old sword supposed to have peculiar powers. At the head of her band of soldiers she rode boldly into the city of Orleans, while a feigned attack of the garrison drew off the attention of one part of the English army, and the rest stood looking stupidly on, believing her to be a witch. A few days later, having succeeded in inspiring the French garrison with a portion of her own courage, she led them against the English fortifications surrounding the city. The attack was successful; and the enemy were so disheartened, and so terrified at the idea of her supposed mysterious powers that it was thought it more prudent to raise the siege. From this time Jeanne Darc (Joan of Arc, in English) is known by the title of the Maid of Orleans.*

In thus delivering the city of Orleans, only half of Jeanne's work was done; she was yet to crown the king at Rheims. The lazy, selfish Charles VII. had to be dragged to the place by the most urgent persuasions; but she did get him there at last and he was crowned in the old cathedral. Then she begged to be allowed to go home and to be once more a simple peasant girl. But she was too valuable to be spared, and was forced, sorely against her will, to continue in the military service.

After a while the enthusiasm in regard to her died out, especially when it was found that she did not always lead the army to victory. It was about two years after her first appearance at Orleans that her last battle was fought. The French army had been defending the town of Compiègne against the English, and after a fight outside the

---

*Or'le-ans; pronounced in three syllables, accentuating the first.

walls had hastily retreated within the gates. Among the few who did not succeed in getting in was Jeanne. It was said that the governor did this on purpose, but it may not have been so. She was taken to the Burgundian camp (for Burgundy was still in alliance with the English) and was afterward given up to the Duke of Bedford for a sum of money. As she was only a prisoner of war, and could not, in common decency, be punished for defending her country against its enemies, the cruel plan was devised of turning her over to the bishops to be dealt with as a heretic. After a year of suffering from the fiendish devices of her tormentors, she was burnt alive in the market-place of Rouen; the French bishop of Beauvais and the English Cardinal Beaufort looking on with satisfaction. "Jesus!" was the last word that passed her lips.

The miserable, selfish wretch, Charles, king of the country for which she had done all this, knew just what was going on and did not lift a finger to save her. It has been said in excuse that he had never believed in her so-called mission. Perhaps not, but he had made use of her so long as she served his purpose, and he knew that she believed in herself. As for the English—the people who had dug up Wycliffe's bones and burned them forty-five years after his death, and roasted Lord Cobham alive over a slow fire, were not likely to be much moved or shamed by the inhuman torture of a helpless French peasant.*

The affairs of the English in France did not get on well after this. The Duke of Burgundy deserted them

---

* For a full account of poor Jeanne's most interesting story, see "A Short History of France," Chapter XV.

and went back to France, his natural ally; the Duke of Bedford died, worn out with hard work at forty-five years old; and in 1453 the last English soldier, with the exception of the garrison at Calais, was driven from the soil of France.

The Hundred Years' War was at an end. Begun in injustice, continued by oppression, revived through ambition, it closed in humiliation and disgrace, leaving both countries the poorer in men and money and good feeling, and the richer in nothing but dear-bought experience.

We have followed the war in France to its completion, but must now go back some ten years to look at the affairs of England during that time. King Henry VI. had grown up to be a man; a mild-tempered, inoffensive person, completely ruled by others, and having no wish to act or think for himself. As was unavoidable in such a case, the stronger natures about him engaged in perpetual warfare for the control of affairs; and of these his uncle the Duke of Gloucester (called "the good Duke Humphrey) and Cardinal Beaufort were the principal.

In order to gain the consent of the king of France to Henry VI.'s marriage with Margaret of Anjou, the Duke of Suffolk, Henry's ambassador, offered to give up the provinces of Maine and Anjou, which the English still held in that country. Gloucester, of course, disapproved of such an unheard of arrangement, and his opposition made Margaret his enemy for life. She was a beautiful girl of fifteen, and possessed of a spirit and determination far beyond her years. She and Suffolk soon formed a close intimacy, and the ruin of Gloucester was resolved upon. He had before this time been attacked through his wife, who was accused of witchcraft. It was declared that she had in her possession a wax figure of the king, prepared with magic ceremonies, which she caused slowly to melt away before a fire; and that as it diminished the king's health and strength were decaying in like proportion. She was condemned to do penance by walking on three different days through the streets of London wrapped in a white sheet with a lighted taper in her hand, and then to be shut up in prison for life. About two years after Margaret's arrival in England the Duke of Gloucester was murdered, as was supposed, by Suffolk's orders; and the queen's minister became so unpopular that to save his life, Henry sent him out of the country. As he was crossing the water to Calais, a large ship called "Nicholas of the Tower," came in sight, hailed Suffolk's vessel, and ordered him to come on board. He was received with the ominous words, "Welcome, traitor!" and lowered into a little boat which carried an executioner, a block and a rusty sword. Here he was directed to kneel down, with the assurance that he should be fairly dealt by; and with half a dozen blows of the sword his head was cut off, after which his body was cast ashore on Dover sands.*

One more outbreak of lawless violence closes this part of our history. The common people of Kent, under a leader called Jack Cade, rose in rebellion against the wretched misgovernment which prevailed throughout the country, and in the "complaint" which they presented to the Royal Council, we notice a remarkable difference from the demands of Wat Tyler's time. There is no question now of villainage or serfage; Lollardism is not

---

* For a poetical account of these circumstances, see Shakspeare's play of "King Henry VI." Second Part, first three acts.

even mentioned; the cry is only for less wasting of the public money, for freedom of elections, and for a change of ministers. The council would not listen to the "complaint," and the rioters gained a victory over the royal forces at Sevenoaks, in Kent, after which they proceeded to London and there committed excesses enough in a month to send the whole 20,000 to the gallows if it had been worth while. Their leader, a low Irishman, took the name of Mortimer, claiming some connection with the royal family, though sometimes calling himself Jack Amend-all; he put on the clothes of a nobleman whom the rioters had killed, and paraded through London with a gilt helmet and a blue velvet gown over his armor, calling out "Mortimer is now lord of this city." His men attacked the Tower, taking from it Lord Say, the minister most disliked, who had been sent there for safety, and, after dragging him through the streets, struck off his head. Unlike the rebels under Wat Tyler, these began to plunder the city; and the government becoming thoroughly alarmed offered a reward for Cade's head, which was soon brought to them, after which the rebels dispersed.*

In 1453, the year of the abandonment of France, King Henry, who had always been weak, was seized with some strange disease which reduced his mind to total inactivity, while physically he seemed in good health. This singular state lasted for about fifteen months, when he suddenly recovered, but knew nothing that had passed in the interval. His mental condition encouraged another claimant to the crown, and for thirty years to come England

---

* There is a vivid description of this uprising in Shakspeare's Second Part of "King Henry the Sixth," Act IV.

was a scene of conflict between the rival families of York and Lancaster.

Henry VI.'s so-called reign lasted nearly forty years; about three-quarters of it is covered by the war with France; then comes Jack Cade's rebellion; and the remaining part is occupied by that great quarrel so unnecessary and so destructive, called the Wars of the Roses.

CHAPTER XXI.

THE WARS OF THE ROSES.

THE Wars of the Roses have been well called "England's great business in the fifteenth century." This being the case, in studying the history of that century, we must try to understand the state of things which led to this "business."

The three kings who came after Richard II., namely, Henry IV., Henry V., and Henry VI., were descended from John of Gaunt, Duke of Lancaster, and are therefore called Lancastrians. Now all this time, the York branch had, by the rule of primogeniture,* a better right to the throne. The Parliament, however, (and the old Witanagemot before it) had always claimed the right of deciding who should be king of England, and therefore when it set aside Edmund Mortimer, of the York line, and crowned Henry of Lancaster (Henry IV.), expected to settle the matter once for all. And there might have been a succession of Lancastrian kings to this day if all

---

* The right of the first-born to inherit.

the sovereigns had been made after the pattern of Henry IV. and Henry V. But with an incapable king and a wretchedly misgoverned nation came a temptation to the Duke of York to take matters into his own hands and claim a crown which would certainly have been his but for the decision of the Parliament.

Richard, Duke of York, was a man of mark. He was brave, able, kindly in disposition, and moderate in action. He had already filled the high post of Protector during the king's illness, and was through that favorably known to the nation at large. With the king's recovery had come new ministers, and York, bringing forward accusations of misgovernment against them, demanded reforms. Gentle King Henry VI. said, when he came to himself after his fifteen months of darkness, that "he was in charity with all the world, and so he would that all the lords were." The lords, however, were very far from being in charity with each other. The most of them were selfish, avaricious, jealous, grasping after power; the welfare of the country being the last thing that interested them. As was natural in the days when a man of high position kept in his pay bands of armed retainers, the different factions soon came to open fighting; and the first battle between the Yorkists and the Lancastrians was fought at St. Albans, May 22d, 1455.

If the Duke of York (who had gained the victory, but had as yet made no claim to the crown) could have looked forward to the events of the next thirty years, would he have assembled that body of soldiers "to protect himself against his enemies"? Such a prophetic vision would have shown him his own gory head set up over the gate of his city of York; three of his four sons dying violent deaths; eighty princes of the royal blood and almost all the ancient nobility falling on the battle-field or through revenge of the party at the moment in power, and not less than a hundred thousand men of lesser note giving up their lives in twelve pitched battles—and all for what? Surely, he would have drawn back in awe from the fearful picture, and sacrificed even what he called his rights rather than be the author of so much misery.

It was not until three years after the battle of St. Albans that the Duke of York brought forward his claim to the throne. Up to this time he had professed the utmost loyalty to King Henry. But in 1458, what the city chronicler calls "a dissimulated unity and concord" was brought about, and all the rivals went together to old St. Paul's Cathedral, where the queen and the Duke of York walked hand in hand, and the worst enemies promised to make up and be friends. The next year, however, the fighting began again.

It is not worth your while to learn the names of all the battles in this confusing war, so we will notice only the important ones. In the battle of Northampton, the Earl of Warwick, the most powerful nobleman in the kingdom, appeared on the Yorkist side. He is said to have fed 30,000 persons daily at his various castles, and is called "the king-maker" from his achievements in setting up and pulling down kings. Queen Margaret fled after the battle, but her husband was taken prisoner and conducted to London. A Parliament was called at which it was decided that King Henry should keep the crown during his life-time, and that at his death it should go to the true heir, the Duke of York. The king showed a gleam of spirit when the decision was made which left out of the question the rights of his son. "My father was king," he said; "his father also was king; I myself have worn the crown forty years from my cradle; you have all sworn fealty to me as your sovereign, and your fathers have done the like to mine. How, then, can my right be disputed?" His was perhaps the right, but the other side had surely the might, and he was obliged to submit.

There was one person who had no intention of submitting, and that was Margaret of Anjou, who raised an army of 20,000 men and defeated the duke at Wakefield, near York, He himself was killed in the action. It is said that the queen had his head cut off, crowned with a paper crown, and set on one of the gates of York. She was a woman whom success made mad. After the battle of Wakefield, she gave permission to her army to plunder the northern counties, and they availed themselves of it to the full. Churches, monasteries, and private dwellings went down before them, and Margaret's name became detested throughout the north. To the credit of the time it must be said that this was the only instance of its kind during the war.

In the second battle at St. Albans, Queen Margaret was victorious. We have now one of those strange contradictions with which these wars are filled. The Duke of York's eldest son, the Earl of March, who had taken command of the army after his father's death, went at once to London, and then, as if the battle had been a victory for him, was proclaimed king at Westminster under the title of Edward IV., the Parliament consenting, and the people filling the air with joyous acclamations, March 4th, 1461.

This date is generally considered to mark the end of Henry the Sixth's reign. He lived for ten years longer; sometimes hiding away from his enemies, sometimes imprisoned by them; always the same gentle, patient spirit, hating the bloodshed and cruelty of which he was made the central figure, but powerless to prevent them. He had never been popular with the people, who could better appreciate military talent than saintly piety, and who readily adopted as a leader the spirited young son of York. Edward IV. was now in his twentieth year.

Queen Margaret, still struggling desperately for her husband and her son, soon collected another army, and with these gave Edward battle at Towton, in Yorkshire. Edward issued orders to his soldiers to give no quarter. A whole long day and night and far into the next day did the cruel fight go on. At last the Lancastrians began to give way; their enemies followed, slaying without pity, and when the fight was over, more than thirty thousand Englishmen lay dead on English ground, killed by their own countrymen. There has been no other such battle in England, before or since.

At the next Parliament called by Edward IV., Henry and Margaret and all who adhered to them were declared traitors, and the crown settled on the family of York. The king was crowned at Westminster; his next brother, George, was made Duke of Clarence, and the youngest, Richard, Duke of Gloucester. A fourth son, the Earl of Rutland, a boy of fourteen, had been killed in cold blood after the battle of Wakefield by "the black Lord Clifford." Queen Margaret went twice to

France, to ask help from her cousin, the crafty and selfish Louis XI. He gave her fair words, but very little assistance, and she had the mortification of seeing Edward's ambassadors received with distinction. When in England she wandered about with her husband and her little son, always the same energetic woman, in prosperity or adversity. After one of her battles, she was going through a forest with her child when she was attacked by a band of robbers, who took away her money and jewels. While they were quarrelling over the division of the booty she slipped off, and was flying, faint with hunger and weariness, when she saw another robber approach, who, she supposed, belonged to the same band. The idea came to her of throwing herself upon his generosity, and going loftily up to him she said, "Here, my friend, is the son of your king. I trust him to your loyalty." The man was won by her confidence, and guided her and the boy to a place of safety.

After the battle of Hexham, Margaret became once more a fugitive, and Henry was carried a prisoner to London, led three times around the pillory on horseback with his feet tied to the stirrups, and then thrust into the Tower. At the same time, Edward sated his vengeance with the punishment of the Lancastrian nobility. Executions followed one another with frightful rapidity, and the ruin of the whole party seemed to be at hand when affairs took another turn. The great Earl of Warwick had been so long used to being the first man in the kingdom that he had forgotten that other people could have wills as well as himself, and now as the royal family were reaching an age when it was time for them to be married, he made plans for them as if he had been their guardian.

Having arranged several suitable marriages for them in his own mind, he was much offended when he found that the king had secretly married Elizabeth Woodville, the widow of a Lancastrian knight, Sir John Grey, and was loading her relations with wealth and honors. At the same time, Edward was unwise enough to show himself unfriendly toward the Earl of Warwick and his brothers; and the earl in a fit of disgust went over to Margaret's side, taking with him the Duke of Clarence, King Edward's brother.

Clarence was a most miserable creature; false, weak, dissipated, and treacherous; but he made a useful tool for Warwick's purpose. The king-maker had no son to inherit his vast estates, but he had two daughters, one of whom he married to this same Duke of Clarence, and the other to Prince Edward, son of Henry VI. and Margaret of Anjou. Clarence changed sides three or four times, and the end of it was that he and Warwick at length got up a great army, with the help of the king of France, and marched to London with the joyful cry, long unheard, "God bless King Henry!"

The hapless Henry had been a prisoner in the Tower four years when this change came in his fortunes. Those who went to bring him out to ride through the streets as king "found him nought worshipfully arrayed as a king, and nought so cleanly kept as should beseem such a prince. They had him out and new arrayed him, and did to him great reverence;" and for a while he was king again. Edward fled to Holland, so poor that he was obliged to pay for his passage with a fur-lined gown, promising to do more for the captain when he should be better off. He was soon again in England, however, and the battle of Barnet was fought; Warwick the king-maker was slain, and the poor dethroned Henry was led back to the Tower.

Margaret made one more effort. She was collecting an army, with good prospects of success, when Edward surprised her at Tewkesbury, before she could effect a junction with a large force, promised her under the Earl of Pembroke. The Lancastrians were completely defeated. Queen Margaret and her son were taken prisoners (1471). The young Edward, son of Henry of Lancaster, was brought to the Yorkist King Edward, who asked roughly how he dared to take up arms against him. The prince boldly answered that he came to recover his own and his father's inheritance. At this the king brutally struck him on the face with his iron gauntlet, and the Yorkist lords standing by,—the accounts say the king's brother Richard, Duke of Gloucester, was one of them—thrust their daggers into his heart. The unhappy mother was sent to the Tower, but she did not see her husband. The chronicler says, "That night, between eleven and twelve of the clock was King Henry put to death, the Duke of Gloucester and divers of his men being in the Tower. And on the morrow he was chested and brought to Paul's, and his face was open, that every one might see him."* Margaret of Anjou had made a brave fight, but she was conquered. She was kept for five years a prisoner in the Tower, and then her cousin Louis XI., king of France, ransomed her for 50,000 crowns, and took care

---

* "Ye towers of London, England's lasting shame,
   With many a foul and midnight murder fed,
   Revere his consort's faith, his father's fame,
   And spare the meek usurper's holy head!"—Gray.

of her for the rest of her life. In Scott's novel, "Anne of Geierstein," the unhappy woman appears again on the scene; "neither wife, mother, nor England's queen."

CHAPTER XXII.

EDWARD IV. THE LITTLE PRINCES IN THE TOWER.

THE battle of Tewkesbury ends the first part of the Wars of the Roses. The White Rose was supreme. The hunted Lancastrians fled in all directions, many of them in extreme poverty. A wounded man writes to his mother from his hiding-place to beg for some money, "for, by my troth," he says, "my leechcraft and physic and rewards to them that have kept me have cost me since Easter-day more than five pounds, and now I have neither meat, drink, clothes, leechcraft, nor money." Philip de Comines, the statesman, soldier, and historian, says that he saw the Duke of Exeter, in Flanders, barefoot and begging his bread from house to house, and that other great English lords whom he mentions were in greater misery than common beggars. Strange to say, the Wars of the Roses produced very little effect on the prosperity of England.*

---

* De Comines, the Flemish writer quoted above, whom Macaulay calls one of the most enlightened statesmen of his time, says, "England has this peculiar grace, that neither the country, nor the people nor the houses are wasted, destroyed or demolished." He says the calamities of war fall only upon the soldiers, and especially on the nobility. "In my opinion, in all the countries in Europe the government is nowhere so well managed, the people nowhere less obnoxious to violence and oppression, nor the houses less liable to the desolations of war than in England."

A traveller gives us a peep into the court-life of that day. "A great lord from Bohemia," we are told, was allowed to sit in a corner of the queen's dining-room while she ate her dinner, and gives an account of the ceremony. "The queen sat on a golden stool alone at her table, and her mother and the king's sister stood far below her. And when the queen spoke to one of those they kneeled down before her, and remained kneeling until the queen drank water. And all her ladies, and even great lords, had to kneel while she was eating, which continued three hours." One can scarcely wonder that the king escaped from such wearisome slavery as this, and indulged his own tastes elsewhere; and vicious tastes they were. There was, however, a nobler side to Edward's reign. As Edward III. a hundred years before, had been the patron of Chaucer, so Edward IV. was the patron of William Caxton. It was a happy day for England when the first printing-press was set up at Westminster by Caxton (1474). The mariner's compass, too, had now come into general use, and ships no longer needed to feel their way, as of old.

The workmen of that time were obliged to be industrious, whether they would or not. For six months in the year, from March to September, every laborer and tradesman must be at his work before five in the morning, and must not depart until between seven and eight in the evening. During this time he could have half an hour each for breakfast and dinner, and an hour for his "noon-meat." From May to August he was to have half an hour of the day-time for sleep. The law took much note of the working men. The "Statute of Apparel" forbade their wearing any clothing that cost more than two shillings "the broad yard." They could wear no furs nor scarlet cloth, and only such persons as had £20 a year might wear damask or satin or gilt girdles. Of a piece with these regulations were those relating to commerce. The Duke of Burgundy ordered that all woollen cloths wrought in England should be banished out of the lands of the said Duke; and Edward, finding that this took away the foreign market from his cloth-weavers, forbade the bringing into England of anything made within the dominions of the Duke of Burgundy. These two acts are among the earliest developments of that part of our political system which is called "protection to home industry."

King Henry VI. took great interest in learning.* He founded at Eton a school, still in existence, where boys prepare for the universities; and he planned a college at Cambridge which, if he had been able to carry out his idea, would have been one of the grandest in the world. The exquisite chapel, which, two centuries later, Sir Christopher Wren, the great architect, used to go once a

---

* An anecdote which shows the taste of the time is related by Anthony à Wood, an English antiquary who lived in the seventeenth century. During the wars of the Roses, scholarship was at so low an ebb that learned men were sometimes obliged to beg their bread from door to door. Two of these, we are told, came to the castle of a nobleman who, understanding from their credentials that they had a taste for poetry, commanded his servants to take them to a well, to put one into the one bucket and the other into the other bucket, and let them down alternately into the water, and to continue that exercise till each of them had made a couplet of verses on his bucket. After they had endured this discipline for a considerable time, to the great entertainment of the baron and his company, they made their verses, and obtained their liberty.

year to look at, was the only part finished by Henry. Queen's College, also at Cambridge, had two queens for its founders who bore no love to one another; Margaret of Anjou and Elizabeth Woodville, queen of Edward IV.

The charming art of letter-writing was cultivated most successfully during this period by the Paston family, of whom all, father, mother, sons, and daughters wrote frequent letters to one another, which, fortunately for us, have been preserved. They talk in these letters about all sorts of things, public as well as private, and some of our most important information comes from this source. In studying of times when there were no newspapers, such records are invaluable.

The twelve years of Edward's reign after the battle of Tewkesbury were, fortunately, uneventful ones. He roused himself once sufficiently to invade France, but was bought off by Louis XI. at the Treaty of Pequigny. The money for this expedition he raised by means of forced loans (never repaid), humorously called "Benevolences."

A more tragic occurrence than the French war took place at home. Edward in some way became suspicious of his brother George, the "false, fleeting, perjured Clarence," as Shakspeare calls him, and had him tried by Parliament and sentenced to death. The sentence was carried out so secretly that no particulars have ever been known. The old story that the miserable, drunken creature, being desired to choose the manner of his death, said he would be drowned in a cask of Malmsey wine, is a pure invention.

Edward IV. was just preparing for another invasion of France when he died, at forty-two years of age, worn out with dissipation. He had been king of England for twenty-two years. He was the first to reëstablish that kind of despotism which shows itself in governing by one man's will, disregarding the will of the people. It had been practised by the Normans and the early Plantagenets, but for almost two hundred years circumstances had favored an approach to government by representatives. It was two centuries later before the question was set at rest, never again to be opened.

Edward IV. left two sons, Edward V., not yet thirteen, and Richard, Duke of York, about eleven years of age. Besides these there were five daughters. At the time of his father's death, the young king Edward was in Wales with his uncle, Lord Rivers, who was called the most accomplished nobleman in England. Edward IV. had left his brother Richard, Duke of Gloucester, regent of the kingdom, and the first use Richard made of his power was to arrest Lord Rivers and the queen's son, Lord Grey, and have them thrown into prison. He then himself took charge of the young Edward and brought him to London.

The queen dreaded her brother-in-law more than anything else in the world; and when Richard, putting off Edward V.'s coronation, had himself made Protector (a title implying much more power than that of regent), she was so terrified that she took refuge in the Sanctuary at Westminster* with her daughters and her younger son. Richard obliged her to give up her son, and then secured Lord Hastings, who he found could not be bought by any bribes. He called a Council at the

---

* This Sanctuary, now pulled down, was a building near the Abbey, built especially as a place of safety for persons in danger.

Tower, at which he appeared remarkably jovial, laughing and joking with the Bishop of Ely and asking him for some of the fine strawberries in his garden. Then he went out for a few minutes and came back, apparently in a state of fury. He frowned and glowered and looked so grim that every one sat silent, wondering what dreadful news he had heard. Suddenly he turned upon Hastings, and, accusing him of impossible crimes, declared that he would not dine until the traitor's head was brought to him. Then he struck his fist furiously on the table and screamed out "Treason!" at which signal armed men rushed in and carried off the unfortunate nobleman, who was not allowed to say a word; his head was struck off on a log of wood that happened to be lying on the Tower green, and Richard went on with his dinner.

This strange scene is hard to believe, but the authority for it is unquestionable. The Bishop of Ely himself told it to Sir Thomas More, one of the most truthful of men, who has related it in his "Life of King Edward V."

At nearly the same time with the Hastings tragedy, another was enacted at Pomfret Castle, where Lord Rivers, the queen's brother, and Lord Grey, her son by her first husband, were put to death. As the persons most faithful to Edward IV.'s sons were now disposed of, Richard made arrangements for a theatrical display which he thought would be very impressive. The Duke of Buckingham, whom Richard made use of as a tool, came with the Mayor of London and a party of friends to Baynard Castle, where the Protector was living, and desired to have speech with him. Richard then appeared on a balcony, and Buckingham, standing in the street below, urged him to accept the crown, giving reasons which it is not worth while to repeat here. Richard begged that they would excuse him. He had no wish to be king, he said; he would rather see his nephew, his brother Edward's son, on the throne; but when Buckingham assured him that the people of England would never allow young Edward to reign, and that if Richard refused it would put them to the trouble of finding some one else, he at last consented, and was soon afterward crowned, with his queen, Anne of Warwick, in the midst of a splendid assemblage of people, and went off on a triumphal journey.

And where was the real king all this while? Safe lodged in the Tower with his little brother, but not in the royal apartments, where he had been placed while preparations were making for his coronation. These had been given up to the use of Richard and Anne, who went from them in state to be crowned at Westminster. It is said that the boys were removed to a dismal little bedroom in what is still called "The Bloody Tower," but nothing about it is certain. Here is the story as it has come down to us, told afterward by two of the actors in it: Richard, finding that the lieutenant of the Tower, Sir Robert Brakenbury, was not to be depended on for a murder, ordered him to give up the keys for one night to Sir James Tyrrel. Brakenbury dared not disobey, and at the dead of night Tyrrel went with two ruffians, servants of his own, named John Dighton and Miles Forrest, and stood at the foot of the winding stair-case leading to the young princes' bedchamber, while the men went up to do his bidding. They found the two boys sleeping quietly together, and being men of great size and strength, they smothered them with the bolster and pillows of their bed. They then showed the bodies to Tyrrel, who had them thrown into a pit under the stairs, and had stones heaped upon them; but when King Richard returned to London he did not approve of the place, and directed that they should be buried somewhere else in the Tower; where, the witnesses did not know.

But we know; at least we think we do. In 1674, nearly two hundred years after the murder, some workmen, in making repairs there, found a box containing the bones of two boys, apparently of the age of Edward V. and his little brother; and the king of that time, Charles II., had them buried in Westminster Abbey, where you may see their tomb to this day. A monkish chronicle of the time announces the event very simply. "And the two sons of King Edward were put to silence."

Edward V. died in his thirteenth year, and owned the name of king for thirteen weeks (1483). If you wish to see a poetical account of his death read it in Shakspeare's play of "Richard III." act 4, scene 3.

CHAPTER XXIII.

THE LAST PLANTAGENET. THE FIRST TUDOR.

THE personal appearance of Richard III. is variously described, his enemies speaking of him as monstrously deformed, and others describing him as good looking, though having one shoulder higher and thicker than the other. His portraits justify the latter description.

Richard had a bitter sorrow in the loss of his only son, who died suddenly at eleven years old. The mother died soon afterward, and the popular feeling against Richard was so strong that he was accused of poisoning his wife in order that he might marry his niece Elizabeth, Edward IV.'s oldest daughter; but this seems doubtful. It is true that in view of her probable death, and while her health was declining, he made an offer of marriage to Elizabeth, saying he was quite sure his wife would be dead by February. The proposed marriage, however, never took place. The Earl of Warwick, son of Richard's brother Clarence, not being very strong-minded, was allowed to live, carefully guarded in a gloomy castle in Yorkshire.

The Duke of Buckingham, who had helped Richard to the throne and whom he had loaded with favors, was still unsatisfied, and, when Richard delayed or refused some request, he formed, with other disaffected nobles, a conspiracy to dethrone him and give his crown to Henry, Earl of Richmond.

This nobleman was a Lancastrian, his mother being a great-granddaughter of John of Gaunt, by his third wife, Chaucer's sister-in-law. His father, Edmund Tudor, was son of Sir Owen Tudor, who married Katherine, the widow of Henry V. (That circumstance, of course, had nothing to do with his claim to be king of England; but it gave him some Welsh blood in his veins.) The first attempt did not succeed. Richmond was driven back to France by contrary winds, and Buckingham, deserted by his men, took refuge with an old servant; but being betrayed for the reward offered by Richard, he was delivered up, and beheaded without a trial.

Richard now felt that nothing could disturb his possession of the throne which had cost him so much to win. His enemies, however, were not idle. Henry Tudor's mother (still called Countess of Richmond, though she had married Lord Stanley after her first husband's death) had been indefatigable in raising men and money for him; and as Richard was celebrating the festival of Epiphany, January 6th, 1485, "in his royal robes and with his crown upon his head," he received intelligence that Richmond was about to make another invasion. He said he was glad of it, as it would give him a chance to crush all his enemies at once; but it was noticed that he gave to Nottingham Castle, where he was staying, the name of the Castle of Care. He had a man put to death for making this rather rude but harmless rhyme:

> "The Rat, the Cat, and Lovel our Dog,
> Govern all England under the Hog."

Ratcliffe, Catesby, and Lovel, (whose coat-of-arms bore a dog,) were three of Richard's chief friends; while the wild boar on his own crest stood for the hog in the couplet.

All things being ready for his enterprise, Henry Tudor crossed the sea, this time safely, and landed at Milford Haven, in Wales, from which place he marched eastward, his army increasing all the while like a rolling snowball, until he met that of Richard on the field of Bosworth in Leiscestershire.

The battle was sharp and short. Richard fought like a tiger, bitterly mortified to see in Henry's army many of the men whom he had counted among his best friends, especially the two Stanleys, one of whom, Sir William, is said to have gone over to Henry's side after the battle began. Fighting furiously, he was cut down with many wounds and trampled under foot by the horses. His crown, which he seems to have been very fond of and to have carried with him into the battle, was found under a hawthorn-bush; Sir William Stanley picked it up and placed it on the Earl of Richmond's head, crying out, "Long live King Henry the Seventh."

That night, in the course of burying the dead, a small, bloody corpse was thrown carelessly across a horse, "like a calf or a hog," the chronicle says, "the arms and head dangling on one side, the legs on the other,"—all its fine clothing gone and the red wounds scarcely to be distinguished for the mire that covered them—and buried in the church of the Gray Friars, at Leicester. Henry VII. had a monument placed over the remains, but monument and church were alike swept away in the wholesale destruction of the monasteries by his son, Henry VIII.

Comparatively few persons lost their lives in this closing struggle of the Wars of the Roses. It is because Bosworth Field forms a dividing line between the old and the new order of things that it is counted among the most noteworthy battles of English history. With the last Plantagenet died out the ascendency of the feudal nobility in England. The Tudor monarchs, from Henry VII. to Elizabeth, loved peace and loved money. Glory, unless it was very easy to come by, they did not covet, and they generally limited their warlike operations to defending themselves when they were attacked. The reign of violence was passing away; the reign of thrift was coming in its stead.

Richard III., arbitrary though he was, made some

wise laws, and if he had come innocently to his throne he might have ranked among England's benefactors. One of his statutes declares that "There shall be no hindrance to any artificer or merchant stranger, of what nation or country he be, for bringing into this realm or selling by retail or otherwise, any manner of books, written or imprinted." His parliaments were the first to make laws in the English language, all previous legislation, since the time of William the Conqueror, having been in Norman French. Richard was the first to appoint a foreign consul, and the first to employ couriers for other than military purposes. In a time of peace and with a longer reign, the country would have taken many forward steps under his government. He was only thirty-two years old at the time of his death.

No period of England's history, from the time of Chaucer to the present moment, has been so barren of literary production as the fifteenth century. The few poets who wrote anything worth mentioning were all Scottish, the captive king, James I., standing at their head. The learned Sir John Fortescue wrote a book in praise of British laws, and Reginald Pecock attacked the Pope's infallibility; William Caxton translated many books, and Sir Thomas Malory made up from the old chronicles a book which he called "The Morte d'Arthur;" but literature, properly so called, was absent from the industries of England during this troubled time. The two most accomplished men in the country, the Earls of Rivers and Worcester, fell under the axe by Richard's orders, and in the times when it was uncertain how long a man's head would remain on his shoulders, it became of less consequence that it should be filled with learning.

A further step was made toward personal freedom in Richard's time by his freeing all the "villains" still remaining in bondage on the royal domains. The Wars of the Roses had practically put an end to serfdom, however, before this time. Some of the great families freed their serfs themselves, in order that they might fight the more willingly; and some families were so diminished by war that there was no one left to take account of the the villians, who thus became their own masters. It is strange, after all this bloodshed, to see how little feeling of bitterness remained on either side. The people did not even form two political parties; and when the Lancastrian Henry Tudor married the oldest daughter of the Yorkist Edward IV., the old feud seemed to be disposed of. Gray makes his bard say:

"Above, below, the Rose of Snow
Twined with her blushing foe we spread;"

and a chronicler of the times says that by the hand of the Archbishop of Canterbury "was first tied together the sweet posy of the red and white roses."

Henry's tranquility did not last long. A priest at Oxford, named Simons, declared that a pupil of his, a baker's son, whose real name was Lambert Simnel, was no other than the young Earl of Warwick, who was reported to have escaped from the Tower. The boy was instructed in his part by Simons, and by him taken to Ireland, where he was joyfully received, and was crowned in Dublin. The Earl of Lincoln, a member of the royal family, took his part and raised an army for him; the Duchess of Burgundy (sister of Edward IV.), sent over a body of men under Martin Schwartz, and these joining Lincoln a battle was fought at Stoke in which the rebels were defeated.* The real Earl of Warwick was brought out of the Tower and exhibited, and Simons, who confessed his imposture, was thrown into prison, where he soon died. Simnel was made a scullion in the king's kitchen, in which honorable position he washed dishes and waited on the servants until he was promoted to the office of king's falconer.† (1487.)

Five years later another imposture was attempted. Perkin Warbeck, a young Fleming‡ of engaging manners and good education, was instructed to personate the Duke of York, the younger of Edward IV.'s sons, under the pretext that this prince had escaped the fate which overtook his brother. Perkin presented himself before the Duchess of Burgundy, who gazed long and earnestly into his face, and then with a burst of joy and affection embraced him as her long-lost nephew. As she is supposed to have instigated the plot, her surprise must have been overwhelming. She called him "The White Rose of England," and supplied him liberally with money. The Irish were shy of him, remembering Lambert Simnel,

---

* Lincoln and Schwartz died on the battle-field, but a curious story is told of Lord Lovel, one of the confederates. He disappeared at the time of the battle and was never seen or heard of again. Just two hundred years afterward, at his country-house of Minster Lovel in Oxfordshire, an underground chamber was discovered, in which was found the skeleton of a man seated in a chair, with his head leaning on a table. It is supposed that Lovel took refuge in this chamber, and, not being able to get out, was starved to death through neglect of his attendants.

† One who takes care of the hawks, which in those days were trained to pursue on the wing and kill other birds, as sport for their masters.

‡ Native of Flanders.

but the king of Scotland took up his cause and married him to Lady Catherine Gordon, daughter of the Earl of Huntly.

Perkin did not show the traditional bravery of the House of York. He raised an army in Cornwall, but on hearing of the approach of the king's troops, deserted his own and took refuge in a sanctuary, leaving his followers to their fate. He was persuaded to give himself up, and, after some attempts to escape, was finally shut up in the Tower. Here he formed with the Earl of Warwick, who had been for fourteen years a prisoner, a plan of escape; and Henry, seizing the opportunity, had Perkin hanged at Tyburn, while the earl, as a death suited to his royal birth, was beheaded on Tower Hill (1499). He was the last descendant, in the direct male line, of the noble house of Plantagenet, which had given kings to England for more than three hundred years (1154–1485).

We have now come to the closing year of the great fifteenth century; that one which had seen printing and gunpowder made as common as the monk's quill and the man-at-arms' pike were in former times; had seen the mariner's compass open a way across the ocean, and America given to the world by Columbus; had seen Vasco da Gama accomplish the long-desired discovery of a route to India around the Cape of Good Hope; had seen the Moors driven out of Spain by Ferdinand and Isabella, and the Turks enter Europe through the gate of Constantinople; had seen France and Spain take the form of consolidated monarchies instead of groups of quarreling provinces; and had seen the power of the old feudal nobility in England broken down and its warlike barons become the obedient subjects of a monarch. The knight in heavy armor was gone; he no longer called to his aid a troop of stout bowmen and with them rose in arms for or against the king. A statute of Edward IV. had ordered the disbanding of all armed retainers, and Henry VII. took care that its provisions should be carried out.*

CHAPTER XXIV.

THE SIXTEENTH CENTURY. HENRY VIII.

IT has been said of Henry VII. that he had two ruling passions, avarice and hatred of the House of York. The latter extended, apparently, even to his queen, whose coronation he deferred until compelled to it by the murmurs of the people. When it was performed, he said she should have all the glory of the occasion, so he remained in a closely latticed box between the altar and the pulpit in Westminster Abbey, and watched the ceremony from that place.

---

* Lord Bacon, who wrote the life of Henry VII. gives an instance of this. The king had been making a visit to the Earl of Oxford (to whom he was under the greatest obligations for services rendered in time of need) and was entertained in a truly princely manner. When he was leaving the castle two long lines of liveried soldiers were drawn up, making a lane for him to pass through. "These are surely your menial servants, my lord?" said the king. "May it please your grace," replied the earl, "that were not for mine ease. They are most of them my retainers, that are come to do me service, but chiefly to see your grace." "I thank you for your good cheer, my lord," said Henry, "but I may not endure to have my laws broken in my sight. My attorney must speak with you." And he spoke to such good purpose that the earl was glad to get off for a fine of 15,000 marks (about $50,000).

Henry's expedients for getting money were as ingenious as their success was complete. He knew he had only to announce a war with Scotland or France to open the purses of his subjects; and having thus obtained vast sums of money for this purpose, he would make the other party pay roundly for a peace, "thus getting gain from both his enemies and his friends." A device of his favorite minister, Cardinal Morton (in Richard's time Bishop of Ely), was to demand "benevolences" from two classes of persons; from those who lived handsomely and spent a great deal of money, because their wealth was apparent; and from those who lived poorly and plainly, because their economy must have made them rich. This was jokingly called "Morton's fork," on one prong or other of which every one must be impaled. But by far the greater part of this wealth came from the people who were "ground in Empson and Dudley's mills." Richard Empson and Edmund Dudley were two judges who made it their business to search out old and forgotten laws, and then, by means of spies and informers, to find out rich men who had broken these laws, throw them into prison without a trial, and keep them there until they paid a heavy fine.

Henry made his younger son Warden of the Scottish Marches and Lieutenant of Ireland when he was only two years of age; too young, one would think, to earn the salary attached to these offices. Such practices, and many more, kept his coffers always full; and he seldom parted with his money except from necessity or for some personal gratification. The queen seems to have been very economical, so that she might have the more to give away. She made handsome allowances to her three married sisters, in order that they should not be dependent upon their husbands, while she herself wore gowns that were "mended, turned, and new-bodied." When the gowns were frayed out around the bottom she had them hemmed up, paying the tailor twopence for each job. Her shoes cost only twelve pence a pair, and had tin buckles instead of silver ones; but when poor people "brought her presents of early peas, chickens, strawberries or roses," they were always liberally rewarded.

Henry VII.'s oldest son, Prince Arthur, was married at sixteen to Catherine of Aragon, the youngest daughter of Ferdinand and Isabella, who brought a rich dowry with her from Spain; his oldest daughter, Margaret, was married when still younger to James IV., king of Scotland. Prince Arthur lived only a few months after his marriage; but the thrifty Henry had no idea of sending back the young widow and her dowry, so he proposed to the bride's father that she should marry his second son, Henry, who was seven years younger than herself. After great objections on the part of Ferdinand, this plan was at length agreed to; and as Prince Henry was only eleven years old, the marriage was to be deferred for some years, the lady and the dowry remaining in England.

When Henry was about to die, he did some generous things with the money which he could no longer use, and he granted pardons to some criminals. Having thus made his peace with Heaven, he died in the twenty-fourth year of his reign and the fifty-fourth of his age (1509). He left two architectural monuments behind him; one a costly palace at Richmond, which has not much interest for us now, and the other the beautiful chapel at Westminster Abbey, still called by his name.

England had never been so prosperous as under Henry the Seventh. His extortions, outrageous as they were, affected chiefly the rich and not the main body of the people. Commerce and manufactures flourished, and the king had a share in the discovery of America by fitting out the ship in which John and Sebastian Cabot explored the coast of Labrador (1498). If this expedition did not bring in immediate returns, it at least furnished England with her ground for claiming, a century later, the whole Atlantic coast.

Henry VII. did not reward his explorers very sumptuously, as we learn from his carefully-kept accounts, where there is an entry of ten shillings to be paid to the discoverer of "the new isle" (Newfoundland), and another of five shillings to the same person. He came near having the honor of being the patron of Columbus, but the brother whom the great Genoese sent to ask aid from England was taken by pirates, and before he recovered his liberty, Queen Isabella had befriended Columbus, earned the gratitude of the world,

"And built herself an everlasting name."

Among Henry's few spendings for public purposes was the building of a huge war-ship, called the "Great Harry," which when finished was so clumsy that it could not be used, but which is considered the foundation of the present English navy.

The Dutch scholar, Erasmus, who lived in England during Henry VII.'s time, and who came from a clean country, was shocked at the condition of English houses, even of the better sort. "The floors," he says, "are mostly of clay, and strewn with rushes. Fresh rushes are periodically laid over them, but the old ones remain as a foundation for perhaps twenty years together." The condition of the lower layers under these circumstances we will leave to the imagination.

Erasmus had good reason to remember the English custom-houses, for when he sailed from Dover to return to his own country, the king's officers took away all his money except six angels, the largest amount any one was allowed to carry out of England. All sums obtained in this way went, of course, directly into the king's pocket.

Henry VIII. came to the throne (1509) with the fairest prospects that ever opened before an English king. The rival lines of York and Lancaster were united in him, so that strife on that ground was impossible; the country was at peace with all the world, and the treasury was full. He himself, now eighteen years old, was handsome, strong, skilful in all manly exercises, and full of hope and high spirits. He was as lavish in spending money as his father had been eager in gathering it together; and the great hoard left by Henry VII. was soon used up in court gayeties. Henry now married the Princess Katherine of Aragon, his brother's widow, to whom he had been betrothed for seven years.

The first public act of his reign was one of the grossest injustice. Popular clamor demanded the punishment of Henry VII.'s two judges, Empson and Dudley; but as they had acted only under the king's orders, and kept strictly within the letter of the law, it was hard to know of what to accuse them. Finally a charge was trumped up against them of having conspired to take the young king prisoner and form a new government. Nothing could be more absurd; but the accusation was made, and they were both beheaded, though none of the ill-gotten wealth procured by their means was ever given back.

The first excitement from outside the kingdom came from a war with France. Rome, Spain, and Venice had formed what they called a "Holy League," against France, though its only holiness was the name of the pope; and Henry's astute father-in-law, Ferdinand the Catholic, made a cat's-paw of him to further his own ends. Henry soon invaded France on his own account, the Emperor Maxmilian of Germany serving under him for pay like an ordinary soldier. There was a battle fought at Guinegate, near Calais (1513), called "The Battle of the Spurs,"* because the French used their spurs so freely in running away. Henry took the towns of Terouenne and Tournay, but went home again without following up his victory.

Before he reached England an event had occurred in his own country which has been made forever famous by the pen of the great magician, Walter Scott, in "Marmion." This was the battle of Flodden Field, where Henry's brother-in-law, James IV. of Scotland, lost his life (1513). King James had made an alliance with France, and invaded England with the whole strength of his army, including the flower of his nobility. After an obstinate battle the Scots were defeated.

> "Their king, their lords, their mightiest low,
> They melted from the field as snow,
> When streams are swollen and south winds blow,
> Dissolves in silent dew."

---

* Sometimes called "The Second Battle of the Spurs," the first having taken place at Courtrai, in Flanders (1302), where the knights' gilt spurs were picked up by the bushel and hung as trophies in the great church.

Peace with Scotland and France soon followed, and Henry cemented it by marrying his youngest sister, Mary, a girl of sixteen, to Louis XII. of France, who was fifty-two years old and in very feeble health. The Princess was already betrothed to Charles Brandon, Duke of Suffolk, one of the most gallant of English knights, but this made no difference to Henry. His self-will always overruled every consideration, whether of sympathy, honor or truth; and she was forced to submit. In less than three months her husband died, and not long afterward she married Brandon in Paris, with the consent of the new king, Francis I. Henry professed to be very angry at this, but the money and jewels which his sister brought back from France soon reconciled him to the match.

With all King Henry's obstinacy and self-will, he was gradually falling under the influence of a man stronger-minded than himself, who was destined to shape his course of conduct for many years. This was Thomas Wolsey, one of the most remarkable men of his age or of any age, who had risen from a very humble station, (it is said that he was the son of a butcher at Ipswich,) to be Bishop of Lincoln and Archbishop of York, and finally to receive a cardinal's hat from the pope. He was a man of extensive learning and varied accomplishments, and in addition to wit and gayety and most agreeable manners, possessed a talent for statesmanship which soon made him, unconsciously to the king, his director in all public affairs. Henry made him Chancellor, and Wolsey followed the practice of the age in living in the utmost splendor and luxury. Henry loaded him with offices that brought him both honor and profit, but the Cardinal's grasping nature was never satisfied, and he contrived constantly to add to his immense fortune. As chancellor, his administration was strict and impartial; in private life his character was blameless; but avarice and ambition obscured his better qualities and prepared for him a miserable end.

In 1519, the Emperor Maximilian died, and the empire, being elective, became a tempting prize to the one who could secure it. The choice fell upon Charles I. of Spain, grandson of Maximilian and also of Ferdinand the Catholic, in opposition to Francis I. of France, who ardently desired to be emperor. The successful candidate is known thenceforth in history as the Emperor Charles V.

Francis was very angry at his defeat, and both he and Charles courted the favor of Henry VIII. Their methods were as different as their characters; Francis got up the superb tournament called "The Field of the Cloth of Gold;" Charles secretly bribed Wolsey to take his part by promising to use his influence to have him made pope. In the end, Charles prevailed; but the tournament, which was arranged under the direction of Wolsey, was the most splendid entertainment at which the courtiers of either nation ever wasted their money. It lasted eighteen days, and more was squandered on it, as was said by those who remembered the economical days of Henry VII. and Louis XII. than either of those wise monarchs would have spent in a year. The wooden palace, built to lodge the king of England and his suite, extended round a square court, each side of which was over three thousand feet in length. The cardinal had a splendid train of retainers, and each English gentleman took as many followers with him as his purse could provide with gorgeous equipments. Nearly three thousand tents, most of them covered with silk or cloth of gold, were erected on the plain adjoining the principal buildings, and many a man "sold his land to buy his horse"; that is, ruined himself that he might present a fitting appearance at the festival. "Many of the nobles," says an eye-witness of the glittering scene, "carried their castles, woods, and farms on their backs." Francis, who was the host on this occasion, was not behindhand with his hospitality. Sumptuous feasts were provided; fountains ran wine; and thousands of persons who came to see the show were fed at the king's expense: "Insomuch," says the historian Hall, who was present, "that there were vagabonds, plowmen, waggoners, and beggars that for drunkenness lay in routs and heaps." The negotiations carried on during the tournament came to nothing, and after Henry's return to England the royal rivals never met again.

CHAPTER XXV.

HENRY THE TYRANT; ALSO "DEFENDER OF THE FAITH."

HENRY VIII. had not yet begun to show his darkest side to his people; they knew him to be extravagant and wilful, but the cruel jealousy which can only be satisfied with blood, he was yet to exhibit.

Edward Stafford, Duke of Buckingham, was a distant relation of the king. His father was beheaded by Richard III. for treason, and the heads of three generations of his family before that had been killed in the Wars of the Roses; and now that York and Lancaster were one, it seemed as if the fifth in descent might live out his life peaceably. But taking advantage of an unguarded expression of Buckingham's to the effect that he would be the next in the line of succession if the king should die without children, Henry ordered him to be executed on as false a charge of treason as ever sent a subject to the block.

The old question of religion now came up again. A German monk named Martin Luther had taken up the work which John Wycliffe left unfinished a hundred and fifty years before, and boldly attacked some of the principles and practices of the Roman Church, especially the sale of indulgences, or remissions of penalties for sins committed. Tetzel, an agent of Pope Leo X., was then hawking these indulgences about, in order to supply Leo with money for building the Church of St. Peter at Rome, and Luther thundered forth denunciations of the unchristian practice. Henry had been brought up a good Catholic, and Luther's utterances seemed to him monstrous. In his zeal he wrote a book against these heretical doctrines, for which the pope gave him the name of "Defender of the Faith." In Latin (the language then used by the governments of Europe in their communications with one another) the words are "Fidei Defensor;" and as all English sovereigns have inherited the title from Henry VIII. you may still read them on some of the coins of Queen Victoria (Fid. Def.).

After the death of Leo X., two successive popes had been elected without a voice being raised in Wolsey's favor. He thought that the emperor (Charles V.) was treating him very badly, and induced Henry to break off his alliance with him and take up the cause of Francis I. who had just been taken prisoner by Charles at the battle of Pavia. Henry readily consented, but turned the matter to his own advantage by demanding an enormous present payment in money from France, and a yearly pension during his life. When Francis was released, he and Henry joined together to liberate the pope, who was also a prisoner, Rome having been taken and sacked by the brutal soldiery of Charles V. These matters being settled, Henry was at liberty to look after his own affairs.

He had now been married to Katherine of Aragon for eighteen years. All their sons had died, and only one child remained, the Princess Mary. Outwardly, Henry was as loving as ever, but he had for a long time been secretly turning over in his mind the possibility of getting rid of his wife. He professed to feel doubts as to whether his marriage with her had been lawful, as she was his brother's widow; but Pope Julius II. had given permission for the marriage, and in those days that was enough to decide any question. Henry, however, had a young lady in his mind, Anne Boleyn, one of the queen's maids of honor, whom he wished to put in Katherine's place, and his scruples became stronger and his conscience more tender than ever. He applied to the pope, Clement VII., for a divorce, and the latter, not wishing to offend him, gave him promise of a favorable answer, but managed to put off the matter, in various ways, for several years. He first sent Cardinal Campeggio to look into it, in connection with Cardinal Wolsey, The two legates (as the pope's ambassadors are called) opened a court for hearing the case. The king answered promptly to his name; the queen refused to appear, and the two cardinals talked about it and about it until finally the pope broke up the court and said the king and queen must come to Rome and have the case tried there.*

Henry was enraged beyond measure at this insult, and was trying to make up his mind what he should do next, when Dr. Thomas Cranmer, of Cambridge, suggested that it would be a good plan to send to the great universities of Europe and ask their opinion on the question, "Is it lawful for a man to marry his brother's widow?" Henry was delighted with this proposal, and sent at once for Cranmer, whom he had never seen; and finding that the doctor was going to be a useful instrument in carrying out his projects, instantly took him into his service and loaded him with favors.

As Cranmer's influence rose, Wolsey's declined. He had not, the king thought, shown himself zealous enough in the matter of the divorce, and he had not pointed out a way to end the difficulty, as Cranmer had; and the friend and counsellor of twenty years was thrown over in a moment. He was banished from the court, and the Great Seal (which denoted his office as Chancellor) was taken away from him; while Anne Boleyn, who hated him because he did not approve of the king's marrying her, made Henry promise never to see Wolsey again. The cardinal was accused, by the king's orders, of treason, because he had held a court in England as legate from the pope, which was against English law;

---

* For an account of the trial in London, which follows history very closely, see Shakspeare's "Henry VIII." Act II. scene IV. Also the scene following, for the queen's interview with the cardinals.

though Henry himself had commanded it, under his own hand and seal, and appeared before it as a suitor. All the cardinal's houses, lands and goods were declared forfeited, and his life was granted only by the king's mercy. His enormous wealth, amounting in value to several millions of dollars, was swept at once into Henry's coffers; his palaces of Hampton Court and York House (now Whitehall) were confiscated, and he was sentenced to retire to his Archbishopric of York, a disgraced and banished man. His spirit was utterly broken. The French ambassador wrote of him: "His face has shrunken to half its natural size, and his misery is so great that even his enemies can not help pitying him." In his retirement he appeared dignified and composed, and won all hearts by his kindness and generosity. But Anne Boleyn's spite was not yet gratified, and within a year Wolsey was summoned to London on a charge of treason. Fortunately, he did not live to get there, and Henry was spared the last disgrace of bringing his head to the block. The cardinal was taken sick on his way to London, and died at Leicester Abbey (1530). His last recorded words were, "If I had served God as diligently as I have served the king, He would not have given me over in my gray hairs." He had lived a selfish and grasping life, and the consciousness of it came to him too late.

Among Wolsey's good deeds was the founding of a college at Oxford. Each of the great universities of England consists of many colleges, which have been added at different times as there seemed to be a necessity for them. Wolsey's was called Cardinal's College, and was unfinished at the time of his disgrace. The king immediately seized it, but afterward allowed it to be completed with funds which the Cardinal had set aside for that purpose, and changed the name of it to Christ Church College.

Henry married Anne Boleyn privately, without waiting for the divorce that was so slow in coming. After the answers arrived from the universities to which he had appealed, and which were generally favorable to his wishes, he had a divorce pronounced by Cranmer, whom he had made Archbishop of Canterbury when a vacancy occurred. This measure was followed by a series of acts passed by a Parliament called for the purpose, freeing England from the dominion of the pope. The king was declared to be the supreme Head of the Church in England, and all persons were forbidden to pay tribute to the pope or in any way acknowledge his authority, under penalty of a charge of high-treason. Sir Thomas More, a learned, wise and excellent man who had been made Chancellor in Wolsey's place, gave up the Great Seal rather than to countenance what he considered an act of iniquity.* For refusing to take the oath acknowledging the king's supremacy and declaring his marriage with Katherine to be unlawful, Sir Thomas More and John Fisher, Bishop of Rochester, were sent to the Tower. After an imprisonment of more than a year, and a most unfair trial, they were both beheaded (1535). Fisher

---

* Sir Thomas More was the greatest author of his time. He wrote a book called "Utopia," which was really a keen satire on the existing government of England, but a satire so delicately conveyed that it gave no offence even to the jealous king. More's ideas on the social system and the labor question were hundreds of years in advance of his age.

might possibly have escaped, but the pope, just at this time, imprudently proposed to make him a cardinal. "The pope may send him a cardinal's hat," said Henry, "but he shall have no head to wear it on;" and soon after the honor was conferred upon him, the king made good his word by ordering him to the block.

Paul III. had still in his hands the old weapon of excommunication, which he had used with such effect in the time of Henry II. and his son King John, and he soon hurled it forth against Henry VIII. But all it could do was to increase Henry's rage against Rome, and in order to deal a last blow, he began breaking up the monasteries, beginning with the smaller ones. The excuse for this was the evil life led by many of the monks, and the exactions of the church, which ate away the substance of the poor. The abolition of the monasteries caused great distress among the idlers who had been fed at their doors, and among the peasants who had been used to pasturing their cattle on the commons belonging to them; and the discontent arising from these causes brought on a rebellion called, "The Pilgrimage of Grace," which was suppressed by the Duke of Norfolk, the same who, as Earl of Surrey, had gained the battle of Flodden.* After this, such monasteries as were not voluntary given up were taken by force, their immense

---

* The king wrote to him, "You shall in any wise cause such dreadful execution to be done upon a good number of the inhabitants of every town, village and hamlet that has offended, as well by the hanging of them up in trees as by the quartering of them and the setting of their heads and quarters in every town, as they may be a fearful spectacle to all hereafter as would practise any like matter."

revenues falling into the king's hands, and their houses and lands being given to his favorite courtiers or absorbed into his private possessions. A special spite was shown in regard to the tomb of St. Thomas à Becket at Canterbury. As he was considered to be the arch-offender in upholding the supremacy of the Church, his name was struck from the calendar of saints, his shrine was torn down, the rich gifts of four hundred years being seized by the king; the coffin was emptied of its contents and the bones were dispersed to the winds.

Henry's chief agent in the destruction of the monasteries was Thomas Cromwell, a man of immense ability, who is credited with having first suggested to the king the doctrine of his own supremacy in matters of religion. Cromwell had been the private secretary of Cardinal Wolsey until the fall of that minister, and under his pitiless rule blood flowed like water whenever the slightest opposition seemed to threaten the king's absolute dominion. One of the strangest things about Henry's reign is the fact that no matter how outrageous were his assumptions, he always found Parliaments ready to do his will. At one time, when he had borrowed large sums of money from his subjects, for the repayment of which he had given bonds and other securities, the Parliament generously annulled all his obligations, and his unfortunate creditors could only "pocket the loss." So long did what Shakspeare calls "the divinity that doth hedge a king," impose upon the most intelligent nation in Europe!

CHAPTER XXVI.

HENRY'S WIVES. THE ENGLISH BIBLE. EDWARD VI.

WE must now go back several years to take up some details of Henry's private life which have a bearing on history. Queen Katherine had died in her house at Kimbolton, and Queen Anne had given birth to a princess named Elizabeth, after the king's mother. But Henry, who grew more fickle and capricious every year, had seen among Anne's maids of honor a young lady named Jane Seymour, who attracted his admiration, and from that moment his only thought was how he might get rid of Anne, as he had done of Katherine. Charges of misconduct were brought against her, and witnesses procured to swear to them (an easy matter) so the pretty young queen was beheaded on Tower Hill. "My neck is but a little one," she said; "it will not give the executioner much trouble." Henry now called a Parliament (for the one which made laws against the pope had been dismissed after sitting seven years) and made them say that the princesses Mary and Elizabeth could not lawfully be queens of England; so when a little son was born to Queen Jane he was very much delighted.

Nothing can be more erroneous than to call Henry the Eighth the author of the English Reformation. He was the enemy of the pope, and through his means some reforms were effected in the practices of the Church of Rome in England; but the belief which finally settled down into English Protestantism was the belief, not of Henry the Eighth, but of Luther.

Neither must it be supposed that because Henry VIII. quarrelled with the pope and plundered the monasteries, he was a convert to the Protestant doctrine. On the contrary, he caused a law to be passed by Parliament that all persons who did not believe in six articles of faith set forth by himself, and which contain the substance of the Roman Catholic belief, should suffer the penalties of heresy. The "six articles" went by the name of "The Whip with Six Strings;" but it was more terrible than a whip. It meant burning at the stake for those who refused to subscribe to the doctrines. These were, Transubstantiation;* that the laity should partake only of bread and not of wine at the Holy Communion; that private masses ought to be said for the dead; that confession to priests was necessary; and two others which forbade the marriage of priests and nuns.

So the burnings, hangings, rackings,† torturings, went on; all who believed in the Reformed religion were liable to them, and all faithful Catholics who questioned the king's supremacy were in danger of losing their heads. Among the former class of victims was Anne Ascue, a young lady belonging to the court, whose fate excited much sympathy. She was burned alive, after being first inhumanly racked. Of the other class, a shameful instance was that of Margaret, Countess of Salisbury, sister to the young Earl of Warwick who was beheaded by Henry VII., and daughter of Clarence, Edward IV.'s brother. Her son, Cardinal Pole, was in Rome with the pope, and from there wrote very hard

---

*The change of the substance of the bread and wine into the actual body and blood of Christ.

†A horrible kind of torture.

things against King Henry; and as the latter could not get hold of the cardinal, (though he invited him to come to England and discuss the matter!) he seized his mother and brother, and as many others of the family as he could lay hold of, and had them killed for corresponding with him. The countess was the hardest to deal with. She refused to lay her head on the block at the executioner's bidding; that was for traitors, she said, and she was no traitor; she moved it swiftly from side to side, this woman in her eightieth year, and finally, with two men holding it down by force, the axe after many blows severed it from her body. She was nearly related to the king.

Queen Jane Seymour died soon after her son's birth, and Henry began to look out for another wife. A certain Duchess of Milan, who was approached on the subject, said that if she had two heads, one should be at his majesty's service; but that having only one, she preferred to keep it. Finally Cromwell picked out a Protestant princess, Anne of Cleves, whose picture by the famous painter, Holbein, pleased the king. But when the lady herself came, Henry found her plain-looking and stupid. She knew not a word of any language but German, which he did not speak; and she had no accomplishments. So she was soon divorced, on some shabby pretext, and the king's wrath fell on Cromwell. The unfortunate minister, whose only fault had been untiring devotion to the king's wishes and interests, was accused of treason and beheaded. Anne of Cleves was comfortably pensioned off, and lived in England until her death, surviving her inconstant husband ten years.

Henry next married Katherine Howard, a relative of

the Duke of Norfolk. She was really a bad woman and there was little difficulty in getting her head cut off soon after her marriage. His sixth wife was Katherine Parr, widow of Lord Latimer, who conducted herself so discreetly, and proved such a good nurse to the miserable diseased monster that she outlasted the king himself.

A war with Scotland is the only foreign event of importance during the remainder of this reign. James V., son of Henry's sister Margaret, had married a Catholic wife, and was much influenced by her family, the Guises, a set of powerful French nobles. This made Henry dislike him, and border warfare had been going on for some time between the two countries, when the Scottish king suddenly sent an army into England, which was defeated at the battle of Solway Moss. James, a low-spirited and timid person, took to his bed on hearing of the disaster; and being told that he was the father of a little daughter, sighed out, "The crown came with a lass and it will go with one."* He died five days afterward, and Henry at once began negotiations for marrying the infant Princess Mary to his son Edward. This being refused, an aimless war was carried on with Scotland and France for about three years, when, after an enormous waste of money and very little fighting, both sides were ready for peace.

Several translations of the Bible were made in Henry VIII.'s reign. William Tyndale published at Antwerp (1526) an English version of the New Testament, and Miles Coverdale made the first translation of the entire

---

* David Bruce, son of Robert I., had no sons. His daughter Marjory married Walter Stuart, and thus became the ancestress of the Stuart kings of Scotland.

Bible (1535). Four years later, a copy of Cranmer's or "The Great Bible" was, by the king's order, placed in every parish church in England.* A part of the church service was also translated by Cranmer from Latin into English, thus helping to establish a truly national church.

Nothing needs to be added to a record of the deeds of Henry the Eighth. Tyrant and murderer, the slave of his passions, the capricious ruler of the destinies of others, our disgust overpowers every other feeling in thinking of him. Yet even this wretch has found apologists; and there are historians who dwell on his energy, his courage, and his vigor of mind; but when these are applied to hateful purposes they lose their lustre in our eyes. It has often been a matter of wonder why, in spite of his monstrous tyranny, he should have been popular with the great mass of the people. With them he was "Bluff King Hal" to the last. In the first place, it was hard to shake their idea of the sacredness of the crown; and then, his cruelties fell almost entirely upon the higher classes. If the poorer ones opposed his will, as in the "Pilgrimage of Grace," they too felt the weight of his hand; but it seldom happened that his interests and theirs were brought into direct collision.

Henry has been called a patron of learning. He founded Trinity College in Cambridge, and encouraged the "New Learning" as the study of Greek was called, though the credit of that belonged more to Cardinal Wolsey and to some eminent men in the universities themselves. The greatest author of the age, Sir Thomas More, was sent to the block for being a good Catholic;

---

* It is from this Bible that the version of the Psalms in the present English Book of Common Prayer is taken.

the finest poet, Lord Surrey, met the same fate because he was a distant relative of the king's, and Sir Thomas Wyatt, also a poet, came very near having his head cut off on the charge of having been a lover of Anne Boleyn's. These three were the most famous writers of Henry's time. John Heywood wrote dramatic pieces of small value, of a kind called "Interludes," and the historians, Fabyan and Hall, added their chronicles to the growing mass of English annals.

Henry died after a reign of 38 years (1547) in the fifty-sixth year of his age.

Edward VI., son of Henry VIII. and Jane Seymour, was ten years old at the time of his father's death. Lord Hertford, the young king's uncle and brother of Lady Jane, was made Protector with the assistance of a council. The new council was composed mostly of Protestants, and as the young king had been brought up in the same belief, the reformed religion was established at once. The law requiring adherence to the Six Articles was repealed, together with all those directed against what was still called "Lollardy," and the Book of Common Prayer was completed by Cranmer and made the established service of the Church. An act was passed allowing the marriage of the clergy, while another repealed the statutes against heresy; and though the English mind had not yet arrived at the great doctrine of toleration in religious matters, the blood penalty for wrong believing fell for a time into disuse.

The change of religion was not accomplished without some disturbance. In several parts of England the people rose in rebellion, demanding the restoration of the mass, and other religious observances to which they had been accustomed; but these were soon put down, and all acquiesced, outwardly at least, in the new forms of worship.

Determined to carry out Henry's intentions of uniting the kingdoms of Scotland and England by marriage, the Protector (now created Duke of Somerset) led an army into Scotland and defeated the Scots at the battle of Pinkie. He did not, however, secure the young queen, who was soon afterward betrothed to the Dauphin of France.

Somerset hurried back from Scotland at the news that his brother, Lord Seymour (who had married Henry VIII.'s widow, Katherine Parr), was forming a party against him. He succeeded in making the Parliament pass a bill of attainder * against Seymour, and the latter was beheaded. In a few years, Somerset himself suffered the same fate. It was not difficult in those times of an irregular and uncertain hold upon power, to find charges against almost any man who conducted public affairs, and Somerset had undoubtedly been arbitrary, taking more upon himself than if he had been indeed a king.

John Dudley, Earl of Warwick (son of Henry VII.'s minister), who had been made Duke of Northumberland, now saw his way clear to succeed to the Protector's power, and never rested until Somerset had been brought to the scaffold (1552). Edward VI., while his uncle's trial was going on, was amusing himself at tournaments, balls, and banquets, it being just at the time of the Christmas holidays; and on the 22nd of January there is a business-like entry in the journal which he kept, and which

---

* An act of Parliament declaring a person guilty of treason and condemning him without trial in any court of law.

is most valuable for historical reference, "The Duke of Somerset had his head cut off upon Tower-hill, between eight and nine o'clock in the morning." This was his mother's brother, and a man who, as far as we know, had never been otherwise than kind to him.

King Edward was now drawing near his end. He was so evidently in a consumption that Northumberland began to make plans for keeping the control of public affairs in his own hands by marrying his fourth son, Guilford Dudley, to Edward's cousin, Lady Jane Grey. The king, intensely interested in the reformed religion and dreading that a Roman Catholic should rule his country, was easily persuaded to set aside his sisters in his will, and declare Lady Jane the true heir to the crown. Shortly before Edward's death, the duke, finding that the physicians were doing him no good, turned him over to the care of an ignorant woman, under whose treatment he grew rapidly worse, and died (1553) after a reign of six years, in the sixteenth year of his age.

Edward VI. was a studious boy, very religious, and had apparently an amiable disposition. He was fond of his half-sister, Elizabeth, who was only a few years older than himself, and was a Protestant, besides; while with the gloomy Mary he had very little sympathy. What kind of king he would have made if he had lived to grow up is a question which can not now be settled.

CHAPTER XXVII.

LADY JANE GREY. BLOODY MARY. CALAIS.

LADY Jane Grey (for so she is always called, though by her marriage she became Lady Jane Dudley) was a granddaughter of Henry VIII.'s second sister, Mary, Duchess of Suffolk. She was probably the best educated woman in England, except the Princess Elizabeth, and was as lovely in character as she was cultivated in mind. She had no desire to be queen, but yielded to the wishes of her father-in-law and of her own father. Northumberland's proclamation of her was received in ominous silence, and one poor boy called Gilbert Pot had his ears first nailed to the pillory and then cut off, for "speaking words" about the new queen. Queen Mary, meantime, instead of being "quiet and obedient" as Northumberland advised her to be, collected an army at once and prepared to march to London. The duke thought of resisting; but seeing how much superior in numbers her army was to his own, changed his mind and joined in hurrahing for her. Mary mounted the throne. Northumberland was arrested and sent to the Tower, as were also Lady Jane and her husband and many of her supporters. Most of the latter were pardoned, but the duke was executed after a short trial, while Lord Guilford Dudley and his wife, the ten-days queen, were left in prison under sentence of death.

If Jane had had even a fair showing of right on her side, there is little doubt that many Protestants would have flocked to her assistance and the country would have been convulsed by civil war; but Edward VI.'s attempt to place her on the throne was so clearly a usurpation that they had no sympathy with it. The law-abiding instincts of the nation asserted their superiority over their preferences, and there was never for a moment any chance that an unlawful cause should triumph.

The queen's first care was to restore the Roman Catholic religion. The bishops who had been turned out by Henry for denying his supremacy were at once recalled, while several of the most noted of the reformed ones, among others, Cranmer, Hooper, Ridley, and Latimer, were thrown into prison. All the statutes of Edward VI.'s reign regarding religion were repealed in a lump, and Mary sent word to the pope that it was the first wish of her heart that the country should be "reconciled" with the Church of Rome. The Parliament passed an act annulling the divorce pronounced by Cranmer between Henry VIII. and Katherine of Aragon, thus putting it beyond a doubt that Mary was England's lawful queen.

Mary was now thirty-seven years old, in poor health and on that account very plain-looking. Notwithstanding this, she occupied a proud place among the monarchs of Europe, and her cousin, Charles V. of Germany (son of her mother's sister Joanna) sent at once to propose a marriage between her and his son Philip, who was eleven years younger than herself. The House of Commons expressed in the strongest terms their disapprobation of such a marriage, upon which Mary, who was determined that it should take place, dissolved the Parliament. The new laws reëstablishing the Roman Catholic religion were now openly enforced; the mass was celebrated everywhere and a convocation of the clergy declared the marriage of priests unlawful. All the married clergy were turned out from their livings. These things alarmed the non-Catholic element of the people, who anticipated measures still more distasteful when there should be a foreign prince fastened upon them. A rebellion was accordingly raised against Mary by Sir Thomas Wyatt the younger, son of the poet. Wyatt was taken prisoner and executed, with about thirty of his followers; and the rebellion proved fatal to the innocent Lady Jane, and her boy-husband. She declined to see Lord Guilford before their execution, for fear it should unnerve them both. She saw him walk to the scaffold, and then saw his body taken out of a cart, with the head wrapped in a cloth, but shed no tear. The old narrative concludes in these words: "She tied the kerchief about her eyes; then feeling for the block, said, 'What shall I do? Where is it?' One of the standers-by guiding her thereto, she laid her head down upon the block, and stretched forth her body, and said, 'Lord, into thy hands I commend my spirit.' And so she ended."

The Princess Elizabeth was arrested at the same time, but after being shut up in the Tower for a month was released and sent to Woodstock, where she long remained a prisoner. Hollinshed, one of the chroniclers of the time, relates how when once upon a time she heard a milkmaid in her garden singing pleasantly, she wished she too were a milkmaid, as she would then lead a merrier and happier life than her present one. But she never for a moment forgot her royal blood, or condescended to ask for mercy. None of Henry VIII.'s children lacked spirit or courage.

It was while Elizabeth was still at Woodstock that Philip of Spain came to England, with many chests of Spanish silver, and was married amid great rejoicings. The Londoners new-gilded the great cross in Cheapside, and pulled down every gallows in the city on which still hung the decaying bodies of "Wyatt's rebels." After the marriage, a trivial incident showed how strong was the party spirit that separated Romanists from Protestants. A certain conduit in Gracechurch Street under which the royal party was to pass, was decorated with a portrait of Henry VIII. holding a Bible in his hand on which was written "Verbum Dei" (the Word of God). Gardiner, Bishop of Winchester, sent for the painter, "and with vile words calling him traitor, asked why, and who bade him describe King Henry with a book in his hand, as aforesaid. The painter humbly apologized, and said he thought he had done well. 'Nay,' said the bishop, 'it is against the queen's Catholic proceedings.' And so he painted him shortly after, in the stead of the book of Verbum Dei, to have in his hands a new pair of gloves."

It was not long before other straws showed which way the wind was blowing. A Parliament was got together in the queen's interest, in which an address to the pope was voted, declaring their sorrow for all past proceedings against him; and the legate, Cardinal Pole, gave the kingdom absolution, and received it again into the bosom of the Catholic Church. On one point the Parliament was perfectly firm. It would not take away the Abbey lands and goods which had been granted by Henry VIII. to individuals. This is not to be wondered at, as many of their own number were now in possession of this very property.

There was nothing about Philip to attract the English. He was so haughty and reserved that he took no notice of the salutations of even the highest nobility, and so hemmed in by formal rules of etiquette that it was impossible to approach him. He was the most unpopular man in England.

A reign of horror was now to open in that country which has affixed forever the epithet of "Bloody" to the name of Henry VIII.'s oldest daughter. By the renewal of the laws against heresy, every Protestant in England was made liable to be burnt at the stake, and the prisons were soon filled to overflowing. The first victim was John Rogers, a clergyman, whose wife and ten young children were present at the stake to witness his sufferings. He was burnt at Smithfield, a place then in the suburbs of London, but now in the heart of the city, where a "Martyrs' Memorial" has been erected, which keeps alive the memory of their constancy and their fate. Hooper, Bishop of Gloucester, was taken to his own cathedral city to end his life. The flames consumed him very slowly; but while lingering in frightful agony, he remained calm and quiet; and died, we are told, "like a child in its bed."

Another of the early martyrs, Rowland Taylor, rector of Hadleigh, could not put aside his spirit of humor even at the last dreadful moment. While going to the stake he remarked, "the worms in Hadleigh church-yard will be deceived, for the carcass that should have been theirs will be burnt to ashes." At the stake, a brutal man threw a fagot at him, which wounded him so that the blood ran down his face. "Oh, friend," said he, "I had harm enough; what needed that?" and he died calmly, like the others.

Gardiner and Bonner, the queen's principal agents in this deadly work, were constantly urged on by Mary and her council to more zealous efforts. Among the individual cases which stand out from the crowd of less distinguished but equally heroic martyrs, are the two bishops, Ridley and Latimer, who suffered death together, chained to the same stake. Ridley was a man in the prime of life; Latimer was more than eighty years old. He said to his brother martyr as they stood waiting for the fire to be lighted, "Be of good comfort, master Ridley, and play the man! We shall this day light such a candle, by God's grace, in England, as shall never be put out."

The most illustrious of the victims, Archbishop Cranmer, remained to be dealt with. The queen had a personal reason for disliking him, even if he had not been a heretic, for he had pronounced the divorce between her father and mother; but in addition to this, he had imprudently uttered violent tirades against the Romish Church in the beginning of Mary's reign, and his condemnation was a foregone conclusion. He was not naturally a man of strong character, and long imprisonment and harsh treatment had enfeebled him still further. He recanted, on the promise that his life should be spared. When he found, however, that this was only a trick to increase his disgrace, and that he was first to make a public address in support of the Romish doctrines and then to be led at once to the stake, his courage revived, and he astonished his audience by a full and emphatic declaration of his Protestant belief. He wavered no more, but went cheerfully to his death, and when the fire was kindled, thrust into the flames his right hand (with which he had signed the recantation) and held it there for some time, saying, "This hand has offended." Such executions had an effect contrary to the one anticipated, and, as has been said, "Each martyrdom was equal to a hundred sermons." It is computed that two hundred and seventy-seven persons, including four children, suffered death by fire during the last three years of Bloody Mary's reign.

Queen Mary was always devotedly fond of her husband, though he treated her with neglect and indifference. For him she declared war against France, a country with which England was at peace, and sent several thousand soldiers there to help him. A great battle was fought at St. Quentin, where the Spaniards were victorious; but the English soldiers were sharp enough to see that they were not fighting the battles of England, and they grumbled and growled so much that Philip was glad to get rid of them and send them home again (1557). The next year the Duke of Guise, uncle of Mary Queen of Scots, and the finest soldier in France, longing to revenge the disgrace of St. Quentin (from which battle he had been absent), determined to retake the town of Calais.* This fortress was supposed to be impregnable, but it was poorly guarded, for the English were lukewarm in carrying on the unacceptable war, and did not supply the governor with the soldiers needed. The Duke of Guise, too, was a general who knew how to take advantage of the weak points of his enemy; and in eight days the fortress which it had taken Edward III. eleven months of hard work to acquire, was retaken and became again a possession of

---

* For a further account of this war, see "A Short History of France," p. 178.

France (1558) after having belonged to England for two hundred and eleven years.

The people of England were so indignant at the folly of the queen in entering into this causeless war that they almost forgot to be mortified at the disaster to their arms, and when Philip offered his help to get Calais back again, Parliament said they were too poor to spend any more money on it. But to Queen Mary, already broken in health, it was like a death-blow. "When I die," she exclaimed, "the word 'Calais' will be found written on my heart."

She did not live long after this shock. Mortification at the neglect of her husband, who never came near her again after having drawn her into the French war, aggravated the fever she was suffering from; and she died at forty-two years of age, after a short and dreadful reign of less than five years (1558). Cardinal Pole (who had been made Archbishop of Canterbury in Cranmer's place) died twenty-four hours afterward.

Queen Mary's reign did good in a certain way, namely, by showing the outrages which such principles as hers lead to, and by preventing Englishmen from ever again bowing under a yoke so degrading.

One gleam of commercial interest lights up the dark monotony of this reign. Some English navigators, in sailing along the northern coast of Europe, discovered a passage to Archangel, on the White Sea, which led to the Czar of Muscovy's* sending ambassadors to ask the friendship of England. This is the first appearance of the Russian nation in the courts of Western Europe.

---

* Muscovy is the old name for Russia.

CHAPTER XXVIII.

ELIZABETH. MARY QUEEN OF SCOTS.

WITH a sudden turn, England whirled around to Protestantism on the death of Mary. The great fabric of Popery, which Mary had so labored to build up, vanished almost in a moment when her vigorous, energetic, popular sister took her place on the throne. As the Spanish ambassador, Feria, whimsically said in a letter to Philip: "There is not a heretic or traitor in all the country who has not started as if from the grave to seek her with expressions of the greatest pleasure." These remarks did not at all hinder Philip from writing to ask his sister-in-law to marry him, offering at the same time to obtain a dispensation from the pope for that purpose; but she put him off civilly, being too quick-witted not to see that such a marriage would be a repetition of her father's with Katherine of Aragon, an example she had no wish to follow.

Elizabeth had been brought up from her very babyhood in adversity. This fact, with her natural discretion, helped her to say and do, at least in the early part of her career, always the right thing at the right moment. Popularity came to her without an effort. On arriving in London from her country house at Hatfield, where she was living when she received the news of her sister's death, she was welcomed with uproarious joy. She was now twenty-five years old, tall, well made, and of a pleasing countenance.

Not one of the bishops, who were all, of course, Romanists, was willing to perform the ceremony of coronation. At last the Bishop of Carlisle was prevailed upon to set the crown upon her head. She did not make enemies by taking immediate action on this refusal; but they were soon afterward required, by act of Parliament, to take the "Oath of Supremacy," and those who did not meet this test were deposed and their places gradually filled by Protestants. It is estimated that nearly ten thousand of the inferior clergy took the oath acknowledging the queen to be head of the Church.

On the morning after the coronation, as Elizabeth was going to chapel, one of the courtiers addressed her in a loud voice, reminding her that it was the custom for a new sovereign to release some prisoners, and saying that there were four or five for whom he begged this favor, namely, the four Evangelists, Matthew, Mark, Luke, and John, and also St. Paul, who had so long been shut up in a foreign tongue that they were unable to converse with the people. Elizabeth gravely answered that it were best to inquire of them whether they wished to be released or not. The matter was referred to a convocation of the clergy, by whose authority a new translation of the Scriptures was ordered. Matthew Parker, the new Archbishop of Canterbury, a truly good and learned man, was entrusted with carrying this out, and caused a version to be prepared called "The Bishops' Bible," which appeared in 1568, and was the authorized one until superseded by that now in use by us. The queen at the same time commanded that the church service should again be read in the common tongue; and this liturgy, being in the main the same with the second one of Edward VI. (1552) is the one still used in England, and, with slight change, in

America. At the same time with the law regarding the queen's supremacy, was passed another called the Act of Uniformity, which required the liturgy of the English prayer-book to be used in religious worship, and forbade all ministers to adopt any other form. These two acts, of Supremacy and Uniformity, settled the question of a national religion. For the queen's assistance in carrying out these measures, she was empowered by Parliament to name such commissioners, either laymen or clergymen; and out of this grew the famous Court of High Commission, of which we shall hear again.

Queen Elizabeth showed especial good judgment in the choice of her ministers. William Cecil, afterward Lord Burleigh, was made secretary of state, and continued for the forty years from the beginning of Elizabeth's reign to his death in 1598, to be her prime minister. Sir Nicholas Bacon, father of the still greater Francis Bacon, was appointed lord keeper of the great seal.

The spirit of the whole reign was shown in the first speech of Bacon to Parliament. He said he trusted that "contumelious and opprobrious words such as heretic, schismatic, papist, would be banished out of men's mouths." Every thing that was done about religion was distinguished by moderation, and the great change was effected quietly. The first Parliament held after the coronation begged the queen to choose a husband for herself (which would have been no difficult matter, as nearly every royal bachelor or widower in Europe wished to marry her), but she answered very firmly that the height of her ambition was to have inscribed on her tombstone that a queen, having lived and reigned so many years, died a virgin.

Her royal cousin, Mary, Queen of Scots, now became for a short time queen of France by the death of her father-in-law, Henry II. She and her young husband, Francis II., foolishly took the title of king and queen of England, and Elizabeth, very indignant, sent an army to Scotland to help the party organized there against Mary and her French advisers. Scotland was a strongly Protestant country, and the people were determined that Romanism should not get the upper hand there as it had done in England under Mary. John Knox, the famous Puritan preacher, used the whole force of his eloquence against the popish party, and the Roman religion was abolished in Scotland, except that it was permitted to the queen herself to hear mass with her household. It was also agreed that she should no longer use the title of queen of England. Just at this time her husband died, and she was obliged, most unwillingly, to return to her native land. On leaving France, she had her couch spread on the deck of the vessel, so that with the last ray of light she could still see that beloved country, and in touching language she bade it farewell. She was received in Scotland with such enthusiasm as would naturally be shown to a beautiful young widow of nineteen, with gracious and winning manners; but nothing could make her countrymen forget that she was a papist.

The first dozen years of Elizabeth's reign were passed in profound peace, except for the slight disturbance with Scotland. With the help of her able ministers she paid off a large part of the public debt; restored to its full value the coin, which had been greatly debased during Edward VI.'s time; introduced the manufacture of gunpowder and brass cannon, and built so many ships that she was called "the queen of the northern seas." She promoted trade and manufactures, and was to some extent a patron of literary men, though she was very careful of money and always managed to make other people spend it when possible.

Queen Elizabeth had some very mean qualities as well as many great ones. She was extremely vain, and loved flattery so much that no one could gain her favor without using adulation to an extent which now seems disgraceful.

> "Till [her] relish grown callous, almost to disease,
> Who peppered the highest was surest to please."

The queen's greatest favorite, Robert Dudley, earl of Leicester, came of a family distinguished for its bad qualities. He was the son of that Duke of Northumberland who had ruined the life of Lady Jane Grey, and grandson of the unjust judge of Henry VII. He was base enough to do anything to keep the queen's favor, and there was even a report that he had killed his wife, Amy Robsart,* in the hope of marrying Elizabeth. But nothing could be proved against him, and, mean-souled as he was, he continued to be her favorite till the day of his death.

The Queen of Scots married her cousin, Lord Darnley, a handsome but weak and low-minded youth, some years younger than herself, whom she soon grew tired of and treated with contempt. "Unless she was freed of him," she said, "she had no desire to live." There was in her court an Italian musician named David Rizzio† whom

---

*See Sir Walter Scott's novel of "Kenilworth."
†Pronounced Ritzio.

Mary had made her private secretary, and with whom she was on terms of intimacy that displeased her husband. Darnley formed a conspiracy with some Scottish lords to murder the favorite. They entered the queen's room as she was at supper with him and others of her attendants, and stabbed Rizzio to death in her presence. The stain of his blood may yet be seen on the floor of Holyrood palace. Not long after this, Mary gave birth to a son who received the name of James. He became the sixth Stuart king in succession bearing that name, and we shall meet him in English history as James the First of England and Sixth of Scotland.

Mary was furiously angry against all who had taken part in the murder of Rizzio, and loaded her husband with insults or treated him with haughty neglect. Darnley not long afterward was found murdered, and suspicion fell upon the Earl of Bothwell, a worthless and dissipated person who was in high favor with the queen; and, as she married him soon after Darnley's death, it is natural to think that she did not disapprove of the crime. She was forced to dismiss Bothwell, who became an outcast, and died, insane, ten years afterward.

Mary was now virtually a prisoner. After the battle of Carberry Hill, which she lost, she was conducted back to Edinburgh between two of the confederate lords, while the air rang with the curses of the infuriated rabble, who looked upon her as the murderess of her husband. A banner was carried before her on which was painted the body of Darnley lying under a tree with a child kneeling beside it, and the motto, "Judge and avenge my cause, oh Lord!" When she awoke the next morning, the same banner was hung up in front of her window. The same day, she was taken to the castle of Lochleven, situated on a small island in the lake of that name, where she was obliged to sign an agreement to resign the crown to her son and to appoint the Earl of Murray, her half-brother, regent of the kingdom during James's minority. The young prince was crowned by the name of James VI. and the Parliament, voting that the queen was an accomplice in Darnley's murder, condemned her to imprisonment. She effected her escape from Lochleven Castle in a very romantic manner,* and, raising an army, fought one commanded by the regent, near Glasgow, where she was completely defeated. Flying southward with all possible haste, she got on board a fishing-boat which landed her on the same day in England, and from Carlisle she sent a message to Elizabeth asking for her friendship and protection. The English queen replied that she must first have proof that her cousin was innocent of the crimes charged against her. With Mary's consent, a sort of trial was held in London, at which both her friends and enemies offered testimony in the case; but it came to nothing, and she remained for nineteen years a prisoner in the hands of Elizabeth.

All through the last half of the sixteenth century, the question of religion, in some form, was the cause of excitement and turmoil. From the time that the Roman Church ceased to be catholic—that is, universal,—the struggle between its doctrines and other forms of belief was incessant; and as people had not then learned the great lesson of toleration as it is called, in other words

---

*For a truthful description of this escape see Sir Walter Scott's novel of "The Abbot," Chapter XXXV.

of allowing each one to keep his own belief unless he can be *persuaded* to accept a better one, the result was strife and bloodshed instead of peace and good-will. In France a deadly civil war was going on between the Catholics and the Huguenots (French Protestants); in the Netherlands, Philip II. of Spain, formerly the husband of Elizabeth's sister Mary, was persecuting his Protestant subjects by burning, torturing, beheading, and burying alive those who would not conform to his own religion; and in England two parties had arisen among the Protestants themselves whose feelings against each other were as bitter, though not as bloodily expressed, as those of either party against the Catholics. On one side stood the English Church established by law, with a ritual or form of service, and on the other the Puritans, those who thought the Church not yet sufficiently purified from what they called the abominations of Rome, and who wished a simple kind of worship, without set forms or a dress peculiar to the clergy.

Elizabeth had already sent some help to the Huguenots in France, when the horrible "Massacre of St. Bartholemew,"* occurred, in which many thousands of them were murdered. This outrage, together with the no less frightful occurences in the Netherlands, kindled a flame of indignation in England which was fanned into fury by events in that country which, to the excited minds of the people, threatened them with similar dangers.

---

* See "A Short History of France," p. 189.

CHAPTER XXIX.

PLOTS. THE NAVIGATORS. MARY STUART.

THE disturbances caused by religous differences, while agitating different countries in different ways, made themselves most strongly felt in England through the plots formed by the Catholics against Elizabeth's government. The conspirators were encouraged in these by a bull of excommunication issued against her by Pope Pius V. declaring her title null and void, and absolving her subjects from their allegiance. These events bore fruit in a plan made to marry the English Duke of Norfolk, a Romanist, to the Scottish Queen Mary, seize and imprison Elizabeth, by the help of Spanish soldiers who were to land in the country, and proclaim Mary queen of England. The plot was discovered, and Norfolk and others were executed.

The discovery of the methods used by Mary and her friends made it necessary to watch the captive queen very closely, though in spite of the vigilance used it was found impossible to prevent her from having constant correspondence with the outer world.

During all this time, the wars of religion in France were growing fiercer and the persecution in the Netherlands more horrible. In one way, these were both of benefit to England; they drove to her shores a great body of well-taught workmen, who were welcomed in the manufacturing districts and found ample occasion there for exercising their skill. The queen paid off with interest the entire public debt, part of which had been accumulating since her father's time; and this was so unusual a practice with the crowned heads of Europe that it gave the stamp of stability to her government.

The people of the Netherlands were still struggling for their liberty, and had more than once asked Elizabeth to be their queen, feeling that with her help they could get rid of the atrocities of Spanish rule. She declined, but sent them some troops (1585), under the command of her favorite, the Earl of Leicester. A person more unfit for the office of commander could scarcely have been found. Leicester had neither military talent nor experience, while Philip's general, Alexander of Parma, was the first captain of the age. Thrilling deeds of heroism were performed by individual commanders, and the common soldiers fought bravely; but the queen's parsimony led her to leave the army for months at a time without pay, and then their condition became so scandalous that there was nothing the Dutch desired so much as to get rid of them.

The fate of Sir Philip Sidney, "the mirror of knight-hood," the most accomplished man of the time, was especially sad. He perished in an unwisely-planned attack on the enemy near Zutphen, in Holland (1586). We give a story of his generosity in the words of his friend, Lord Brooke: "Passing along by the rear of the army and being thirsty with excess of bleeding, he called for some drink, which was presently brought him. But as he was putting the bottle to his mouth he saw a poor soldier carried along who had eaten his last at the same feast, ghastly casting up his eyes at the bottle; which Sir Philip perceiving, took it from his head before he drank, and delivered it to the poor man with these words:

'Thy necessity is yet greater than mine.'" Such is the stuff that heroes are made of; a whole character is told in this little tale.

Meanwhile, England's explorers and navigators were not idle. Francis Drake was the second person to sail around the globe (1577-1580), the Portuguese under Magellan having accomplished the same feat nearly sixty years before. Drake, on his way, took many rich Spanish prizes, though there was no open war between England and Spain at the time. The queen, instead of reproaching him for this breach of the law of nations, knighted him, and allowed him to give her a banquet at Deptford on board the ship which had made the successful voyage. Another navigator, John Davis, in trying to find a northwest passage to the Pacific, discovered the strait which bears his name; Sir Martin Frobisher found another in the same part of the world which is also called after him; and Sir John Hawkins, one of the boldest of those adventurers, has the unenviable reputation of having been the first Englishman to engage in the African slave-trade. All these were mere sailors, brought into notice by their enterprise, perseverance, and courage. There were others, however, of a higher social rank, who did their share in exploring new countries and unknown seas. Among these were Sir Walter Raleigh and his half-brother, Sir Humphrey Gilbert. The latter, before setting out on his last voyage, received from the queen a gift of a small gold anchor guided by a lady, as a token of her esteem. After many adventures, and the loss of the largest ship of his little fleet, he started to return to England; but during the voyage a storm arose and separated his vessel, the Squirrel, from her consort.

Before they parted he called out to those on the other ship, "We are as near Heaven by sea as by land!" The Squirrel was never seen again.

Sir Walter Raleigh's is one of the most brilliant figures in the Elizabethan gallery. He seems to have been a born courtier, as well as an adventurer, for there is a story that on his first meeting with the queen he threw down his rich cloak in a muddy path that she might not wet her feet. If he did not do this he might have done it, and probably would have done it if the opportunity had occurred. At any rate, he stood high in the queen's favor, and he had the privilege of naming the new land, which he called Virginia, in honor of the Virgin Queen.* He sent out a colony which settled on Roanoke Island, near North Carolina (1585), but it did not thrive, and the next year, when Sir Francis Drake came along, the colonists were glad to return with him to England. Raleigh was not yet discouraged by his ill-success. The following year he sent another colony to the same place, providing it with all things necessary; but at the end of three years it had entirely disappeared, and he had already spent so much money on it that he was obliged to give up any further attempts at colonization.

We have now arrived at what Motley calls the tragedy of Mary Stuart: "A sad but inevitable portion of the vast drama in which the emancipation of England and Holland, and through them of half Christendom, approached its catastrophe." Mary's whole life in England had been a torment to Elizabeth. Her partisans were constantly intriguing with the agents of foreign

---

*This name was originally given to the whole Atlantic coast, from Maine to the Spanish settlements in Florida.

countries to try in some way to compass Elizabeth's death, and the assassination of the patriot and statesman, William of Orange (1584), encouraged hopes of success in such attempts. In 1586, some Roman Catholic priests in the seminary at Rheims, in France, had worked themselves up to a pitch of frantic fanaticism, and thought it would be a noble deed to destroy Elizabeth, restore the Catholic religion, and place the Queen of Scots on the throne. They found a ready accomplice in England in Sir Anthony Babington, a young man of family and fortune, who entered eagerly into their plans and drew into the conspiracy many Romanists of position and wealth.

It happened, however, that these plots were not kept so secret but that they came to the knowledge of Sir Francis Walsingham, one of the queen's secretaries of state; who by means of his spies knew every step as soon as it was taken. He allowed the conspiracy to go on until all the evidence was collected necessary to convict the actors in it. A traitor in the castle where Mary was confined received and passed on to her the letters addressed to her (which were sometimes concealed in a box conveyed in a barrel of beer), and she answered them, never dreaming that they were leading her to her own destruction. At last, when the plot was fully ripe, the conspirators were seized, tried, and condemned, the evidence against them being so complete that no defence could be made.

Elizabeth hesitated long before taking the final step with regard to Mary. Not only the Parliament, but all Protestant England, clamored for the death of the Scottish queen, and Elizabeth, yielding at last, ordered her to be tried at Fotheringay Castle (to which place she had been removed after the discovery of Babington's conspiracy), by a court held there for the purpose. Before this court, which was composed of both Catholics and Protestants, she denied everything; declared that the letters to Babington in her own handwriting had been forged; denied that she had ever received any from him, and defended herself with great spirit and ingenuity, but without avail. "The daughter of debate" was condemned, and adjudged worthy of death.

Parliament ratified the finding of the court, and the people in general were so wildly happy over the verdict that they rang the bells and lighted bonfires, and went about London streets shouting for joy. Elizabeth, however, though she may in her secret soul have desired Mary's death, was painfully perplexed. She hesitated long before signing the death-warrant, and after this had been done and the fatal paper sent on its way, she tried to lay the blame on her ministers, especially on her unfortunate secretary, Davison, who was thrown into prison and heavily fined for doing his plain duty in the matter. If Elizabeth had boldly taken upon herself the responsibility of her own actions, defending the death of Mary as a necessity of state, she might have been blamed but she would not have been despised. As it is, there is something contemptible in her being willing to share the profit but not the odium of the transaction. "Willing to wound and yet afraid to strike."

Four months passed between the condemnation and the execution of Mary Stuart (October, 1586—February, 1587), and in this time the kings of France and Scotland interceded for her in vain. Her son, James VI., blustered a good deal, but was easily pacified. He was now twenty-one years old and might have shown some spirit; but he was of a timorous disposition and did not choose to quarrel with his powerful neighbor. The remonstrances from France passed over Elizabeth as the idle wind.

Mary Stuart, like many persons who have done ill in their lives, never appeared to more advantage than in her last hours. She was beheaded in the great hall of Fotheringay Castle, where a scaffold had been erected covered with black cloth, an executioner dressed in black velvet standing beside it. Sir Andrew Melville, her ambassador to England in the days of her youth and beauty, was with her to the end. She had wished to have the services of a priest, but this was refused, and instead the Dean of Peterborough exhorted her to become converted to the Protestant faith. She told him not to trouble himself about her, for that as she had lived a Catholic she would die one; and she began to pray in Latin while he was praying in English, neither one taking any notice of the other. Afterward she prayed in English for Christ's afflicted church, for her son and for the Queen of England. The Earl of Kent, one of the functionaries on this occasion, told her to "leave those trumperies." A cloth was pinned over her face by her maids; and then, groping for the block, as Lady Jane Grey had done, she laid down her head, and two strokes severed it from her body. Her little dog, who had stolen upon the scaffold unperceived, was found nestling among the folds of her gown, and refused to leave her dead body.

And this was the end of beauty without principle, passions without self-restraint, and ability without truthfulness. If Mary Stuart's intellect had been guided by a desire to do right, and her beauty accompanied by sincerity and tenderness, there would be a fragrance around her name that would be only the sweeter for her misfortunes. As it is, we can pity her sorrows, but we must condemn her crimes.

Mary died in her forty-fifth year, having been nominally queen since she was five days old, and having reigned after her return from France about seven years.

CHAPTER XXX.

THE ARMADA. IRELAND. DEATH OF THE QUEEN.

PHILIP II. of Spain had for three years been making preparations for the conquest of England, when the "Invincible Armada,"* at last fully equipped for sea, sailed out of the port of Lisbon,† June, 1588. There had been a detention on account of the death of the admiral, who was succeeded by the Duke of Medina Sidonia, a brave soldier, but totally unacquainted with the sea. No expense had been spared; there were 130 ships, the greater part of them larger and heavier than had ever been used in European warfare, carrying 33,000 men and 3,000 cannon. The Armada had been more than a month on the way, and the English thought it was not coming at all; when it was seen from the Lizard,‡ one bright day in July, crowding all sail to enter the English Channel.

---

* Armada, the Spanish term for a large war fleet.
† Portugal belonged to Spain from 1580 to 1640.
‡ The most southern point of England.

While the Spanish fleet was in preparation, Sir Francis Drake had been hovering off the coast of Spain, and had taken a hundred ships near Cadiz, beside destroying great quantities of provisions and ammunition. In England, all the available vessels had been made ready, partly by the use of public money and partly by free gifts from the cities and seaport towns. The ships were very small compared to those of the Spaniards, and carried not much more than half as many men. Lord Howard of Effingham was in command of the English fleet; Drake, Hawkins, and Frobisher were among his captains, while Raleigh was in charge of a land force. A camp was formed at Tilbury, near London, and the queen rode among the troops encouraging and animating them. "I know that I have but the body of a weak and feeble woman," said she, "but I have the heart of a king, and of a king of England!"

The Spanish fleet advanced up the Channel in the form of a crescent, seven miles from tip to tip. Lord Howard had scarcely time to get out of Plymouth harbor before it passed; and fearing that he could not attack the whole fleet to advantage, he contented himself with lying in wait for such vessels as should be separated from the rest, and in this way captured two of the largest galleons, one of which was loaded with treasure. For several nights, beacon-fires had been lighted on various parts of the southern coast, to give notice to the inhabitants of the Spaniards' approach.* By constantly annoying the

---

* "Swift to east and swift to west the warning radiance spread—
High on St. Michael's Mount it shone, it shone on Beachy Head.
Far o'er the deep the Spaniards saw, along each southern shire,
Cape beyond cape, in endless range, those twinkling points of fire."
—Macaulay, "The Armada."

enemy, hanging on the rear of the fleet and darting in and out with their light and easily-managed vessels while the clumsy Spanish ones were trying to get into position, the English did much damage to the enemy.* One night Howard took eight of his least valuable ships, and, filling them with combustibles, set fire to them and sent them adrift among the Spanish galleons; the latter were seized with a panic, and cutting their cables they fled in confusion; the English pursued them, and the next morning found them in all haste speeding away from Calais, where they had taken refuge.

The Spanish admiral did not dare to return with his demoralized fleet through the Channel. He turned northward and made the best of his way through the German Ocean† to the Orkneys, followed and harassed by the English; and had not the ammunition of the latter given out, they might have captured the whole Spanish fleet. A violent tempest overtook the Armada after it had passed the Orkneys, destroying or crippling many vessels; and another drove a part of it on the coast of Ireland, where such men as reached the shore were butchered by the natives. Less than half the ships that had sailed so proudly out of Lisbon, two months before, ever again saw the coast of Spain. The Invincible Armada was conquered (1588).‡

The joy, the exultation, the heartfelt gratitude of the English may be imagined. Thanksgivings went up from

---

* Lord Howard wrote to Walsingham, "Their force is wonderfully great and strong, and yet we pluck their feathers by little and little."

† The North Sea.

‡ See Kingsley's novel, "Westward Ho!"

every church in the land, and the love and admiration for the queen rose almost to idolatry. On one of the medals struck to commemorate the great deliverance was a good parody of Cæsar's famous despatch. The English one ran: "Venit, vidit, fugit."*

The queen's pleasure in this victory was tempered by a private grief. The Earl of Leicester, perhaps the only person for whom she ever felt a real affection, died soon after the last Spanish sail disappeared from English waters. His place in her favor was apparently taken by his step-son, the Earl of Essex, a young man of agreeable manners and many accomplishments, and not lacking in fine qualities, though reckless and ill-balanced. Upon one occasion, he so far forgot himself as to turn his back upon her with an insulting laugh when she refused to comply with his wishes. Elizabeth had her own way of treating such offences, and gave him a box on the ear with her jewelled fingers, telling him to "go, and be hanged." After this interchange of courtesies Essex retired from court, and was with difficulty persuaded by his friends to make friends again with his royal mistress.

Meantime, the war with Spain went on. Eight years after the failure of the great Armada, the city of Cadiz was taken and plundered, under the direction of Essex.† In 1598, Philip II. died, and though no definite peace was made, there was little fighting done during the remainder of the queen's life-time.

---

* He came, he saw, he fled.

† Lord Macaulay says of this, that it was "the most brilliant military exploit achieved on the continent by English arms during the interval which elapsed between the battle of Agincourt and that of Blenheim" (1415-1704).

The Irish were at this time still half-savage, and had never become reconciled to English rule.* The Earl of Tyrone, a native chieftain of great ability, headed a rebellion against Elizabeth, and had already given much trouble when Essex, at his own request, was sent to take command in Ireland. He was not able to bring the war to a conclusion, though he made a truce, during which he left his post, contrary to the queen's express orders, and hastened to London, where he presented himself before her without being announced.† The queen was so startled that she received him graciously, at which he expressed himself much comforted; but when she had had time to think it over she was very indignant at his presumption, and ordered him to be confined to his own house. He, as well as every one else about the court, expected that he would soon be restored to his old position as her favorite. He was set at liberty, but the queen refused to see him. Every account from Ireland brought fresh news of his misgovernment there, and he was too popular with the English people to be secure from her jealousy. When he asked for a renewal of his monopoly of sweet wines she refused to grant it, saying (though not to him) that "an unruly beast must be

---

* Henry VII.'s solution of the problem as it existed in his time, was ingenious. When the Earl of Desmond boldly defied the English government, some one in the council said, impatiently, "All Ireland can not rule this man." "Then he shall rule all Ireland," said the king, and made him Lord Deputy.

† The chronicle of the time says: "He stayed not till he came to the queen's bedchamber, where he found the queen newly up, with her hair about her face. * * 'Tis much wondered at that he went so boldly to her majesty's presence, she not being ready, and he so full of dirt and mire that his very face was full of it."

stinted in his provender." He was unwise enough to make the remark that "the queen was an old woman as crooked in her mind as she was in her body." Busybodies took care to report this speech, which, being made about the vainest woman in Europe, was not likely to increase her good temper. The hot-headed favorite now became a rebel in good earnest. He formed, with a few other persons as foolish as himself, a conspiracy against the queen's government, which was discovered and the chief offenders executed. It was a long time before Elizabeth could make up her mind to sign the death warrant of Essex, and when it was done she regretted it for the rest of her life.

Lord Mountjoy, the successor of Essex in Ireland, found everything there in the worst possible condition, but managed so well that in three years the rebellion was at an end. Yet the submission of Tyrone brought no joy to the queen. Life had lost its zest. Her people no longer greeted her appearance with rapture, as they had done at Tilbury Fort or on one of her earlier "progresses."* They looked on in silence, and she missed the old enthusiastic welcome. For a while after Essex's death the queen kept up the old habits—hunting, dancing, travelling, playing on the "virginals" (a kind of ancestor of the modern piano), and trying to feel that nothing had changed; but age was creeping upon her, and she was not in sympathy with the more serious temper of the nation. A story is told, not on the best authority, but generally believed, of a bitter experience that came to her some time after her favorite's death. She had given him a ring (so it is said), promising that if he ever

---

* Royal journeys through different parts of the kingdom.

got into trouble and would send her the ring, she would help him. Not receiving it, she came to the conclusion that Essex's obstinacy and "highmindedness" had prevented his appealing to her, and therefore allowed him to be executed. A month or two before her death, the Countess of Nottingham, being on her own death-bed, sent for her and confessed that Essex had intrusted her with the ring, and that her husband, who was a political enemy of Essex, had forbidden her to carry it to the queen. Upon this, Elizabeth shook the dying woman in her bed, crying, "God may forgive you, but I never will!" Such is the story. There are several circumstances against it, but a ring, said to be the one about which the tale is told, is still in existence.

Elizabeth's last weeks were very sad ones. She would sit speechless for days together, in the deepest melancholy; and once called for a sword, with which she made aimless motions, as if she were guarding against an attack. Sir Robert Cary, her kinsman, visited her, and says: "She fetched forty or fifty great sighs, which surprised me, for in all my lifetime I never knew her fetch a sigh except when the queen of Scots was beheaded." She refused to go to bed, but sat, propped up with cushions, and took no notice of any one. Once she was roused into a moment's exhibition of the old spirit, when Sir Robert Cecil (who was the son of Lord Burleigh, and succeeded him as prime minister) told her she "must" go to bed. "Must!" she exclaimed. "Little man, little man!* thy father, if he had been alive, durst not have used that word!" When the old question of the succession was brought up, and the name of Lord Beau-

---

* Cecil was hump-backed and of very small stature.

champ* (a distant relative of her own) was proposed, she said, "I will have no rascal's son, but a king." "Rascal" meant a common person; with her, a subject. When she was asked if it should be the king of Scots, she put her hands above her head, to signify a crown, it was said, but could not speak. After this she sank into a lethargy, and died unconscious, March 24, 1603, in the seventieth year of her age and the forty-fifth of her reign.

This great queen was so wise about some things and so foolish about others, so large-minded and yet so mean, at once so keen-sighted and so blind, that one needs to study her character from many points of view to get a correct idea of it. She loved England with her whole heart; and though wilful and capricious, like her father, did not let these faults interfere with the people's interests. She lacked refinement, and was perfectly indifferent to truth when falsehood would serve her turn better, while her temper was never restrained except by policy.† Abusive and profane words were always at her command, and she never scrupled to use them. Her appetite for flattery was insatiable. Nothing could be too gross for her; at least in social life. If any one tried it at the council-board, he was soon reminded that they were met there for business. Her vanity, even when she was an old woman, made her so jealous of other women that her courtiers often kept their marriages secret for fear of exciting her wrath. Leicester, Raleigh, and Essex, all mar-

---

* Pronounced Beech'am.

† The Earl of Huntington complained, in a letter still preserved in the British Museum, that on the occasion of some quarrel she "pinched his wife very sorely."

ried without her knowledge and lost her favor by it for a time; and in some other instances she punished cruelly persons who had presumed to marry before getting her leave. She was extravagantly fond of dress, partly, perhaps, because she had thought it more prudent to curb this taste in her youth. We read that when the ladies in Edward VI.'s time went to meet Mary of Guise with their hair "frounsed, curled, and double-curled," she altered nothing, but "kept her old shamefastness." So she made up for this when she could do as she pleased. Just after her death one of her friends wrote, "She made no will, neither gave anything away, so that they which shall come after her shall find a well-furnished jewel-case and a rich wardrobe of more than two thousand gowns, with all things answerable." Her extreme parsimony, which prevented her giving away the wardrobe full of rich dresses which she could not use, did not keep her from constantly adding to this immense stock. And, indeed, it has been observed since the days of Queen Elizabeth, that persons who spend lavishly on themselves are often the most penurious when it comes to spending for others.

Yet after all, notwithstanding her faults and follies, Elizabeth was a great queen; perhaps the greatest in authentic history.

CHAPTER XXXI.

16TH CENTURY SUMMARY. JAMES I.

WHAT had the sixteenth century accomplished for England? For one thing, it was more humane at its close than at its beginning. We no longer read of three hundred heads at a time exposed on London Bridge, as was seen by a German traveller in Queen Elizabeth's time. Never again were a hundred thieves condemned to the gallows at once in a single county. The care of the poor had now become part of the public business. "Sturdy beggars" were punished as before, but the old and the helpless were provided for by requiring the well-to-do to give for their support.

The struggle went on between the kingly prerogative, or privilege, and the growing sense of the rights of the people as represented by the House of Commons. Little by little the Tudors had to give way, though we find Elizabeth trying, almost to the end of her life, to control the utterances of Parliament. The habit of respect for royalty was so strong that it required a bold man to bring forward a bill on any topic which the queen had forbidden to be touched; and when one attempted it, he was very likely to land in prison.

The feeling of old-fashioned loyalty was weakening, year by year. The poor man who, when Elizabeth had ordered his right hand to be struck off for some trivial offence, waved his hat over his head with the left and shouted "God save the queen!" was a type of the class that has never appeared since the Tudors ceased to reign. The gilding was rubbing off from the statues of kings, and men saw that after all they were but clay.

Domestic comfort had advanced somewhat since Henry VII.'s time, though most of it would have appeared "cold comfort" to us. "Hang out your lights!" was still shouted by the watch at nightfall, for there were no street lamps. Almost everybody had chimneys, though not, perhaps, the very poor, as these additions were still considered a luxury. When the queen went in to her dancing-hall, the passage thither was covered with hay, "as was the custom of the court," an observer tells us. We still admire the Elizabethan style of architecture though we modify it internally for the sake of convenience. Gray names some of its features with good-humored satire when he writes of Sir Christopher Hatton's house as having

> "Rich windows that exclude the light,
> And passages that lead to nothing."

Another very wealthy man, Sir William Hollis, spent his money in boundless hospitality. For the three winter months his house was open, and any man might come and stay three days without declaring his name. Sir William would never dine until one o'clock (common people dined at eleven, and very great ones at twelve), because, he said, a friend might come twenty miles to dine with him, and he "would be loth he should lose his labor."

The young gentlemen of the time liked to travel occasionally (nobody ever thought of a young lady's travelling!), and when one came to Lord Burleigh for a license to do so, he would first question him about England; "and if he found him ignorant, would bid him stay at home and know his own country first"; an admirable test of one's fitness for travelling.

A new impulse was given to commerce by the charter granted by Queen Elizabeth to the East India Company (Dec. 31, 1599). It was at first only a trading company, but we shall see it develop into a vast empire.

In manufactures, great progress was made during the century, and England exported large quantities of cloth to the continent. A pair of knit silk stockings was presented to Queen Elizabeth which pleased her so much that she never afterward wore cloth ones. Pins were also invented, ladies having previously used clasps or skewers. Great sums were expended on rich clothing, and writers complain that in this respect the poor aped the manners of the rich. Cottagers' daughters "are so impudent, that albeit their parents have but one cow, horse or sheep, they will never let them rest till it be sold, to maintain them in their braveries." Queen Elizabeth did not object to having such things said about the poor, but when the Bishop of London preached before her on the vanity of decking the body too finely, she told her ladies that if the bishop held more discourse on such matters she would fit him for heaven, but he should walk thither without a staff, and leave his mantle behind him.* In other words, he should lose his bishopric.

One practice in the reign of Elizabeth which we should be ashamed to think of as possible, was the unblushing begging of rich people for things that would make them richer. The queen had many such things in her gift; sinecures (offices with salaries but no duties), monopolies, forfeited estates, benefits of all sorts for which there

---

* In allusion to his pastoral dress.

was an endless stretching out of open hands. She said once to Sir Walter Raleigh:

"When, Sir Walter, will you cease to be a beggar?"

"When your gracious majesty ceases to be a benefactor," replied the ready courtier.

The great writers of Queen Elizabeth's reign need a book to themselves. Shakspeare, Ben Jonson, and Marlowe were among its dramatists; Spenser and Sidney among its poets; Hooker and Bacon among its prose-writers. Thomas Sackville, afterward Lord Buckhurst, but best known as the author of "The Mirror for Magistrates" and "Gorboduc" (the first English tragedy), was among her most trusted councillors. Roger Ascham,* one of the most learned men in England, was Queen Elizabeth's tutor. His fine treatise on education was published in her reign. The queen had some literary aspirations and wrote one very poor sonnet; but her most important writings were her business letters, where she often breaks out into metaphors and is very fond of proverbs. In writing to an ambassador, instead of telling him to burn her letter as soon as he has read it, she says, "Let this memorial be only committed to Vulcan's base keeping, without any larger abode than the reading thereof, yea, and with no mention made thereof to any other wight. * * * *Seem not to have had but secretary's letter from me.*" This is Queen Elizabeth, to the life. It is evident that the ambassador did not obey her injunction on the first point, whatever he may have done as to the others.

James I. lost no time in setting out for London when the queen's death was reported to him. He was acknowl-

---

* Pronounced As'kam.

edged king without opposition, chiefly through the efforts of Sir Robert Cecil, whom he retained as prime minister and created Earl of Salisbury. On his way from Edinburgh he bestowed the honor of knighthood upon two hundred and thirty-seven gentlemen who were presented to him, thus bringing the time-honored institution into derision. James was, in fact, so contemptible a person in all ways that affected the honor and welfare of his people, that the English nation soon became disgusted with him, and his reign was one long struggle between their sense of right and his determination to have his own way. He was most unkingly in his looks and manners. He had goggle eyes and weak legs, and a habit of holding his mouth open so that people could see his tongue while he was talking. As he talked a great deal and said many foolish things, his failings were very conspicuous. He had an immense amount of book-learning, but very little practical common sense, as was shown by his announcing that kings ruled by divine right, and that whatever privileges the subject possessed were due to the condescension of the king. When a man sets out with such a stupid idea as this in an intelligent country like England, we may be sure that the people will make it very uncomfortable for him.

James soon made himself so disagreeable by his vulgarity, his greed for money, and his insolence, that a conspiracy was formed within the first year of his reign to dethrone him and place his cousin, Lady Arabella Stuart (daughter of Lord Darnley's brother) on the throne. This was discovered, and some of the actors in it were executed, while James pardoned others after they had laid their heads on the block. We should scarcely remember this plot but that Sir Walter Raleigh was accused of being concerned in it. There was not evidence enough to convict him, yet he was sentenced to death and left in the Tower for twelve years—a singular way of administering justice. Sir Edward Coke, the attorney-general, was a bitter enemy of Raleigh, and behaved on the trial with a brutality that has made his name infamous. In the same year (1604) James made peace with Spain, thus ending the long war between the two countries. He also was proclaimed king of "Great Britain, France, and Ireland," though properly there was no sovereign of "Great Britain" until after the union with Scotland (1707). The absurd use of the title "King of France" was kept up for two hundred years longer, not being dropped until the nineteenth century.

The year 1605 is memorable as that of the gunpowder plot. The Roman Catholics had expected great favors from James I. (who was so bitterly opposed to Puritanism that they thought he would naturally go to the opposite extreme) but on finding that the severe laws against themselves were re-enacted by James's first Parliament, a few persons formed a plan for getting rid of the king and the Parliament together. They hired a building adjoining the Houses, and, from the cellar of this, dug with incredible labor a passage through a wall nine feet thick into the vault under the Parliament Chamber. In this vault they stored thirty-six barrels of gunpowder, which they covered with fagots, so that the whole looked like a great wood-pile. Parliament was to be opened on the 5th of November;* and on the previous day, Lord

---

* "Remember, remember the Fifth of November,
The Gunpowder Treason and Plot."—Old song.

Monteagle, a Roman Catholic peer, received a mysterious letter warning him to keep away from the session on that day, "for though there would be no appearance of any stir, yet I say they shall receive a terrible blow this Parliament, but shall not see who hurts them." Lord Monteagle instantly gave warning to the authorities; and they, judging from the words used that an explosion must be meant, sent to examine the vaults. There they found a tall, dark man with slow matches and touchwood in his pocket, just coming out of the door, and in the cellar a dark-lantern with a lighted candle in it. The man turned out to be Guido Fawkes (commonly called by the English name, Guy) who gave a false name, but was made to tell his real one by cruel torture. The plan had been to blow up the entire Parliament, Lords, and Commons, together with the king and his oldest son, Prince Henry, who would be present at the opening. They seemed to have very vague notions of what would come next, but expected, somehow or other, to have a new set of laws made which should favor the Catholics. The chief conspirators, among whom were Sir Everard Digby and Robert Catesby, both belonging to families of distinction, were executed. Most of the Catholics in England looked with horror on the plot, and several of them, like Lord Monteagle, gave their help in unearthing it.

In 1607, an event occurred which seemed of very little importance to the English world of that time, but which is a notable fact in our own history; the first permanent English settlement was made in America, at Jamestown (so called in compliment to King James I.), by Captain John Smith and his companions. The king gave the colonists a charter which allowed them to make their own laws, under a governor appointed by himself. From this time we date English rule in America.

Now began the long struggle between King James and his Parliaments which forms the most striking feature of his reign. He called one together only when he needed money; the Parliament regularly demanded that he should reform some of the old abuses of the government, especially the Court of High Commission, and give up some ways of raising money which the Commons thought it high time to do away with. James was obstinate and they were firm, according to our way of looking at it; they voted him only about half as much as he needed to carry on the government, and reminded him that all taxation without consent of Parliament was null and void. Then he dissolved the Parliament and went on raising money illegally; but with all his efforts he could not get as much as was needed for his boundless extravagance. Court life was spent in costly pleasures, and his palaces were the scene of a continual round of balls, masques, and feastings, which the low tastes of James and his queen, Anne of Denmark, turned into drunken revels. He could not live without a "favorite"; some man who could entertain him, while the king would go about with his arm round the favorite's neck, "slobbering over him," as we are told, and kissing him in his disgusting fondness, calling him by pet names, and scandalizing all decent people by his behavior. The sums squandered on these degraded objects of his infatuation are beyond belief. On one occasion he gave his friend Carr an order on the treasury for £20,000. Lord Salisbury (Robert Cecil) had the money counted out in silver and spread out in a room where the king was to meet him. "Whose is that money?" asked James. "It was yours until your Majesty gave it away," answered the minister. This "object lesson" had the desired effect. James swore that the favorite should have only a few hundreds of it, and kept the rest himself. The reform was not permanent, however, and the grasping and the wasting went on as before. Carr, who had been created Duke of Somerset by the king, wished to marry the wife of the Earl of Essex (son of Queen Elizabeth's favorite), who for this purpose obtained a divorce from her husband. This was opposed by Sir Thomas Overbury (one of James's courtiers), who tried vainly to prevent the marriage. Somerset and his wife caused Overbury to be poisoned, and were afterward sentenced to death for the crime. If they had been poor people they would have died on the gallows; but being "noble," James only banished them from his royal presence and gave them an income of $20,000 a year. There is poetical justice in the fact that they were very unhappy, and hated each other cordially for the rest of their lives.

CHAPTER XXXII.

THE BLOODY HAND. RALEIGH. TRANSLATION OF THE BIBLE.

KING JAMES, like most extravagant persons, was always short of money; and an ingenious courtier suggested a way to replenish his finances* by creating a title of honor between the knights and the lowest order of nobility, the barons.

---

* Pronounced fin*an*-ces—accent on the second syllable.

These new dignitaries were to be called baronets. They would be addressed by the title "Sir," like knights, and their wives would be called "Lady;" the difference being that the title was hereditary. The king caught eagerly at the idea, and made as many baronets as could be found willing to purchase the privilege, each one being required to pay a thousand pounds to the king, besides fees to various officers. James wished to bestow the honor on two hundred gentlemen; about half that number availed themselves of the offer. A scheme of colonizing the province of Ulster, in Ireland, with English settlers, who were to take possession of the land forfeited by rebels, was the excuse for this device for raising money. The infant colony, it was said, needed a military guard to protect it from its savage neighbors; but the money raised by the sale of baronetcies did not go to Ulster; it remained in the king's pocket. The arms of Ulster were a bloody hand, and this, being adopted for the new order, has been the crest appropriated to baronets ever since.

The death of Lord Salisbury (1612) removed the principal check upon James's extravagance, and his government became even less respected than before. Henry, Prince of Wales, the king's oldest son, died soon afterward from a fever. This young man was very fond of Sir Walter Raleigh, whom he often visited in the Tower; and it is reported that he said nobody but his father would keep such a bird in such a cage. James had now only two children left; Prince Charles, who afterward became King of England, and the Princess Elizabeth, married to the Elector Palatine, a German sovereign ruling over a territory nearly corresponding to the more recent Grand Duchy of Baden. It is through this princess that the present royal family of England take their title to the throne.

After the dismissal of Somerset, King James took up a new favorite, George Villiers, who was, like Carr, handsome and agreeable, but had far more ability and daring. He spoke out his mind with great freedom, and soon acquired unbounded influence over his master. This made him hated by other courtiers, who could get nothing from the king without first securing the favor of Villiers, and distrusted by the Parliament. James advanced his favorite from one dignity to another until he made him Duke of Buckingham, thus securing for his benefit the title of one of the proudest families in England.

All this time, Sir Walter Raleigh had been languishing in prison. It is said that his imprisonment was not severe and that his wife was allowed to be with him. He was very industrious, and not only wrote the "History of the World" during his confinement, but amused himself with experiments in chemistry, in which he was very skilful. Though he was now sixty-three years old, he was full of vigor and enthusiasm, and in an evil hour he persuaded the king to allow him to go to Guiana, in South America, where, he said, he knew of some gold mines. Gold always opened a way to James's heart; he consented to release Raleigh, though without pardoning him, and sent him out on his quest.

What was called Guiana in Raleigh's time included what we now call Venezuela, and it was somewhere on the Orinoco that Raleigh expected to find the mine. As the country belonged to Spain, the English could have no right to enter it except peaceably, and Raleigh was warned that there must be no fighting. The expedition proved a failure; no gold mine was found, and Raleigh's son was killed in an encounter with the Spaniards.

The Spanish minister in London, whose brother had been killed at St. Thomas (a Spanish fort taken and destroyed by one of Raleigh's captains while Sir Walter was ill on his own ship), now demanded the punishment of Raleigh for having attacked Spain in time of peace. The mean, cowardly James, wishing to marry his son to a Spanish princess, determined to sacrifice Raleigh; and instead of accusing him of his real offence, which was carrying out the king's wishes with too much zeal, he had the baseness to order the execution of the sentence passed against him fourteen years before. Raleigh met his death bravely and calmly, saying of the axe that was to behead him, "'Tis a sharp remedy, but it is a cure for all ills." No action of James's reign, though he committed many disgraceful ones, has left so deep a stain upon his name as this (1618).

In 1620, we come to another of those landmarks of time which stand out so distinctly in our sight—the sailing of the "Pilgrim Fathers" in the Mayflower. These emigrants belonged to that class of Puritans called "Brownists" from their founder, or "Separatists," because they wished to separate themselves entirely from the Church of England. Driven from their own country by persecution, they settled for awhile at Leyden, in Holland, and then, stopping for a short time in England, sailed from Plymouth, in Devonshire, to Plymouth, in Massachusetts Bay.

Frederic V., the Elector Palatine, who had married James's daughter, Elizabeth, was at this time (1620) in trouble from having accepted an invitation from the Protestants of Bohemia to become their king. He was defeated by the legitimate claimant; and all Europe was looking on, expecting that James would send help to his son-in-law, whose cause was well understood to be the cause of Protestantism. The king's theories, however, did not permit that. According to them, the Catholic King of Bohemia was so by Divine right; therefore, his subjects must not try to get rid of him and take a Protestant in his place. This added to James's unpopularity in England, and he soon came to an open quarrel with the Commons. They became more out-spoken than ever, and when James told them that they had no rights except such as he chose to allow them, they answered with spirit that the rights and liberties of the people of England were quite independent of the king, and that they had, and ought to have, freedom "to propound, treat, reason, and bring to conclusion" whatever concerned the welfare of the country. This is exactly the spirit of the "Declaration of Rights" by our own Continental Congress, and of all the other sturdy utterances which preceded and led up to our Declaration of Independence. James was furiously angry. He sent for the journal of the House of Commons, and tore out the record of the offensive resolution. "I will govern according to the common weal," said he, "but not according to the common will." He dissolved the Parliament; but it was like shutting up a smouldering fire. It is checked for the moment; but sooner or later the flame will burst forth, and the ruin will follow all the more surely.

One measure had been carried through by this Parliament which we can not even now think of without pain. This was the impeachment, for bribery and corruption, of Francis Bacon, Viscount St. Albans, Lord Chancellor of England; the "wisest, brightest, meanest of mankind," as Pope calls him. It was not that he had been more corrupt than others, but that Parliament was determined to make an example, and unfortunately Bacon was open to some charges of this kind. The bribes he had taken had been few, but they were enough to convict him. This truly great man, occupying the highest position it was possible for a subject to hold in England, was degraded from his office, sentenced to pay a fine of £40,000, and to be imprisoned during the king's pleasure. The latter punishment was remitted by James, but the far greater one, the loss of his good name, could not be spared him. He lived five years longer, a retired life, devoted to study and scientific pursuits, happier, perhaps, than he had been in the feverish struggle for wealth. His extravagance had undone him.

Disappointed in getting money from Parliament, James now began intriguing with Spain for the marriage of his son, Prince Charles, to the Infanta (princess) of that country—a measure which he knew to be most distasteful to his subjects. "I must have money," said this worthy king, "and if my people won't give it to me, I must get it from Spain in the shape of a dowry." After some negotiation with the Spanish court, the prince, or, as his father delighted to call him, Baby Charles, set off for Spain with Buckingham, whom the king nicknamed "Steenie,"* and they travelled there in disguise under the names of John and Thomas Smith. As their coming had not been announced, much surprise was felt in Spain

---

* Sir Walter Scott's novel, "The Fortunes of Nigel," treats of life in England under James I.

at so un-royal a proceeding; but they were politely received, and Prince Charles was allowed to see the Infanta. The negotiations came to nothing, and the visitors went back to England very much displeased. Buckingham, who had behaved at the Spanish court with such insolent familiarity as to disgust every one who saw him, pretended, on his return, that he had prevented the match, and Prince Charles, the most untruthful of men, supported him in this statement. James was inconsolable at the loss of two millions of gold crowns, which he was to have had with the Infanta, but the Commons, thankful to get rid of the marriage at any price, immediately voted him a large sum of money, and all seemed to be prospering when the king was attacked by an ague, and died after a few days' illness. He was in the fifty-ninth year of his age, and had reigned twenty-two years in England.

It is hard to be just to James the First. His personal qualities were so disagreeable and many of his notions so foolish that they obscure his better qualities. He had not the rough strength of the Plantagenets nor the dignity of the Tudors. He was personally a coward, and wore a thickly padded coat for fear some one should stab him; at the same time he was slovenly in his habits and an habitual profane swearer. In government, he seemed to lack all sense of responsibility, his vanity making him believe that it was enough for him to will a thing to make that the only thing possible to be done. His friends called him the British Solomon; Henry IV. of France said he was "the wisest fool in Europe." Among other efforts to interfere with people's personal rights was his trying to prevent the use of tobacco, which had by this time grown into great favor. James was very fond of writing books, and in his "Counterblast to Tobacco" describes the use of that weed as being a custom "loathsome to the eye, hateful to the nose, harmful to the brain, and injurious to the lungs." King James's own contributions to learning are now merely matters of curiosity; the great addition to the stock of the world's literature in his reign was the translation of the Bible made by his order and published in 1611. This is the "Authorized Version"—the one now in common use. Forty-seven learned men were employed on it for four years, and by its means our English language has been fixed in its present form.

Many famous dramatists and poets lived in James I.'s reign, some of them belonging also partly to Elizabeth's. Shakspeare did not die until 1616; Bacon and Raleigh come in both centuries. Names of lesser note must be learned in connection with English literature. Among men of science perhaps next to Bacon, stands Dr. Harvey, discoverer of the circulation of the blood. It is said that he lost practice by putting forth so absurd an idea.

CHAPTER XXXIII.

CHARLES I. "THE THOROUGH." THE LONG PARLIAMENT.

SOON after his accession, Charles I. brought home his bride, Henrietta Maria, the daughter of Henry IV. of France and sister of Louis XIII. She was only sixteen, and brought in her train a great company of French courtiers, and twenty-nine priests, so that the English were at once prejudiced against her.

Charles was now twenty-five years old (1625). A Parliament was promptly summoned, for James had left the country without money and in debt. The first demand of the Commons was for a redress of grievances; they demanded stricter laws in regard to religion, and wished to know for what purpose the king was going to use the money he asked for. Haughtily declining to answer this, he disolved the Parliament (1625), and proceeded to levy taxes on his own authority, in defiance of the laws. Buckingham undertook an expedition for the relief of the Huguenots in La Rochelle,* but it was a complete failure, with no result but an immense increase of debt (1627). The Commons sent a "Remonstrance" to the king, in which they complained that the conduct of the war had "extremely wasted that stock of honor that was left unto this kingdom, sometime terrible to all other nations, now declining in contempt beneath the meanest." As they further demanded the dismissal of the Duke of Buckingham, the second Parliament was dismissed like the first (1626). A second expedition was about to sail for France in aid of the Huguenots; Buckingham, in spite of his evident incapacity, being again put in command, when he was assassinated by John Felton, a lieutenant in the navy who was angry at being refused promotion. The king wept; the people shouted for joy. The Earl of Lindsey took Buckingham's place, made another failure, and the starving garrison of La Rochelle surrendered to the Catholics.

One more Parliament (whom Charles, on dismissing

* See "A Short History of France," p. 214.

them, called "a set of vipers") closes the first period of his reign. It presented to the king the famous "Petition of Right," a sort of re-statement of the Magna Charta, which he was forced to sign. He ventured on an imprudent exercise of his prerogative by committing to the Tower several members who opposed his wishes. Some of them were released on bail, but Sir John Eliot, refusing to make any submission, was kept in prison until he died, three years later, of a disease brought on by his close confinement. He is often called the first martyr in the cause of English liberty.

Among the "grievances" of which redress was demanded were two illegal courts; the Star-Chamber, which dealt with political offenders, and the Court of High Commission (dating from Elizabeth's day) which judged ecclesiastical cases. The Star-Chamber had long been in existence, but had never until now been so scandalously misused. Men who were brought before these courts were condemned to punishments far beyond any which would have been inflicted in an ordinary court of justice. Crushing fines, whipping, branding, slicing off of ears in the pillory, and slitting of noses, besides indefinite imprisonment, were among the sentences passed on persons who spoke or wrote anything against the king's majesty or against the established church; and there was no redress.

For eleven years (1629-1640), Charles ruled without a Parliament, and by means which the Petition of Right, signed by himself, had declared to be illegal. His chosen ministers during this time were Thomas Wentworth, who had begun his career as an ardent friend of liberty, and Dr. William Laud, lately made Archbishop of Canterbury. These two men concerted with Charles a system which they called "The Thorough," and which, when carried out, was intended to reduce every man in the kingdom, body and soul, into complete subjection. Wentworth forgot all about the people's liberties after he became chief minister of the king, and Laud had but one wish, that of establishing the English liturgy, by force if need be, throughout the length and breadth of the land.

Being in need of money, Charles now proceeded to levy tonnage and poundage* on his own authority, and also demanded ship-money—a tax for the equipment of a navy—from the whole kingdom. In addition to these he granted monopolies (of course in return for large payments of money) though the Parliament had made all monopolies illegal and had forever abolished them.† John Hampden, a gentleman from Buckinghamshire, refused to pay the ship-money, and brought the matter before the law-courts. His share was only twenty shillings, equal to $5, and he spent at least a hundred times as much in defending the case, which was decided against him; but his resistance awakened people to a sense of their danger. The attacks on their pockets, however, did not press so heavily on the English as the attacks on their religion. James I. had issued a "Book of Sports" which specified certain games as lawful to be played on Sunday. Charles's Parliaments, being strongly Puritan

---

* Duties on articles imported from foreign countries.

† Speaking of the monopolists, who made their own prices for the most necessary commodities, like soap and salt, a member of Parliament said, "They sup in our cup, they dip in our dish, they sit by our fire; we find them in the dye-vat, the wash-bowls and the powdering-tub. They have marked and sealed us from head to foot."

in sentiment, had forbidden Sunday pastimes. The king now issued a proclamation authorizing such sports, which he required every minister to read aloud from his pulpit. One of them did so, and at the close of the reading said, "You have now heard the commandment of God and the commandment of man; obey which you please." Most of the Puritan clergymen refused to comply, and were turned out of their parishes by the Court of High Commission. Many of them took refuge in New England, where they could worship God according to their own consciences. England's loss was America's gain.

At the same period with the Puritan exodus, a different class of religious believers were finding a home on our shores. Lord Baltimore, a high-minded Roman Catholic, wishing to provide a refuge for the persecuted people of his own belief, obtained from Charles (1632) a grant of lands on the shores of Chesapeake Bay, where a thriving colony was established which was named Maryland, after Charles's queen, Henriette Marie. Lord Baltimore was the first to give to the world the noble spectacle of a colony founded on complete religious toleration.

In Scotland, Laud's attempts to enforce Episcopacy were not so successful as in England. He prepared a liturgy for the Scottish Church, modeled on that of England, and a day was appointed for its first use. A large congregation was assembled in the cathedral of St. Giles in Edinburgh, and the dean began to read the service. Instantly cries of "A Pope! A Pope! Antichrist!" filled the air, and an enraged woman named Jenny Geddes flung a stool at the dean's head. The uproar was so great that the meeting broke up in confusion. A covenant was drawn up, signed by great numbers of the

Scots, binding themselves to resist all efforts to interfere with their religion. Charles offered some concessions, but, as usual, was too late, and only succeeded in showing his weakness. The next year (1638), in a general assembly which met at Glasgow, Episcopacy, the Court of High Commission in Scotland, and the Liturgy were all abolished at a single stroke, every one being required to sign the covenant or be turned out of the church.*

So matters wore along until the year 1640, when Charles, having exhausted his resources,† was obliged to summon a Parliament, after an interval of eleven years. He made his demand at once for supplies, but the tiresome Commons declined to consider that question until they had talked over their "grievances." They discussed illegal imprisonments, ship-money, tonnage and poundage, and various other things; and there is no knowing to what length their perversity would have carried them, if the king had not tried his old remedy and dissolved the Parliament after a session of three weeks.

It was a foolish thing to do, and Charles knew this as soon as he had done it. The ill-feeling against his two ministers was increasing every day. Laud was considered no better than a papist. In his zeal, he had restored many of those forms and practices of the Romish Church which were most abhorrent to the Puritans. Crucifixes, vestments, genuflexions, all that belonged to an elaborate ritual,‡ were things without which, in his mind, re-

---

* See Sir Walter Scott's novel, "A Legend of Montrose" for references to the condition of Scotland at this time.

† Pronounced re*sour′*ces; accent on the second syllable.

‡ In regard to Scotland he remarked, "They have no religion there, that I can see!"

ligion could not be; and he went so far that the pope had privately offered to make him a cardinal if he wished to become reconciled to the Church of Rome. But he had no such wish; he simply desired to establish the ritual of the Church of England as he thought it ought to be, and then force every man, woman, and child in the British dominions to conform to it. Wentworth, now created Earl of Strafford, was a tyrant at heart; and all the authors of "The Thorough" were riding post-haste to their own destruction.

On November 3d, 1640, Charles called together his last Parliament. As it sat for thirteen years, it is called in history, "The Long Parliament." Its first business was to send for the poor wretches who were still pining under sentences from the Star-Chamber and the Court of High Commission. Dr. Leighton, a clergyman of the Church of Scotland, who had dared to write against prelacy, and who had now passed ten years of his life-sentence in prison, was brought to London. He had been whipped, pilloried, had his ears cut off and each side of his nose slit, and was branded on each cheek. Mutilated, deaf, and blind, he was set at liberty, and received some compensation in money. William Prynne, a zealous Puritan writer, had put forth a book against the stage, and as Queen Henrietta Maria was very fond of the theatre, this book was taken as an insult to her. He too had lost his ears and was serving a life-sentence in prison when a decree of Parliament released him. The Commons then condemned, under the name of "Delinquents," all who had been in any way employed in carrying out illegal acts, and Laud and Strafford were thrown into the Tower on the charge of treason. Before their trial came on, Parliament passed a law to abolish all images, altars, and crucifixes, in consequence of which Edward I.'s beautiful Charing Cross was torn down, and also the gilded one in Cheapside. The order was carried out so ruthlessly that many things were destroyed beside the crosses, and we miss much lovely stained glass and exquisite carving, the fruit of years of labor on the part of those who thought they were serving God.

While this was going on, Strafford's case was taken up. As there was some difficulty in proving the charges against him, the impeachment was changed to a bill of attainder, where the charge does not need to be proved, but is passed, like any other law, by the Lords and Commons, the king giving his consent. Pym, the leading orator of the House of Commons, brought forward the charge against Strafford, who defended himself with great ability, but was condemned, as had been intended from the beginning. Strafford wrote a letter to the king, generously bidding him consent to his death, if by so doing he could make matters easier for himself; and Charles, always weak where he should have been firm, and obstinate where he should have yielded, basely gave his assent to the execution.

Strafford had not expected that the king would take him at his word, and exclaimed bitterly, "Put not your trust in princes!" but he met his fate with dignity and composure. An eye-witness says that he walked to the scaffold with the step and manner of a general marching at the head of an army, rather than the demeanor of a condemned criminal. As he passed the window of the room where Laud was confined, he knelt down and asked his blessing. The archbishop was kept four years in prison before he followed his friend to the block.

On the same day with the order for Strafford's execution, the king signed the most important bill of the session; namely, one stating that Parliament should not from that time forth be dissolved nor adjourned without its own consent, and that the king was bound to call it together at least once in three years. The Star-Chamber and the Court of High Commission were abolished; and the Houses, feeling that they had done enough for one session, adjourned.

A frightful rebellion now broke out in Ireland, where the natives were joined by the "English of the Pale," [*] and excesses committed too horrible to tell. The king was accused of encouraging this rebellion in order that he might raise money to quell it, and though this seems impossible to believe, Charles's faithlessness and insincerity were so well known that the Commons paid no attention to his denial. They framed a "Remonstrance," setting forth his illegal measures and his various acts of tyranny, and brought out the fact that unless some means could be devised for putting an end to them, their liberty would be a thing of the past. There was a tremendous opposition to the measure. For twelve hours the debate lasted, and, for the first time in the history of Parliament, lights were brought in while it was in session. Members on both sides drew their swords, and only the good management of Hampden kept the peace. At midnight

---

[*] "The Pale" was a district in the eastern part of Ireland which had been occupied by English settlers for hundreds of years. The inhabitants were Catholics, and were more in sympathy with the Irish than with their English masters.

the Remonstrance was passed by a small majority, and the next day copies of it were sent all over England.

CHAPTER XXXIV.

CIVIL WAR. MARSTON MOOR. NASEBY.

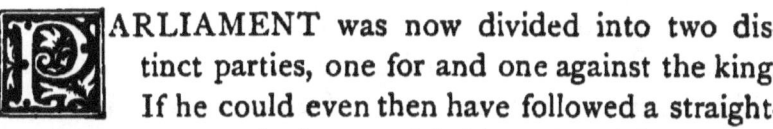ARLIAMENT was now divided into two distinct parties, one for and one against the king. If he could even then have followed a straightforward course, and given up his idea of "divine right," all might have gone smoothly again; but such a course was impossible to him. His one idea was to be able to rule without interference, and he seemed to learn nothing from experience.

While public feeling was in an excited and irritable state, the king ventured on a step which threw all his previous indiscretions into the shade. Accusing of high-treason five members of the House of Commons, including Hampden and Pym, and one of the Upper House, Lord Kimbolton, he sent a sergeant-at-arms to the Commons, demanding that the five members should be delivered into his custody. The members were in their seats, but remained silent when called upon, and the speaker ordered the officer to withdraw. The next day the king came himself and demanded the five members, who had, by direction of the House, absented themselves. Charles asked where they were. The speaker, Lenthall, fell on his knees, saying that he had no eyes to see nor tongue to speak but as the House commanded him. "Well," said the king good-humoredly, looking round the

House, "I see the birds are flown, but I expect you to send them to me as soon as they return." As he passed out he heard cries of "Privilege! Privilege!" which meant that he was infringing upon the rights of the members. On cooler reflection, Charles felt that he had gone too far. He made an apology to the House and withdrew his charges against the members, but he could not calm the excitement he had raised.

The Commons seized the magazine at Hull, and took possession of the Tower of London. They also passed a bill assuming entire control of the militia. This the king refused to sign, and both sides prepared for war.

The enthusiasm for the Parliament, among its supporters, was unbounded. Money poured in for the raising of troops. Immense quantities of plate were sent to be melted up, and so many small articles of personal use were contributed that it was called in derision "the thimble and bodkin war." The queen raised some money in Holland by selling her jewels, and the Royalists were not behindhand in making sacrifices. All felt that the country was preparing for a momentous struggle.

The difference between the two parties now grew more marked than ever. Those on the king's side took the name of Cavaliers, while those belonging to the Parliament were called Roundheads, because they generally wore their hair cropped close. Most of the nobility were royalists, though the Earl of Essex (son of Elizabeth's favorite) was made general of the Parliamentary forces. Having collected as many men as he could, Charles set up his royal standard at Nottingham (1642).

Prince Rupert (son of Charles's sister and the Elector Palatine) began the war by routing a small body of Parliamentary cavalry at Worcester. The first general battle was an indecisive one at Edgehill, where the Earl of Lindsey, the royal general, was mortally wounded. In a battle at Chalgrove Field (1643), otherwise unimportant, the Parliamentary party lost the great patriot Hampden, who was deeply regretted by both sides. His moderation and tact were invaluable in such a struggle; and, had he lived, might have changed the issue of the war.* On the king's side a loss almost equally great was that of Lord Falkland, who was killed at Newbury. Several other battles were fought this year, gained mostly by the Royalists, who were far superior to their opponents in military experience and training. The Parliamentary army, as yet, was made up largely of the enthusiastic but untrained rabble, and had little of that material which afterward made them invincible. By the efforts of Sir Henry Vane (the younger) an alliance was entered into with the Scots, by which their "Solemn League and Covenant" to fight to the death against popery, prelacy (by which they meant the Church of England), superstition, and profanity, was made equally binding on the English. The House of Commons in England swore to observe this agreement, and the name "Covenanter" became a party watch-word, binding the subscribers to one another as with bonds of steel.

All this time there had been serving in the Parliamentary army a man who, though as yet undistinguished, was destined to play a more important part in England than any other man has ever filled there. This was Oliver

---

* A locket was found on Hampden's body, inscribed:
"Not against the King I fight,
But *for* the King and country's right."

Cromwell, a plain country gentleman, who had begun his public life in the Parliament of 1628. His rustic air and ill-fitting clothes caused some of the members to look on him with contempt, and one of them asked Hampden, "Who is that sloven?" Hampden told him, adding, "If we should ever come to a breach with the king, that sloven will be the greatest man in England." Cromwell was Hampden's cousin, and the two men had formed a plan of settling in America. It is said that they had actually embarked, but were forced back by an order of council. Cromwell was a man of an intensely religious spirit and a wonderful power of influencing other men. He soon gained such an ascendency over the solid men of his own party that great numbers of them entered the army, giving it a character of dignity which it had heretofore lacked. Cromwell had entered it as a colonel of cavalry, and had drilled his regiment until his men received and deserved their name of "Ironsides." These Ironsides were all "men of religion." If they were not so before, they caught the spirit of their surroundings and became as ardent in devotion as they had before been in dissipation. "They are a lovely company," Cromwell says. "Not a man swears but he pays his twelve pence." No drunkenness was allowed, nor any of the other vices to which soldiers are addicted; their recreation consisted in listening to a godly discourse, and when they fought, they felt that "the Spirit of the Lord was upon them." If any man proved himself unworthy of belonging to such a body, or was not amenable to discipline, he was dismissed at once. "A few honest men are better than numbers," said Cromwell. In the same letter he writes, "I had rather have a plain russet-coated captain that knows what he fights for and loves what he knows, than that which you call 'a gentleman' and is nothing else. I honor a *gentleman* that is so indeed!"

Charles was daily losing ground. Prince Rupert, a brave but rash young soldier, insisted upon giving battle to the enemy at Marston Moor, contrary to the advice of the Marquis of Newcastle, his superior in command. Here the royal army was completely routed, chiefly by means of Cromwell and his Ironsides. "God made them as stubble to our swords," he wrote to a friend the same evening. Newcastle, in disgust, abandoned the king's cause and left the country.

On the other hand, the divisions in the Parliamentary party itself had now become fatal to any unity of action. At first, those who differed from the Established Church were mostly Presbyterians, but the sect called Independents, to which Cromwell belonged, was rapidly advancing in power and influence. A part of them wished to abolish both monarchy and aristocracy, from which they took the name of "Root-and-Branch" men. Cromwell, wishing to get rid of certain influential members of Parliament, induced it to pass a so-called "Self-denying Ordinance," making it impossible to hold a seat in Parliament and a position in the army at the same time. Acting upon this, many of the members resigned their commands in the army, though an exception was made in Cromwell's favor.

He now set himself about raising the whole army to the standard of his own Ironsides. What he called "The New Model" was introduced into it, maintained by a rigorous discipline and inspired by a religious zeal and fervor never equalled in history. Each officer was a chaplain; the soldiers spent their spare hours in prayer and in the study of the Scriptures, and in their talks together discussed the state of their souls and encouraged one another to greater zeal. They marched to battle singing hymns to the accompaniment of military bands.

The greatest battle of the war was fought at Naseby, where the king commanded in person (June, 1645) and was defeated by Cromwell. During all this time efforts were made to treat with Charles, but his habitual duplicity made any arrangement impossible. At Naseby his cabinet was taken, where letters were found more damaging than the loss of a battle. He was discovered to have been asking for soldiers from abroad, in spite of his most solemn assurances to the contrary; his statements to the queen were exactly opposite to those he made to his enemies, and he boasted of how well he had been able to deceive the Parliament, and how he would crush out all opposition when the power was in his own hands again. At length, hopeless of making terms with them, he fled to Newark and put himself under the protection of the Scots, who were encamped at that place. They required him to sign orders to give up to them all the castles still occupied by his troops, and after a short interval they made an agreement with the English Parliament to deliver him into their hands, on payment of a sum of money due to them for the expenses of the war. The Scots tried to take away from this transaction the appearance of a sale, but the verdict of history is against them, and as a sale it will be handed down to posterity.

"I am sold and bought," said the king, when the two hundred cases of silver which sealed the bargain made their appearance in the Scottish camp.

By this time the most bitter feeling had arisen between

the Parliament and the army—in other words, between the Presbyterians and the Independents. Their hatred of each other was quite as great as that which each felt toward the "Malignants," by which name Cromwell's party called all Royalists who had taken part in the war. The Parliament had the king in charge; the army wanted him; and one Cornet Joyce appeared suddenly before him at Holmby House with a band of troopers at his back, and told Charles he must go with him. "Where is your warrant?" asked the king. "There!" said Joyce, pointing down into the court-yard, where four hundred soldiers were drawn up. "It is written in very legible characters," answered the king, and made no resistance. The Parliament threatened violence when they found they had been outwitted, but Cromwell marched his whole army through London, and things quieted down directly. The king was now removed to Hampton Court Palace, where he enjoyed much freedom, but fearing that harm was intended him, he fled secretly to the Isle of Wight, where he was kindly received by the governor, and lodged in Carisbrook Castle.

CHAPTER XXXV.

PRIDE'S PURGE. EXECUTION OF CHARLES I. DUNBAR AND WORCESTER.

THE Parliament made one more effort to treat with Charles, and offered terms which seemed impossible for him to reject; but being then engaged in secret negotiations with the Scots he refused these, and lost his last chance. They then voted that no further address should be made to him. After a short sojourn in Newport (Isle of Wight) during which still more evidences of his duplicity were discovered, he was removed to Hurst Castle, a gloomy fortress on the Sussex coast, where he anticipated the fate of Edward II. at Berkeley and Richard II. at Pontefract. But assassination had gone out of date in England; and when he hinted his fears to his guards they told him that whatever the Parliament did would be "very public, and in a way of justice to which the world should be witness." It is a curious proof of the strength of loyal feeling even as late as this, that while Cromwell was away fighting the Scots, who were in arms for the king, Parliament reconsidered its former vote and decided to send further propositions to him. The army, however, interfered, and a council of officers sent Col. Pride (formerly a drayman) with two regiments of soldiers to the Parliament House to turn out all members in favor of treating with the king. This expulsion went on until a hundred and forty of them had been sent off, and none remained except about fifty Independents, who could be relied on to execute the orders of the army (December, 1648). This high-handed action was popularly called "Pride's Purge," the body left as a Parliament receiving the name of "The Rump."

Cromwell returned while the "clearance" was going on; he said he did not know of it, but was glad it had been done. The remnant of the Commons next voted that it was treason in the king to make war on the Parliament, and that he should be tried for this offence. The House of Lords, now reduced to twelve members, not wishing to join in this vote, took a recess, hoping to prevent it; but the Commons declared that, the people being the origin of all just power, the Commons of England are the superior authority of the nation, and that whatever is enacted by them has the force of law without the consent of the king or the House of Peers.

In pursuance of this statement, the "Rump" appointed a High Court of Justice for the trial of the king, of which John Bradshaw was president, Cromwell, Ireton, and the chief officers of the army being members of it. The judges had also been appointed to serve on this court, but as they said the proceeding was contrary to law, they were excused from taking part in it.

The king, after leaving Hurst Castle, was brought to London by General Harrison, one of the most violent of the Republican leaders, and lodged in the palace of Whitehall. The trial took place in Westminster Hall; the same room which had seen the dethronement of Richard II., the condemnation of Sir Thomas More, of the Protector Somerset, and of Lord Strafford; the same noble building which, divested of its judicial furniture, now forms the entrance to the Houses of Parliament. The court consisted of one hundred and thirty-five persons, but there were never more than seventy present at any one sitting.

The king, who had come from the palace in a sedan-chair, was escorted in by the sergeant-at-arms, and took his place in the seat set for him opposite the judges. He did not remove his hat, and the sixty-nine judges kept on theirs without rising from their seats. When addressed as Charles Stuart, King of England, and asked for his answer to the charge of being a tyrant, a traitor, and a murderer, the king denied the jurisdiction of the court and refused to plead before it. This continued for three days. Then some witnesses were examined who testified that he had borne arms against the Parliament, and sentence of death was pronounced Jan. 27, 1648-49.*

Only two of Charles's children were still in England; Elizabeth, aged twelve years, and Henry, aged nine. These were allowed to take leave of him, on the day before his death. The young girl remained a prisoner in the hands of the Republicans. She pined away, and died the next year of a slight illness. The son was afterward sent to his mother in France, but did not live to grow up.

The execution was appointed for Jan. 30th, 1648-9, at two in the afternoon. A scaffold was erected outside the window of the banqueting-room of the palace of Whitehall, and out of this the king walked firmly, after spending several hours in devotion. He had meant to speak to the people, but seeing that none but soldiers were within hearing, he addressed himself to the few friends who were on the scaffold with him. Consistent to the last, he said that his people mistook the nature of government; that people are free, not by having a share in the government, but by assisting in its administration. Bishop Juxon, his old friend, attended him. The king gave him his "George"† with the single word "Remember!" He then knelt in prayer for a few minutes, and gave the signal to the executioner by stretching out his hand. His head was severed at one blow, and when the masked executioner held up the "gray,

---

*This date was then called 1648, as the year began on the 25th of April instead of the 1st of January, as at present.

† A decoration belonging to the Order of the Garter.

discrowned head" with the usual formula, "This is the head of a traitor!" a deep groan burst from the crowd around instead of the expected cheers.*

Charles Stuart died in the forty-ninth year of his age and the twenty-fourth of his reign.

No event in English history has been the subject of so much discussion as the judicial death of Charles the First. To the loyalists it was a deliberate murder; to the opposite party, a patriotic necessity. It was brought about by means as clearly illegal as any thing Charles had done; but those who did it justified themselves on the ground of political necessity. It could not have happened in a later age; coming when it did it is generally considered a benefit to the cause of liberty.

In his private life Charles I. was blameless. He was thoroughly refined, had a fine taste in literature, and was a generous patron of art. In all but his public dealings he was scrupulously honorable and gentlemanly. His false notions of the rights and duties of a king made him unfit to be one; while his habitual indecision prevented him from taking advantage of circumstances when they were favorable to him. Added to this, his absolute inability to speak the truth in political matters, took away his last chance of regaining his hold upon the affections of his people.

The death of the king made a re-organization of the

---

*Andrew Marvell, the friend of Cromwell and Charles's political enemy, who was looking from a window at the time, wrote,

"He nothing common did, or mean
Upon that memorable scene;
But laid his comely head
Down, as upon a bed."

government necessary. It was declared treason to acknowledge Charles Stuart (his son) as King of England, and a new seal was engraved with the motto, "The first year of freedom by God's blessing restored, 1648." No name was formally given to the new government, but it is generally called "The Commonwealth." All public business was done in the awkward name of "The Keepers of the Liberties of England." The House of Lords was abolished at the same time, as being "useless and dangerous." A Council of State composed of forty-one members, with Bradshaw as president, was next appointed; but the real power naturally remained with Cromwell. His brother-in-law, Desborough, and his sons-in-law, Ireton and Fleetwood, held important commands in the army. John Milton, the poet, was appointed Latin Secretary to the government. He had come back from his travels in Italy on account of the Civil War, and had already written some political works, and his poem of "Lycidas," which reflected severely on the Established Church. Among other writers of the royalist period were George Herbert and Francis Quarles, religious poets; Sir John Suckling and Richard Lovelace, song writers, Isaac Walton and Sir Thomas Browne, essayists. Thomas Fuller, the Church historian, also lived at this period.

The new government did not at first go on very harmoniously. More than half the Council refused to sign the required declaration that they approved of what had been done, and it was not until after violent disputes that this was dispensed with. Several of the principal royalist generals were beheaded, as were also the ringleaders of a set called "Levellers," a sort of Socialists.

The chief resistance came from Scotland and Ireland. Presbyterians and Catholics were alike opposed to the Independents, who were now at the head of English affairs, and Charles II. was proclaimed in both countries. Cromwell went at once to Ireland, and by a succession of merciless slaughters reduced that country to obedience. He next proceeded to Scotland, where the loyalists had met with a severe loss in the death of the Marquis of Montrose. He was betrayed by a pretended friend and taken prisoner to Edinburgh, where he was hanged with every circumstance of insult that vindictiveness could devise.* Charles II. (we will call him so to distinguish him, though it was ten years before he received that title in England) landed in Scotland soon afterward, and was obliged, in order to be recognized as king, to sign the covenant, and profess many things which he did not believe. Cromwell met the Scottish army near Dunbar. Their number amounted to double that of his own, and his position was a very dangerous one. They advanced on him rashly, and were badly beaten Sept. 3, 1650. Edinburgh surrendered soon afterward.

Charles II. was crowned King of Scotland, at Scone, as his ancestors had been, but he and his subjects did not get on well together. They preached at him a great deal, and required him to pursue a most distasteful way of life; so, seizing his opportunity, he gathered an army hastily together and marched into England, expecting that the Royalists there would join him. In this he was disappointed. Cromwell pursued him and overtook him at Worcester, where, after a sharp fight of five hours, the

---

*See the beautiful poem entitled "The Execution of Montrose," in Aytoun's "Lays of the Scottish Cavaliers."

royal army broke and fled (Sept. 3, 1651). This battle Cromwell called his "crowning mercy." The Scottish army of about 14,000 men were either killed or taken prisoners. Of the captives, 1500 were sold as slaves to the West Indies. The king left his companions without notice, and, accompanied by one faithful friend, Col. Carless, took refuge at Boscobel, a lonely farm-house owned by a man named Penderell. This man received the wanderers with the greatest kindness, dressed them in his own and his brother's clothes and protected them for several days. Charles spent one night concealed among the boughs of an oak tree, which might be still standing if it had not been cut down by tourists. It was called "The Royal Oak," and was long shown with veneration to travellers. The prince had all sorts of adventures. At one time he acted as the servant of Jane Lane, a young lady who rode many miles behind him on a pillion, to bring him to safe quarters. At last he joined his mother in Paris.

Under Cromwell's vigorous and wise government, all prospered with England. Ireton finished the conquest of Ireland, Monk that of Scotland; Robert Blake, the great admiral, captured a Portuguese fleet of richly-laden vessels, because the Portuguese had been helping Prince Rupert. The "Channel Islands,"* the Scilly Islands and the Isle of Man, which held out for the king, were all subdued, the last named being defended by the heroic Countess of Derby, whose husband had been executed by the Parliament.† The English also had trouble with Holland, and to annoy their thriving neighbor they passed

---

* Jersey, Alderney, etc., in the English Channel near France.
† See Sir Walter Scott's novel, "Peveril of the Peak."

the famous Navigation Act, by which all nations were forbidden to import any goods into England except in English vessels or in the vessels of the country producing the goods. As the Dutch did most of the carrying trade in Europe, this was very offensive to them, and the two countries soon drifted into a war in which the English admiral Blake was opposed to the Dutch admirals, Van Tromp and De Ruyter. They fought several battles, with various success, and Van Tromp sailed about with a broom fastened to his mast-head, to indicate that he was going to sweep the English from the sea. Thereupon Blake gathered up all his strength, and defeated him in a three days' battle off Portland. Van Tromp's own ship escaped, but the broom came down from the mast-head.

CHAPTER XXXVI.

THE PROTECTORATE. THE RESTORATION.

AFTER some years, Cromwell became dissatisfied with the Long Parliament, and took a method peculiar to himself of putting an end to it. Dressed in his usual suit of plain black with gray worsted stockings, he took three hundred soldiers to the Parliament House, and, leaving them outside, went in and sat for a while, listening to the debate; then starting up he exclaimed, "This is the time! I must do it!" and began loading the members with abuse. Sir Peter Wentworth answered that it was the first time he had ever heard such language used in Parliament, and was going on when Cromwell interrupted him with, "I will put an end to your prating. Call them in! call them in!" Then stamping his feet (which was the signal for the soldiers to enter), he screamed out, "You are no longer a Parliament! The Lord has done with you! He will have other instruments to do his work!" Two files of musketeers entered the room, upon which Sir Henry Vane said, "This is not honest. Yea, it is against common morality." "Oh, Sir Harry Vane! Sir Harry Vane! The Lord deliver me from Sir Harry Vane!" was Cromwell's only reply. Striding up to the table and laying his hand upon the mace, he cried out, "What shall we do with this bauble? Take it away!" The speaker declining to leave the chair, Major General Harrison said he would help him, and pulled him down by force. Cromwell, still wrought up to the highest pitch of passion, called out to the House, "It is you that have forced me to this! I have sought the Lord night and day that He would rather slay me than put me upon this work!" When his soldiers had cleared the hall, Cromwell locked the door, put the key in his pocket, and marched off to his home at Whitehall.*

The Council of State was dismissed in the same summary way. "We have heard," said Bradshaw, the president, "what you have done this morning at the House. But you mistake, sir, if you think the Parliament dissolved. No power on earth can dissolve the Parliament but itself!"

The Rump had been so much disliked by the people that no outcry was made at this high-handed measure,

---

* The French minister wrote home that there was now written, on the Houses of Parliament, "This House to be let, unfurnished!"

especially as Cromwell, having the whole army at his back, was for the time all-powerful.

Choosing to keep up some of the form of constitutionality, he now summoned, in his own name, a hundred and forty persons, from all parts of England, to frame a new Parliament. There was no pretence of an election. All sorts of people were assembled—Fifth Monarchy men* and those belonging to other fanatical sects—and these gave a character to the Parliament. Among the number was a noisy and ignorant man named Praise God Barebone; and he occupied so much of the time of the sessions with long prayers and speeches, that the assembly was called in derision, "Barebone's Parliament." Its more respectful name was, "The Little Parliament."

Big or little, it was a great failure. Its counsels were confused, its meetings disorderly. Having passed several bills of doubtful wisdom, it crowned its operations, after having been in existence five months, by humbly surrendering to the lord general the powers it had received from him, and appointed a Council of State which conferred on him the office of Lord Protector (1653). His signature was like that of a king, only the first name being used. He wrote "Oliver P." (Protector) as the king had signed "Charles R." (Rex). His unmarried daughters were called the Lady Mary and the Lady Francis Cromwell, and both married into noble families.

When he assumed his title a proclamation was issued by Charles II. (who was wandering about, glad to be provided for by any one who would give him a home), which

---

* Persons who expected a kingdom of Christ to arise which should abolish all human governments. The four preceding monarchies had been the Assyrian, Persian, Grecian, and Roman.

began: "Whereas a certain base mechanic fellow, by name Oliver Cromwell, has usurped our throne,"—and went on to offer a pension of £500 a year to any one who should take his life. It did not do much of either good or harm.

For the first time in the history of England a standing army was established, which was to be entirely under the Protector's control, thus enabling him to form a military despotism if he should be so inclined. All churchmen, Presbyterians, and Royalists, were excluded from the Parliament, and no one could be elected to it who had not an estate of at least £200. Finding that the first he summoned was not disposed to submit blindly to his wishes, Cromwell dissolved it without ceremony, in a storm of angry reproach (1655).

After this, the Protector and his council ruled in the most arbitrary manner, levying taxes at discretion and imprisoning persons on suspicion, much as Charles had done. There was a strict censorship of the press,* and when people tried to obtain their rights by law, their counsel were sent to the Tower.

It was a very moral England that Cromwell ruled over. Drunkenness and vagrancy were suppressed, though not apparently with cruelty, and Sabbath-breaking became very difficult. One man sat in the stocks for three hours for going to a neighboring town to hear a sermon on Easter-day and eating milk and cream with some other young folks, the entertainment costing each person two pence. A tailor is punished for working until two o'clock on a Saturday night so as to finish a garment for some

---

* A supervision which allows nothing to be published without being first examined and sanctioned by the government.

one to go to church in. Profane swearing was followed by some hours in the stocks, and one could not say "Plague take you" without being fined for it.

England had never been more respected abroad than during the reign of the Protector. Foreign powers saw that there must be no trifling with Oliver. He made a treaty with France by which Charles I.'s two sons were required to leave that kingdom, while the two countries joined in a war against Spain. More than one tyrant was forced, by the terror of his name, to cease from persecutions which were the disgrace of Christendom. Blake cruised along the Mediterranean destroying the fleets of Algerine pirates, whose cruel ravages made its waters dreaded by all European seamen. Admiral Penn (father of our William Penn) and General Venables, attacked the Spanish West-Indian Islands; they were repulsed from Hayti, but took Jamaica. The Protector was so angry at the misfortune in Hayti that he forgot to be pleased with the capture of the smaller island. And yet Jamaica is not to be despised as an acquisition.

Blake had many brilliant successes at sea, but died prematurely, worn out by hard work and exposure. He was strongly opposed, politically, to Cromwell's usurpation of power, but said, "It is still our duty to fight for our country, into what hands soever the government may fall." He was the type of a true Christian soldier, and was borne to his grave in Westminster Abbey amid the tears and regrets of his countrymen.

Cromwell had boasted, in the early part of his career, that he would make the name of Englishman as much feared and respected abroad as ever that of Roman had been, and he found himself ably supported in his efforts.

He said once, when negotiations were proposed with Spain, "There is no embassy like a ship of the line." For the first time since the death of Elizabeth, England became formidable to her neighbors. France and Spain, the Moor and the Pope, were obliged in turn to bow to her decisions.

Cromwell called one more Parliament, from which he excluded all not favorable to his measures; but he quarreled with this as with the others, and dissolved it in a towering passion (1658). This Parliament offered him the coveted title of King, but the army opposed this so strongly that he did not venture to assume it. His career was now drawing to a close. He was encompassed by trouble at home; the country was deeply in debt; royalist plots were forming around him, and a book entitled "Killing no Murder," by one Colonel Titus of the army, boldly advised taking him off by violence. The Fifth Monarchy men were making a stir against him, and he lived in so great dread of assassination that he wore armor under his clothes and always carried pistols. He never let it be known by what road he was going to travel, nor slept more than two nights in succession in the same room, fearing to give his enemies a chance to make a plot against his life. His favorite daughter, Elizabeth Claypole, died at this time, and the event threw him into a gloom from which he never recovered.

A gleam of pleasure came to him through the capture of Dunkirk* from the Spaniards, by the combined armies of France and England. The town was, by agreement, delivered to him, and was felt by the English to atone,

---

* A city in French Flanders; now the most north-easterly town in France.

in some measure, for the loss of Calais. This was the last public event of importance in his life-time. He was attacked by a slow fever, which was aggravated by his distress of mind, and on the anniversary of the battles of Dunbar and Worcester, he passed quietly away, September 3, 1658, in the sixtieth year of his age.*

Even Cromwell's enemies were obliged to confess that he was a great man. As regarded the people at large, he was a just and vigorous ruler; his foreign policy was far-sighted and brilliant; his aims, at least in the early part of his career, were of the noblest. But his plan of government had a fatal weakness in it. It was built on the power of the sword. Fortunately, the people of England could be trusted to neutralize or destroy the dominion of any ruler who attacked their liberties; and their descendants in America, when their turn came, showed that the lesson had not been lost upon them.

A noble feature of Cromwell's administration was its spirit of toleration. The Church of England was not interfered with, so long as its ministers did not preach against the government; and even the Jews, the outcasts of nations, would have been allowed, if the Protector had had his way, to return and settle legally in England.† There was such violent opposition to this measure that he was obliged to withdraw it; but the Jews came back by little and little, and in 1656 he permitted them to build a synagogue. George Fox, leader of the new sect calling themselves Friends, called by others Quakers, talked more than once with Cromwell, who is represented to have been favorably impressed by him.

---

*Cromwell is one of the characters in Scott's novel, "Woodstock."
†Edward I. had banished them in 1290.

Cromwell left two sons; Richard, a mild-tempered, inoffensive man, with very little capacity, and Henry, who had shown great ability as Lord Lieutenant of Ireland, and was in every way superior to his brother. Unfortunately it was taken for granted that the elder must inherit his father's title, and Richard Cromwell was named Protector, without opposition, on the day after Oliver's death. A Parliament was called, which immediately got into trouble with the army. General Lambert, a prominent officer, who had been the first to propose the Protectorate, plotted against Richard; and the army, acting under his influence, compelled the latter to dissolve the Parliament. Being urged to support his claim by force of arms, Richard replied, "I will not have a drop of blood spilt for the preservation of my greatness. It is only a burden to me." He resigned his office, and the army controlled everything through a council of officers. General Monk, the ablest man in it, did his best for Richard as long as he remained Protector, but then began secretly to conspire with the royalists, who saw their chance in these divisions. The council of officers recalled those members of the Long Parliament whom Cromwell had expelled in 1653, and as these were mostly Presbyterians, they and the Royalists combined against the Independents. As it was impossible for the members to work in harmony, a new assembly, called the Convention Parliament, was summoned, which opened communication with the king, who was then at Breda, in Holland. Charles sent from that place a "Declaration," in which he promised everything that he thought would be acceptable to the people; and, since no one doubted that he would keep his word, he was welcomed back with expressions of heartfelt joy. He entered London on his thirtieth birthday, May 29, 1660. This event is called the Restoration.

CHAPTER XXXVII.

CHARLES II. TRIPLE ALLIANCE. TREATY OF DOVER.

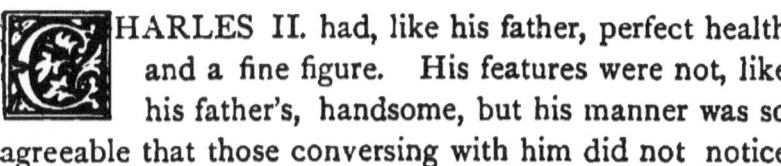HARLES II. had, like his father, perfect health and a fine figure. His features were not, like his father's, handsome, but his manner was so agreeable that those conversing with him did not notice their harshness.

Charles chose his ministers with discretion, taking them, without distinction, from opposite political parties. Edward Hyde, a statesman of ability and integrity, was made lord chancellor and prime minister, under the title of Earl of Clarendon. General Monk, to whom more than to any other person, Charles owed his restoration, was created Duke of Albemarle. James, Duke of York, the king's brother, was made Lord High Admiral. Of the so-called regicides (king-killers), the name given to the judges who tried Charles I., only six were executed. Many of them were dead; some were imprisoned, and a few escaped beyond sea. Two of these, Goffe and Whalley, came to America, and lived for many years in concealment in New England. Many of the Cavaliers were dissatisfied with the "Act of Indemnity and Oblivion," which ended the matter, and said the indemnity was for the king's enemies, the oblivion for his friends.

The Parliament had the childish folly to order that the bodies of Cromwell, Ireton, and Bradshaw should be dragged from their splendid tombs in Westminster Abbey, hung on the gallows at Tyburn for the space of one day, and then buried in a deep pit under it, their heads being cut off and fixed on Westminster Hall. Their estates were also confiscated.

The army was now disbanded, except a few regiments to serve as garrisons and to form a guard for the king. It was the general opinion that the men thus suddenly thrown upon the country would become marauders, or vagrants, but they were formed of too good material for that. They returned quietly to their former occupations, causing scarcely a ripple upon the surface of society; a state of things paralleled by our own experience after the War of the Rebellion.

In religious matters, those who had expected toleration were grievously disappointed. The Church of England was restored, of course; and two new laws were passed; one called the "Act of Uniformity," requiring that every clergyman should be ordained by a bishop and should give up the Covenant, while the other, called the "Corporation Act," made it necessary for every magistrate and every civic corporation to swear never, under any circumstances, to resist the king's authority. More than two thousand clergymen were expelled from their parishes for opposition to the Act of Uniformity.

Laws of a better class were those abolishing the last remains of the feudal system, in the form of certain privileges of royalty which had become intolerable. Instead of them, the king took a yearly sum of money.

When public affairs had somewhat settled down in

England, a new interest began to be felt in the colonies. King Charles, who was always ready to grant a tract of land in America to any one who asked for it, gave to certain persons called "Lords Proprietors" a large territory cut off from the southern part of Virginia, to which was given the name of Carolina (from Carolus, the Latin for Charles). At a later period, an elaborate plan of government called the "Grand Model" was prepared for it. The Grand Model did not work well, however. The people soon grew dissatisfied with it, and early in the next century the tract was divided into two royal provinces called North and South Carolina.

In the third year of his reign, Charles married Catherine of Braganza, a Portuguese princess, who brought him a large dowry in money, besides the city of Tangier in Africa. Though the annalists of that time say that she was "pretty enough," Charles did not admire her, but said, after seeing her for the first time, "Upon my word, they have brought me a bat instead of a woman!" He received her kindly, as he did every one, but soon began to treat her with neglect, bringing into the palace other women whom he openly preferred to her. The court became a scene of the vilest dissipation. The courtiers, both men and women, ridiculed whatever was good and virtuous, so that the better class of persons, of all religious beliefs, withdrew themselves from court. With the main body of the people it was not so; the Puritan leaven was still working among them, and they kept on their way, undisturbed by the scandals of high life. The frivolity of Charles and his associates was of the most expensive sort; and while hundreds of faithful friends who had sacrificed everything for the royal cause were left to languish in poverty, he poured out money like water to satisfy the demands of worthless favorites, and to keep up a round of idle and vicious gayeties. By the advice of Clarendon, he sold the city of Dunkirk to France for £400,000, the minister thinking the king no longer able to support a fortress which required £120,000 a year to maintain. The intention was good, but the result was only to give Charles more money to spend on his infamous pleasures. The English court became the ridicule of foreigners. In one Dutch print the king was represented with his pockets "turned the wrong side outward, hanging out empty;" in another, two courtiers were employed in picking his pockets, while he looked on laughing. To obtain more money from Parliament he picked a quarrel with Holland, and before war was declared, the Duke of York was sent to take possession of New Amsterdam* (1664). The Dutch governor, Peter Stuyvesant, was quite unprepared, so the place was easily captured, as we know from American history. The whole province now forming the states of New York and New Jersey was bestowed on the Duke of York at the same time. He afterward granted New Jersey to two friends of his, Berkeley and Carteret, who in their turn sold it to the Quakers of Pennsylvania.

A more terrible enemy than Hollander or Spaniard now attacked England. This was the Great Plague, which raged with such violence that 100,000 persons died of it in London alone (1665). The red cross, with the words, "Lord, have mercy on us!" marked many a door, and the doleful cry, "Bring out your dead!" sounded every morning as the death-carts took their way

---

* Now the City of New York.

through the desolate streets. With the approach of winter, the pestilence slackened, and the Parliament, which on account of it had been summoned to meet at Oxford, now found leisure to pass the "Five-Mile Act." By this, no dissenting minister who had not taken the oaths of uniformity and non-resistance was allowed to come within five miles of any city, nor of any place where he had formerly preached. There had already been passed a "Conventicle Act," which forbade all persons to meet together for worship in any private house, to the number of more than five in addition to the family. Fines, imprisonment, and transportation were the penalties attached to this offence. The jails were soon filled with men and women who felt that they had no right to refrain from meeting to worship God according to their consciences. In one of those jails, John Bunyan wrote the Pilgrim's Progress; in a hundred others, men as zealous and as earnest, gave their testimony in favor of freedom of worship.

The horror attending the plague had scarcely passed away when the Great Fire again threw the people of London into consternation (1666). Four days it raged without cessation, among the wooden houses of which London was then largely built, and which were at that time as dry as tinder. The fire was at last stopped by blowing up buildings, and it reminds one of modern times and cities to read, in a letter written four days after the flames ceased to spread, "The citizens, instead of complaining, discoursed almost of nothing but of a survey for rebuilding the city of bricks and with large streets." Unfortunately, however, the petty jealousies of proprietors prevented the grand plans of John Evelyn and Sir

Christopher Wren from being carried out, and the streets remained narrow and crooked as before.

It does not give one a very lofty idea of the England of that day to know that when a great monument was built on Fish-street Hill, to commemorate the conflagration, there was an inscription put on it saying that the Roman Catholics set the city on fire; and it is not a little surprising to know that this inscription was allowed to remain there until 1831. Pope refers to it in these lines:

"Where London's column, pointing to the skies,
Like a tall bully, lifts the head and lies."

Meanwhile the war with Holland went on. There was now no Blake to strike terror to the nations, and uphold the honor of England's flag. To save expense, or rather to have more money for his own pleasures, Charles had allowed the navy to run down; and the Dutch, taking advantage of this, sailed up the Thames as far as London Bridge, burning the shipping as they went along. A timely peace put an end to these ravages (1667), but the war added nothing to England's credit.

Angry at this turn of affairs and determined to have a victim, the Parliament, yielding to the murmurs of the people, required of the king the dismissal of Lord Clarendon. Charles was glad to get rid of his minister, who looked with open disapproval on the immoral life of the court; and the faithful services of thirty years went for nothing. The earl was impeached by Parliament, and a sentence of banishment passed upon him. He had perhaps made some errors of judgment, but there was not one of the king's courtiers at once so able and so patriotic. Clarendon's daughter, Anne Hyde, was married to the Duke of York, Charles's brother, who tried to befriend him; but the indolent monarch did what was easiest for himself, and let his minister go. The latter spent the rest of his life in France, writing his "History of the Rebellion," a valuable storehouse of facts, though naturally colored by the earl's political feelings. After Clarendon's fall, a new ministry was formed called the Cabal,* from the initials of their names, Clifford, Arlington, Buckingham, Ashley,† and Lauderdale. With the coöperation of these men, Charles now formed the first famous "Triple Alliance,"—a treaty between England and Holland in which Sweden afterward joined, with the object of restraining the growing power and arrogance of Louis XIV. of France. Samuel Pepys says of it, "It is the only good thing that hath been done since the king came to England." The treaty was arranged at the Hague by Sir William Temple on the part of England, and John De Witt acting for Holland—both distinguished statesmen. Charles himself never liked it, although, for reasons of policy, he had thought best to allow it to be carried through. Holland was a republic, which was enough to prejudice him against it; and he wished to be independent of his Parliament, which he could not be without the help of Louis XIV. Conveying, therefore, to Louis, an intimation of his wishes, the latter sent over the Princess Henrietta, wife of his own brother, the Duke of Orleans, and sister of Charles, who arranged the matter without difficulty. Charles met her at Dover, whither she brought a young Frenchwoman, Louise de Queronailles, to help gain his consent. Under their influence, Charles made a secret and shame-

---

* A set of men plotting together for some bad purpose.
† Better known afterward as Lord Shaftesbury.

ful agreement with Louis, called the Treaty of Dover, and adopted the young lady as one of his favorites. By this treaty, he promised to help Louis in his war against Holland (the very country with which England had formed the Triple Alliance), and to make a public profession of the Roman Catholic religion "at some convenient time." In return, Louis was to pay him a sum of money down and £200,000 a year as long as the war lasted, and to send him help in case of another rebellion at home. Charles remarked that he did not think he was a king so long as a company of fellows (i. e. the Commons) were looking into his actions, and examining his ministers as well as his accounts. So England was sold by its sordid, selfish monarch, who had but one desire in the world—that for unlimited self-indulgence. The agreement was kept a profound secret from all but the few persons whom Charles took into his confidence, for if the people had known of it, either the Treaty of Dover or the king's reign would have ended at once.

CHAPTER XXXVIII.

PLOTS.   HABEAS CORPUS.   DEATH OF CHARLES.

AS SOON as the Treaty of Dover was signed, Charles obtained a great sum from Parliament for fitting out a navy to uphold the Triple Alliance. Then he dissolved the Parliament and kept the money. As it was not enough for his wants (no money was), he suspended payment of the loans made by the goldsmiths and others to the exchequer (treasury),

which caused general bankruptcy and distress in all kinds of business. The king now issued a so-called "Declaration of Indulgence," which granted freedom of worship to all except Catholics, and even to them the privilege of having mass celebrated in their own houses. The jails were opened; Bunyan saw the end of his twelve years' imprisonment; the Quakers could again go about in peace; ministers returned to their congregations, and there were great rejoicings. Some thoughtful persons, however, shook their heads. The king had done this by his authority as head of the church; but the Parliament had made the laws—how could he unmake them? Addresses were made to Charles, signed even by dissenters, to ask that he would withdraw the Declaration. "I would rather suffer the rigor of the law," said one of them, "than see all the laws of England trampled under the foot of a prerogative." A new Parliament took the matter up, and declared that no penal laws could be suspended except by consent of Parliament, so the king was obliged to cancel the Indulgence. One more step on the road to freedom.

Holland was now again attacked by Louis XIV., who expected, with the assistance of England, to make an end of its independence. The chief officer of the little republic was William, Prince of Orange, son of Charles's sister, Mary, and grandson of William the Silent. "Do you not see that your country is lost?" asked the English ambassador, counselling submission. "There is a sure way never to see it lost," answered William, "and that is, to die in the last ditch." He was not driven to this, however. When the French had fairly entered the country, he cut the dykes that kept out the ocean, and flooded the country. Louis's army was obliged to retreat, and Holland was saved.

So strong a prejudice still existed in England against the Roman Catholics that the nation was not satisfied until a Test Act was passed, requiring every person who held any office, either civil or military, to subscribe to the oaths of allegiance and supremacy, to take the sacrament in the Church of England, and to deny all belief in transubstantiation. Upon this, thousands of Catholics gave up their offices, James, Duke of York (Charles's brother and Lord High Admiral) heading the list. Both he and his wife, Clarendon's daughter, had become Catholics after their marriage, though the king insisted that their daughters Mary and Anne (afterward queens of England) should be brought up as Protestants. Anne Hyde, James's first wife, being now dead, he married Mary of Modena,* an Italian princess, and a Roman Catholic, thereby giving great offence to the English.

One of the strangest and wildest delusions known to history now took place in England. A wretched creature named Titus Oates, once a clergyman of the Church of England, but dismissed on account of his vicious practices, pretended to have discovered a plot of the Roman Catholics to burn London, kill the king, massacre the Protestants, and deliver the kingdom into the hands of the French. Just at this time, Sir Edmondsbury Godfrey, a Justice of the Peace, who had heard some of the so-called evidence of the plot, was found dead in a field near London. It is probable that he committed suicide; but the cry went out that he had been murdered, in revenge, by the Catholics, and the popular fury rose

---

* Pronounced Mod'ena.

higher than ever. Witnesses sprang up on all sides to swear to outrageous falsehoods, and it was not until after many victims had perished that the excitement calmed down. The most distinguished of these victims was Viscount Stafford, an old nobleman of the highest character, whose gray hairs could not save him from the scaffold. After a while the prosecutions stopped, but it was long before London recovered from the excitement.

Political affairs are so confused in this reign, so many laws were passed bearing on important subjects, so many public men, conspicious for ability and for good or ill fortune, pass in succession over the scene, that it is impossible, in a short space, to give a clear idea of them. Sir William Temple, the framer of the Triple Alliance, one of the most high-minded of Charles's statesmen, after using his best efforts to bring order out of confusion, retired into private life and devoted himself to literary pursuits. Lord Halifax, known as a "Trimmer," (*i. e.* one who leans to either side as he sees one or the other likely to prevail) was the chief of the moderate men. Shaftesbury, once high in the king's favor, quarreled with him and became one of the most violent leaders of the opposition. Buckingham (son of the one who was stabbed at the beginning of Charles I.'s reign) was the head of the "Cabal" ministry, and did what was in his power to make Charles II. an absolute ruler, independent of Parliament. The poet Dryden wrote of him thus, saying that he,

> "Stiff in opinions, always in the wrong,
> Was everything by turns, and nothing long."

Sidney Godolphin, the man who, Charles said, was "never in the way and never out of the way," was high-minded and patriotic, and so useful that he served under four successive sovereigns, and always with honor. Others, whose names appear in larger histories, like the Earls of Danby and Sutherland, we can only mention here.

Several bills of importance were passed during the winter of 1679-80. One of these was the "Habeas Corpus Act," which restrained illegal imprisonment by requiring, in open court, the trial of a prisoner, so that the cause for which he is shut up may be made known. An "Act for Disabling Papists" was also carried through, in consequence of which no Roman Catholic sat in the House of Commons from that time until 1829, a space of a hundred and fifty years.

As Charles had no children, the Duke of York was heir-presumptive to the throne. A strong effort was made by means of the "Exclusion Bill," to prevent his succeeding, but though the bill passed the Commons by a large majority, the Peers threw it out.

A frightful persecution of the Covenanters in Scotland now took place, under the Duke of York as Lord High Commissioner and John Graham of Claverhouse, a brilliant, hard-hearted general. There had been an insurrection there, and after it was put down, scores of persons were shot or hanged without trial, and torture, which had been abolished in England in 1640, was mercilessly inflicted. The Duke of Monmouth, an illegitimate son of Charles II. by a woman named Lucy Walters, defeated the Covenanters at Bothwell Bridge. The Duke of York took pleasure in seeing the torture administered to "heretics," and would look on complacently at the application of the iron "boot" while the members of his council stole away in horror.

The dread of a Roman Catholic succession and the

indignation against Charles's misgovernment had now become so great that a conspiracy, called, from the place where the members met, the "Rye-House Plot," was formed to dethrone Charles, and put his son, the Duke of Monmouth, in his place. Some of the conspirators really intended to kill the king, as the shortest way of getting rid of him; others wished only to put him under some restraint, so that he would be incapable of further mischief. There were others, including two of the first statesmen in the kingdom, Lord Russell and Algernon Sidney, who had talked over among themselves the evils of the state, and discussed a possible remedy. Some conversation of this kind was reported by a traitor, and on this Russell and Sidney, the latter a man of letters, and author of "Discourses on Government," were condemned to die (1683). With the usual brutality of the time, they were denied the assistance of counsel; both conducted their own defence with ability and spirit; but the result was inevitable. Lady Russell was with her husband during his trial, arranging his papers and handing them to him as he needed them. Both these executions were clearly judicial murders, sentence being given without anything to be called proof of the offence.

The king was now drawing near the end of his career. His last appearance in public is thus described in the words of an eye-witness, Mr. John Evelyn: "I can never forget the inexpressible luxury and profaneness, gaming and all dissoluteness, and as it were total forgetfulness of God, last Sunday evening at Whitehall. The king sitting and talking with several women, a French boy singing love-songs in that glorious gallery, while above twenty of the great courtiers and other dissolute persons were playing cards around a large table, a bank of at least two thousand in gold before them." The next morning the king was struck with apoplexy. He regained his senses and was able to speak, but lived only a few days. Just before his death, his brother James, having cleared the room where he was lying, smuggled a Catholic priest up a private stairway into the room, and Charles received the last sacraments of the Romish church. Soon after this, he died, in the fifty-fifth year of his age and the twenty-fifth of his reign. The people lamented his death very sincerely, for though there was much to be blamed in his administration, they feared that worse was to come.

Charles II. seems to have possessed scarcely any virtue besides a natural courtesy and good temper. He was always agreeable. A witty minister, the Earl of Rochester, once pinned on Charles's door this verse, professing to be his epitaph:

"Here lies our sovereign lord, the king.
 Whose word no man relies on;
 Who never said a foolish thing,
 Nor ever did a wise one."

When this was repeated to Charles, he said it was quite true, for his words were his own, but his actions were his minister's.

The party names "Whig" and "Tory" came into use in this reign, whig signifying one who wished reforms made in the government, and tory a conservative, or one who wished to keep things as they were. The words soon acquired an additional meaning, tories being those who stood out for the prerogative of the king, and whigs those who would uphold the supremacy of the people.

The quarter of a century which ended with the death

of Charles, was a brilliant one for literature. Milton had written "Paradise Lost;" Bunyan, the "Pilgrim's Progress;" Clarendon had told the world about the Rebellion, Butler had satirized the Puritans in "Hudibras", and Marvell had done a like work for the Cavaliers. Pepys and Evelyn had written the inimitable diaries which make the social life of that day as real to us as is that of our own century. Locke was writing his "Essay on the Human Understanding," and Dryden, the dramatist, who died in 1700, had already produced many plays. But perhaps the name which comes nearest to our American hearts is that of William Penn.

His father, Admiral Penn, the conqueror of Jamaica, was seriously annoyed by the discovery that his son, who ought to have been a good courtier, had joined the unpopular sect of the Quakers. Finding that he could not persuade him to change his mind, the admiral turned him out of doors; but having a great respect as well as affection for him, was induced to receive him into favor again. The father had lent a large sum of money to King Charles, and after the admiral's death, William asked that instead of the money the king should grant him some land in America, on which to found a refuge for his persecuted brother-Quakers. Nothing could please Charles better than to avoid, by any expedient, the payment of a debt; and a tract was selected to which Penn gave the pretty name of Sylvania, which means woodland. The king, however, insisted upon the prefix Penn, and from the king's word there was no appeal.

CHAPTER XXXIX.

JAMES II. SEDGEMOOR. THE SEVEN BISHOPS. FLIGHT OF THE KING.

"I SHALL make it my endeavor," said James II. at the first meeting of his privy council, "to preserve the government, both in church and state, as it is now by law established." How he succeeded in his endeavor, we read in the pages of history.

If James could have remained simply a naval commander, a post for which he was well fitted, the English people might have forgotten his desertion to the Church of Rome, and forgiven his questioning Covenanters by means of the "boot." As a king, however, his power to do harm was so much increased that he was watched more jealously than before, and soon gave ample evidence that he needed such watching.

His first public act was to order the collection of customs duties, which could be legally done only by order of Parliament. Then he released from prison, on his own authority, not only Romanists, but other nonconformists, to show that his disregard of law was systematic and not personal. He went openly to mass, a penal offence. On the other hand, all the chief offices remained in the hands of Protestants. Rochester, Clarendon (son of Charles II.'s prime minister, who was now dead), Godolphin, Sunderland, Halifax, occupied the chief places in his cabinet.

It is not to be supposed that the infamous Titus Oates escaped the reward of his crimes when James came into power. He was punished with a ferocity which brought a glow of pleasure to the king's cruel heart. Besides being fined, having to stand twice in the pillory and being sentenced to life imprisonment, all of which he well deserved, he was whipped through the city with unusual severity from Oldgate to Newgate on one day, and then from Newgate to Tyburn two days afterward. On the second day, not being able to stand, he was dragged through the streets on a hurdle, receiving on that day seventeen hundred lashes. The judges meant to kill him with these floggings, as his offence was not one for which he could be hung, but the wretch survived them, and lived through James's reign, standing in the pillory five times a year, until at the accession of a Protestant king, he was liberated and provided with a pension.

The Duke of Monmouth had been in Holland during the last years of his father's life, in disgrace on account of his connection with the Rye-House Plot. Unwise counsellors now urged him to take advantage of James's unpopularity to make a claim to the throne of England, under the pretext that his mother had been married to Charles II. Monmouth, a handsome, amiable youth, but weak in character, caught at the bait. He landed in Dorsetshire, on the southern coast, with scarcely a hundred followers; but the people, disliking the sombre James, and detesting popery, flocked to his standard, and he soon found himself at the head of six thousand men. At Taunton, his adherents thronged the streets, every one with a green bough in his hat; the houses were hung with garlands; flowers were strewn in his path, and a troop of young girls went in procession to offer him twenty-seven standards, worked by their own hands. In a declaration published by Monmouth on landing, in which he abused his uncle, James II., in very discourteous language, Monmouth had said that he would leave his claim to be decided by a free Parliament. At Taunton, however, he assumed the title of king, and issued proclamations dated "from our camp at Taunton, in the first year of our reign." Moving northward, he heard of the defeat and capture of Argyle, who had raised an army for him in Scotland. Affairs began to look dark. One discouragement succeeded another, and in a few days he came up with the royal army at Sedgemoor. The battle was soon decided. Monmouth's army of peasants and miners gave way and fled, the unhappy leader taking shelter in a ditch. Here he was found, almost starving, with only a few raw peas in his pocket. He was taken to prison, where he wrote an abject letter to James, begging for an interview, expressing deep contrition, and accusing the friends who had led him away with false arguments. James had the incredible meanness to see him and let him crawl up to him on his knees, begging for life, and then to dismiss him coldly to his fate. Monmouth was beheaded on Tower Hill, in the thirty-sixth year of his age (1685).

Then began the butchery of his followers. James had chosen for the accomplishment of this task the two fittest instruments in England; Colonel Kirke, whose "Lambs" (a regiment of soldiers so called) had been trained to ferocity by practice among the Moors in Tangier; and Judge Jeffreys, a debased wretch to whom the king held out the promise of the office of Lord Chancellor, as a bait to engage him to do his work thoroughly. Kirke hanged his prisoners in batches without the form of a trial. The story is told that while the bodies were still quivering, he would order the drums to beat, saying that they should have music for their dancing. Such an immense number of persons were quartered that their remains were thrown into great cauldrons of boiling pitch, to get rid of them. Kirke kept no record of his deeds, but it was believed at the time that he hanged a hundred prisoners during the week after the battle. He was recalled in displeasure by the government, not on acconnt of his barbarity, but because all the rich rebels got off by bribing him.

Then came the circuit of Jeffreys. His first trial was of Alice Lisle, an old gentlewoman who was accused of harboring two of the rebels for a night. Jeffreys ordered her to be burnt to death. Such a protest was raised against this that he was obliged to commute the punishment to beheading. A poor woman named Elizabeth Gaunt, guilty of the same crime, was burnt alive. During what was called "The Bloody Assizes," this judge hanged three hundred and thirty persons, besides condemning others to fines, imprisonment, and whipping, and sentencing hundreds to be sold into slavery in the West Indies. In this last horrible traffic, the queen and her ladies joined, and begged for prisoners that they might make money by their sale. The office of Lord Chancellor was conferred on Jeffreys, as the king had promised, in reward for his zeal.

The laws against the Romanists were not repealed, but they were openly violated by the king and by all Catholics. The public discontent being plainly shown at this, James established a camp of thirteen thousand men at Hounslow to keep London in order. In Scotland, he caused a law to be passed punishing with death and confiscation of property all who attended conventicles in the open air, or who preached at them. In Ireland the army was put under the charge of Lord Tyrconnel, who turned out many Protestant officers and added great numbers of Irish Catholics to the ranks. All this showed the English what they were to expect in their own country.

It seemed as if James exerted all his ingenuity to do whatever would be most offensive to the English people. He reëstablished the Court of High Commission; he took money from France, though not so secretly but that he was found out; he sent an ambassador to Rome to express his wish that England might be received into the church as in Queen Mary's time; he forced a Romish priest on one of the colleges at Oxford.* Next, he published a Declaration of Indulgence, stating that non-conformity to the established religion should no longer be punished, and ordered that on a certain Sunday this declaration should be read in all the churches (1688). This ordinance the clergy, as a general thing, did not obey, and seven bishops, including Archbishop Sancroft, presented to the king a humble petition against it. James was enraged at what he called their insolence, and the bishops were committed to the Tower. On their way thither, the banks of the Thames were lined with crowds of persons who knelt and implored their blessing, utter-

---

* The young Duke of Somerset was ordered to introduce the Pope's messenger into James's presence-chamber. "I am advised," he answered, "that I can not obey your Majesty without breaking the law." "Do you not know that I am above the law?" said James angrily. "Your Majesty may be, but I am not," answered the duke, and was dismissed from his post.

ing cries to Heaven for their deliverance. The trial took place in Westminster Hall, the bishops being charged with "publishing a false and seditious libel." They were acquitted, and bonfires, bell-ringings, and illuminations testified to the joy of the people.

In the midst of this excitement, a son was born to the queen. This event completed the general dissatisfaction. While King James's Protestant daughter Mary was heir presumptive to the crown, his subjects bore his tyranny, thinking that when he died there would be a change for the better; but to look forward to having the son of James II. and Mary of Modena reign over them was more than they could bear. Their eyes naturally turned to the Princess Mary and to her husband, William of Orange, who, being himself a grandson of Charles I., was the next heir to the throne after the family of James. An intimation to this effect being conveyed to William, he began to make preparations for an invasion. James was thunderstruck at hearing of this. It had never occurred to him that he could not to the end of his days go on trampling on the liberties of the people, and he suddenly poured forth concessions, relinquishing the things he had insisted on, replacing the officers he had turned out, and trying to make friends with the people he had insulted; but it was too late.

In September, 1688, the Prince of Orange published a declaration which was eagerly read throughout the country, stating that he, from his near relationship to the kingdom, felt it his duty to protect the civil and religious liberty of its people, and denying that he had any further object in view than the calling of a free Parliament. With a fleet of sixty ships and fifteen thousand men he landed at Torbay on the south coast, and marched northward, his army increasing as he advanced. When James took command of his camp at Salisbury,* he found the desertion of his soldiers so extensive that he decided to retreat towards London, thus making his weakness only the more evident.

Besides these defections, the king had others most unexpected to him. Lord Churchill (afterward Duke of Marlborough) who owed everything to James, and who had been loaded by him with favors, went over to the enemy, taking with him many of the officers on whom the king most depended. But this was not the worst. He and his wife had acquired an unbounded influence over the Princess Anne, James's daughter, a weak, dull woman, married to Prince George of Denmark; and the Churchills persuaded this couple also to leave the king and go to the camp of the Prince of Orange.

This last blow seemed to touch James more nearly than any other. He burst into tears on hearing of Anne's escape, and exclaimed, "God help me! My own children have forsaken me!" He sent away his queen and infant son to France; and being convinced, from the intelligence brought to him, that his cause was hopeless, he himself fled, with one attendant, throwing the great seal into the Thames, to prevent its being used in calling a Parliament.

Nothing could have pleased William of Orange and the English people in general so much as to have King James run away, as he had done; and they were all very much disgusted when it was found that he had been captured by some fisherman at Sheerness, as he was

---
* Pronounced Saulsbury.

making his escape in disguise. He was necessarily brought back to London, but every facility was given him for escaping again; and while he imagined himself to be cleverly outwitting his enemies, they were really opening bolts and bars before him, so that nothing could throw him again on their hands. This time he really got away, embarked on a ship which was waiting for him, and hastened to Paris, where he was received with great kindness by Louis XIV., who gave him a splendid establishment at St. Germains, and supported him in luxury as long as he lived.

CHAPTER XL.

REVOLUTION OF 1688. WILLIAM AND MARY.

WE have now arrived at the third of the three great R's of the seventeenth century: the Rebellion, the Restoration, and the Revolution. The latter is commonly known by the prefix "glorious." If the Commonwealth had continued, the events of 1642–49 would have made a revolution; as the old state of things in 1660 was reëstablished, it is known as a rebellion. Revolution is successful rebellion.

William of Orange, whom we must henceforth call William III. of England, was careful to observe all the forms of government. A convention was called (there could be no lawful Parliament, because there was no king to issue the writs for one) in which, after stating the throne to be vacant by the desertion of James, it was decided to offer it to William and Mary for their joint lives, and to William if he should survive his wife. The administration was to be altogether in his hands, To this was added a Declaration of Rights, in which the real worth of the Revolution consists. The points insisted on were these: 1. The king can not dispense with the laws, nor suspend their execution; 2. He can not levy money without the consent of Parliament; 3. Subjects have the right of petition; 4. The king can not keep up a standing army in time of peace without the consent of Parliament; 5. Parliament must be frequently assembled, and elections and debates must be free. Other items were added, still further limiting the power of the crown; and, as Macaulay says, "The highest praise of the Revolution of 1688 is that it was the last."

It was a grand country that William and Mary now took in charge. Though the whole century had been one of political struggle, with an occasional battle like Marston Moor, or Naseby, the general prosperity had gone on with a steady increase. Fields were tilled, mines worked, commerce carried on, manufactures improved; the people were better off, more comfortably lodged, better fed and clothed in 1688 than in 1588. Something like a post-office was established, and it was a matter of pride to say that a letter could be carried three hundred miles and an answer received in five days. This rate of speed was attained by means of relays of post-horses. The government was very jealous of newspapers, but Charles II. allowed the publication of the London Gazette, which has been issued now (1891) twice a week for more than two hundred years. Clubs took, to some extent, the place of daily journals. News passed from mouth to mouth, and a gentleman went to his club to hear the latest items of interest and know what others thought of them, as he now takes up his morning paper.

In point of comfort, there was still much to be desired. The roads from one town to another were almost impassable. The streets of London were unpaved, and were not lighted, except by private individuals, until the last year of Charles II.'s reign. Even then, the dim oil lamps would seem only to make "darkness visible" in comparison to our gas and electricity. Carpets gradually took the place of straw and rushes. There were no circulating libraries; those who wanted to read books must borrow or buy them. The state of education among women is shown by an inscription written by Queen Mary, wife of William III. (who was probably as well educated as most women of her time), in a gorgeously bound Bible, "This book was given to the king and I at our coronation." Foreign princesses were even worse off. James II. records in his journal that when Mary of Modena was told that she was to marry him, she asked who he was. "She had been so innocently bred," he observes, "that she did not know of such a place as England, nor of such a person as the Duke of York."

The enthusiasm with which the arrival of William III. had been hailed, diminished as he was brought into personal contact with the English. He had cold, distant manners, and so little command of the language that he was usually silent in company. The common people distrusted him as a foreigner, and a very large proportion of the better class considered him a usurper. It was plain that his position was going to be a difficult one, and that it would need great judgment and discretion to steer clear of the dangers which surrounded him.

These were just the qualities in which William excelled. He chose his ministers from among the statesmen most trusted by the English people, even though some of them had opposed his being made king. His dearest friend, William Bentinck, a native of Holland, was made a privy councillor, with the title of Duke of Portland.

His first trouble in England arose in connection with the army. Some regiments having shown themselves discontented, William, by the advice of his council, decided to send them to Holland and supply their places with Dutch troops. This made them still more indignant, and they marched northward in open mutiny, with drums beating and colors flying. They were put down by some Dutch regiments which were sent in pursuit of them, and severely punished, while Parliament for the first time passed a Mutiny Bill, placing the army under martial law. Up to this time a soldier was considered a citizen, and even if he struck his commanding officer, he was liable only to the penalty for assault and battery.

Many members of the House of Lords, including Archbishop Sancroft and several other bishops, refused to take the oath of allegiance to William, on the ground of their previous obligations to James. Such persons were called "non-jurors," and, in the case of the clergy, were afterward deprived of their livings.

To emphasize still more the distinction between the non-juring prelates and the loyal subjects of William, a "Toleration Act" was passed, allowing freedom of worship to all who took the oaths of allegiance and supremacy, and denied the doctrine of transubstantiation. This relieved the disabilities of all dissenters except the Roman Catholics. During these debates, the double coronation took place, and as the Archbishop refused to officiate at it, the ceremony was performed by the Bishop of London.

In Scotland, a strong party still held out for King James, at the head of which was Graham of Claverhouse, now created Viscount Dundee. He raised a small force of Highlanders with whom he defeated a much larger number of English in the battle of Killiekrankie, but was himself mortally wounded. The Highlanders, discouraged, dispersed to their homes, Edinburgh Castle, which held out against William, surrendered, and the whole country was reduced to obedience (1689). To gratify the Scotch, William abolished Episcopacy, and Presbyterianism has since been the recognized religion of the country.

James II. had not given up the struggle for his crown. Being supplied with a fleet and army by Louis XIV., he landed at Kinsale, in Ireland, and marched to Dublin, being joined by great numbers of the Irish. The city of Londonderry held out against him and was besieged by his forces for 105 days, during which time the inhabitants suffered the extremity of hunger. A Presbyterian clergyman named Walker put himself at the head of the garrison, whose commander had deserted them, and conducted the defense with skill and energy. Just as it seemed as if the defenders must give up from starvation, relief came from England, and James's general, DeRosen, moved away. The protestant town of Enniskillen was also successfully defended on the field of Newton Butler.

The great battle of the war was yet to come. It was fought in person by the two kings, on the bank of the River Boyne, not far from Dublin. James's army was inferior in numbers to William's, but his position was so strong that he ventured to fight. The king was wounded, a bullet grazing his shoulder, but the English won the day. The loss on both sides was small, considering the important issues at stake. James himself set the example of flight when he saw that the battle was going against him, and his soldiers dispersed, so that when he reached Dublin he was without an army, and took ship as soon as possible for France. This engagement is called "The Battle of the Boyne" (1690).

William returned to London in triumph, after an absence of only five weeks. While he was away a naval battle had been fought with the French off Beachy Head in Sussex, in which the enemy were victorious. The commander, Lord Torrington, was incompetent, and the battle was an ignominious one. There were fears that the French would pursue the beaten fleet up the Thames and threaten London as the Dutch had done in Charles II.'s time; but they only burned the town of Teignmouth and went home. William was extremely angry with Torrington, who had put the Dutch ships where they would bear the brunt of the battle; and though the admiral was acquitted by a court-martial, William would not see him, and ordered him to be dismissed from the service.

One more naval battle finished the war. It was fought off Cape La Hogue in Normandy, King James commanding the French fleet and Admiral Russell the combined Dutch and English one. The latter gained a brilliant victory, and as Louis refused to furnish James with further aid, the deposed king retired to

St. Germains (1691). From this time he disappears in person from English history, though his name was still a rallying word for all discontent, and the plots of his friends never ceased to distract the tranquillity of William's reign.

CAPTER XLI.

GLENCOE. DEATH OF MARY. PEACE OF RYSWICK. DEATH OF WILLIAM III.

THE war in Ireland was not ended by the Battle of the Boyne. Most of the country was still in possession of James's friends; and it was only at the close of the year 1691 that the struggle closed with the Pacification of Limerick. By this it was agreed that the Irish who consented to acknowledge William should be allowed to enjoy their religion and their property, while all others were offered free passage to France. Twelve thousand men under General Sarsfield availed themselves of this offer, and were promised by him that their families should accompany them. When the troops prepared to embark, however, it was found that there was not room enough for all, and hundreds of women and children were left on the shore to die of slow starvation or to beg their way home, there to endure untold misery, deprived of their natural protectors.

Between the two victories, the battle of the Boyne and that of Cape La Hogue, a horrible tragedy took place in Scotland for which William III. is at least partly responsible. The Highland chiefs who had been engaged in the rebellion under Dundee were slow in taking the oath of allegiance to the new king, and one of them, Macdonald of Glencoe, put it off until the last day allowed by the treaty, Dec. 31, 1691. On arriving at Fort William, which he supposed to be the place appointed for taking the oath, he found no one there qualified to administer it, and in great distress of mind made his way, through heavy snow-storms and over steep mountains to Inverary. He had spent six days on the toilsome journey, and with difficulty persuaded the sheriff to allow him to take the required oath. Unfortunately, his deadly enemy, Sir John Dalrymple, Master of Stair, had procured from William an order for the extermination of the Macdonald clan. This miscreant sent a body of soldiers to the peaceful village of Glencoe, where they were hospitably entertained for a fortnight, the Highlanders freely sharing with them everything they had. At a preconcerted time each party of soldiers undertook to murder every male, old and young, in the houses where they were quartered; and in the early morning, after an evening of gayety spent in drinking and playing cards, wild shrieks proclaimed that the work of death was begun. Some forty persons were massacred, including some women who were trying to defend their children. About two-thirds of the inhabitants escaped, though many of these died of cold and hunger while fleeing through the mountains.

William's apologists have tried to excuse him on the ground that he did not know what he was doing in signing the order to "extirpate that set of thieves, if they can be well distinguished from the rest of the Highlanders." But the order itself remains, and is a horrible monument of the brutal use of power.

Among the political changes in William's reign was the establishment of a Cabinet, or Council of Ministers, all chosen from the same political party, and thus acting together. Until this time, each of the king's council had been independent of the others, and their advice was often contradictory. This new kind of ministry proved most efficient in the transaction of public business, and gradually became, what it continues to the present day, a kind of committee of the House of Commons.

Many great public measures were now carried forward. A bill was passed for a triennial Parliament; the censorship of the press was abolished, after which a host of newspapers sprang up, and a national bank was created, which regulated and made permanent the national debt.

The war against Louis XIV., to prosecute which was the great object of the king's life, continued for some years with varying success. William gained some brilliant victories, but lost the battles of Steenkirk and Landen, and his fleet met with reverses at sea. His misfortunes encouraged to renewed efforts the partisans of James, who never ceased to intrigue against him, and who included among their number some of the ablest men in the kingdom. The double-dyed traitor, Marlborough, was again in communication with James, waiting only for an opportunity to bring him back; and the inconstant Sunderland was also suspected of favoring his return. Embarrassed by these difficulties on every hand, William sustained a severe blow in the loss of his wife, who died of small-pox (1694). In later years, he had been devoted to her, though her early married life was far from being a happy one. She was a woman of marked ability, and had been left regent in England during her husband's frequent absences on the continent, always performing the duties of the office with success, even under the most trying circumstances. Mary was only thirty-two years old.

It had long been the queen's desire that the palace at Greenwich, which had never been completed, should be turned into a hospital for disabled soldiers. After her death, William carried out her wishes and Greenwich Hospital became a noble monument of her benevolence and his affection. It is now occupied as a Royal Naval Academy and Hospital-School. Mary had been an excellent wife, supplying by her graciousness of manner and her many agreeable qualities the popular elements which were lacking in her husband's character. Bishop Burnet, a famous contemporary preacher and author, was the intimate friend of both William and Mary, and has left most interesting records of their private life.

The long war between England and France was brought to an end in 1697 by the Treaty of Ryswick. In this treaty, Louis, besides giving up many of his continental conquests, agreed to acknowledge William III. as king of England, and to do nothing that would interfere with his claim. This was a glorious victory for William, and put an end, for the time at least, to the machinations of the Jacobites in England. The settlers in America had good reason to be glad of it, for it marked the close of that period of horror in the colonies known as "King William's War," which included the massacre at Schenectady (1690). But little progress had been made in the colonies during the century that was now closing. Our forefathers, still struggling for a foothold in the new world, were scarcely noticed in the old; although preparing to take, in less than another hundred years, their place in the family of nations.

A singular project was started at the close of this war, for colonizing a part of America very different from the sterile coast of New England. A Scotchman named William Paterson, who had been one of the original founders of the Bank of England, persuaded himself and others that untold wealth was to be had almost for the asking in the fertile regions about the Isthmus of Darien. A company was organized to go to this Land of Promise, but the settlers met fever, pestilence, and starvation, while Spanish guns finished the work that hunger and destitution had begun. Their fort in ruins, their huts burned, the fertile soil that they meant to cultivate filled with their graves, the few survivors found their way to Jamaica or to some port on the Atlantic coast, and the Darien Colony was a thing of the past except in the memory of those who had duped themselves and others with visions of unearned wealth.

Among the foreign visitors of this reign was a young barbarian chieftain who was afterward known as Peter the Great, Czar of Muscovy. He eschewed forms and ceremonies, detested being stared at, and went to sleep at dinner parties given in his honor; but he accomplished what he came for, which was to study the English manner of ship-building. From the ways of these visitors, we get a glimpse of the condition of things two hundred years ago in what is now the Russian Empire. John Evelyn's beautiful country-house at Deptford was hired by the king for his accommodation, because it was near the shipyard; and the great Peter amused himself by driving a wheelbarrow, for exercise, through Evelyn's holly hedge, while he and his followers left the house in such a condition that it had to be completely refurnished.

The history of Kidd, the pirate, belongs to this period.

In the four years of quiet which followed the Peace of Ryswick, William was not without annoyances at home. It was hard for him to steer between the two political parties. The whigs, who had made him king, wished to limit his power; the tories were more to his taste, but many of them were Jacobites. With all his moderation and good sense he was still a Stuart, and would have preferred absolute rule if it had been possible to him. The Commons thwarted and opposed him at every turn, insisting upon cutting down the army contrary to his judgment, and a serious break might have resulted but for an event for which not even the most far-seeing Englishmen were prepared. On the death of James II. at St. Germains (1701), Louis XIV. surprised the world by acknowledging his son, a boy of thirteen, as James III., king of England.

There was no question now of peace. The army was instantly increased again and put on an efficient footing. A Grand Alliance was formed by Germany, England, and Holland, against Louis XIV., partly in consequence of his claiming the throne of Spain for his grandson, Philip, which led to the War of the Spanish Succession, while England had her special grievance in the insult offered to her by the breaking of the Treaty of Ryswick.

Before any active military operations could be begun, William, whose health had long been failing, met with an accident which ended his life. While he was riding in the park his horse stumbled over a mole-hill, and he fell off and broke his collar-bone. Being already very feeble he could not rally from the injury, and died after a few days of suffering, in the fifty-second year of his age and the fourteenth of his reign.

For an estimate of William's character, we may take that of Prince Albert, the lamented husband of Queen Victoria, who said, in a meeting of the Society for the Propagation of the Gospel, "This society was first chartered by that great man, William the Third—the greatest sovereign this country has to boast of."

One conspicuous feature in the advance of the English people from ignorance toward knowledge, from brutality toward humanity, from darkness toward light, is the rise, progress, and decline of the witchcraft delusion and persecution. It began a little before the time of the discovery of America, reached its height about 1692 (the date of the tragedy in Salem, Massachusetts), and exhausted itself ten years later in England, when the last execution took place in that country (1702). In 1484, the pope issued a bill commanding the Inquisition to hunt up and kill all witches. In four years, 600 persons were burned or hanged in the bishopric of Bamberg, and 900 in that of Wurzberg. Five hundred persons were burned in Geneva during four months of 1576, and 1000 in the district of Como in 1524. In 1562, a statute of Elizabeth made witchcraft or sorcery a capital crime, and James I. himself wrote a treatise upon it. During the Long Parliament, 3000 persons are said to have been put to death. The cruelties which fill us with horror in the history of our own country are few in comparison with this fearful list. Even in England, the madness had small sway compared to its ravages in Continental Europe (where it numbered its victims by the hundred thousand), while our own land escaped with only a scorching. And all this for a crime which no one ever did or could commit, for it had no existence.

After being for years a dead letter, the laws against witchcraft were repealed by Parliament in 1736, though in some European countries they have existed to within the nineteenth century.

CHAPTER XLII.

ANNE. ACT OF SETTLEMENT. WAR OF THE SPANISH SUCCESSION. UNION WITH SCOTLAND. DEATH.

HEN it became plain that William III.'s days were numbered, Parliament was obliged once more to take up the question of the succession. The Princess Anne's only child, the Duke of Gloucester, had just died, at eleven years of age, and no further provision had been made. With the approbation of the king, it was decided that Sophia, the wife of the Elector of Hanover, and daughter of James I.'s daughter Elizabeth, should be queen after Anne, if the latter should leave no children. The nearest relative in blood to Anne was, of course, her half-brother, James, son of James II. and Mary of Modena, but as he and all other possible candidates were Roman Catholics, they were out of the question. The Electress Sophia had remained a Protestant and was therefore eligible; and her son

George, now forty years old, would become king at her death.

At the same time with the Act of Settlement, it was provided that every future sovereign must be a member of the Church of England. This put an end to all complications regarding Roman Catholics.

These arrangements having been made, Anne, the sixth and last of the Stuarts (for William and Mary always count as one), became queen (1702). She was then thirty-eight years old. The Duke of Marlborough and his wife continued to be her intimate friends and advisers; and, the tories being somewhat in the ascendant in the new Parliament, a tory ministry was formed, which immediately declared war against France and Spain. The struggle thus entered upon is known by the name of "The War of the Spanish Succession."

Charles II., King of Spain, who had been in failing health for many years, had died in 1700, leaving no children. His eldest sister had married Louis XIV. of France, the latter promising at the same time that the throne of Spain should never be claimed for herself or her descendants. Louis now brought forward a demand that it should be bestowed on his grandson, Philip of Anjou, on the ground that, as his queen's dowry had not been paid, he was not bound by his part of the contract. The Emperor of Germany, who had married the younger sister, brought forward a similar claim for his grandson. England took the side of the emperor, and the war began.

Marlborough opened the campaign in Flanders, where he took several towns; Admiral Rooke conquered the world-famed fortress of Gibraltar (1704), which England still holds; and between 1704 and 1709, Marlborough won the great victories of Blenheim, Oudenarde, Ramillies and Malplaquet, in Germany and Flanders. Blenheim was the first great battle gained by the English on foreign soil since Agincourt (1415). Prince Eugene of Savoy, second only to Marlborough as a general, led the German armies which coöperated with the English in these famous engagements. He also won, alone, a splendid victory at Turin in Sardinia, by which he drove the French out of Italy. After Marlborough's first great success, the English were wild with joy, and heaped honors upon him. He already had a pension for life, and in addition to this and to the thanks of the queen and Parliament, the nation gave him the royal manor of Woodstock, and at a later time erected upon it the superb mansion called Blenheim House, which is still one of England's palaces.

The next year (1705) was distinguished by a brilliant campaign in Spain, the land forces being under the Earl of Peterborough, and the fleet under Sir Cloudesly Shovel, an admiral who had worked his way up from the position of cabin-boy. As he was returning from his second campaign in Spain, the admiral's ship was wrecked off the Scilly Islands, and all on board perished (1707).

The same year saw the long-talked-of "union" between England and Scotland. From the time of James I. they had been two countries under one king, having separate Parliaments and laws. It was now agreed, in spite of intense opposition from the minority in Scotland, that thereafter the Scottish Parliament should be given up, and that the country should be represented by sixteen peers in the English House of Lords, and by forty-five members in the Commons. This measure, affecting a people so tenacious of their independence, caused riots in Edinburgh; but after the union had been fully tried, all classes joined in approving it.

When the queen gave her assent to the Act of Union, she added, "I desire and expect from my subjects of both nations, that from henceforth they act with all possible respect and kindness to one another, that so it may appear to all the world they have hearts disposed to become one people." These are noble words, and they have been nobly acted upon. From this time the formal designation of the whole country has been "The United Kingdom of Great Britain and Ireland."

After the successes of the combined English and German armies, Louis XIV., whose country was almost exhausted, made proposals for a peace. The allies, however, flushed with victory, demanded such terms as he could not grant consistently with his self-respect, and preparations were made for continuing the war.

The trial of Doctor Sacheverell, a clergyman of the Church of England, for a political offence, is worth noticing as characteristic of the times. He was an advocate of non-resistance to royal power; and having preached two intemperate sermons on the subject, the Parliament, in which the whigs were now in power, impeached and tried him for sedition. The populace took up his cause as their own. He was escorted every day from his lodgings to Westminster Hall by crowds of people, and several dissenting meeting-houses were pulled down by the mob in their fury. When a sentence of suspension from preaching for three years was passed on Sacheverell, instead of the severer penalty, their joy was boundless, as he was considered the champion of the established church. The feeling was so strong against the whigs that the queen was obliged to change her ministers, and in the next Parliament (1710) the tories were again in the majority.

The long intimacy between the queen and the Duke and Duchess of Marlborough was now drawing to an end. The Duchess Sarah, a domineering woman who had by her force of character completely governed the queen, grew so intolerably insolent that even the patient Anne ("a crowned slave," she called herself) could endure it no longer. In the early days of their friendship, while Anne was still a princess, she herself had suggested that all ceremony should be dropped between her and her darling friend, and that they should write to one another (which they did constantly) under feigned names. Anne chose the name of "Mrs. Morley," and Lady Marlborough (it was before she became a Duchess) that of "Mrs. Freeman," as being suited to her character. But all their fondness had passed away, and the queen's one desire was to get rid of her ex-favorite. Abigail Hill, afterward Mrs. Masham, a relative of the duchess, whom the latter had placed with Anne to get rid of some of her own duties as mistress of the robes, gradually supplanted her in the queen's good graces, and the duke and duchess were deprived of their places in her household. Marlborough's political enemies, too, were stirring against him (he was at this time a whig), and the tories procured his disgrace, had him recalled from the Continent (where he was planning another campaign that should rival that of Malplaquet) and dismissed him from all his employments. They accused him of cheating the government, which he had undoubtedly done, for his avarice was as great as his passion for military glory and he hesitated at no baseness to gratify it. Upon one occasion, when Prince Eugene was visiting London, the crowd thought he was in a certain sedan-chair in Hyde Park, and began cheering; but when they saw that the person was Marlborough they changed their hurrahs to "stop thief!"

The Marlboroughs had received, honestly, from the queen and the parliament, grants amounting to the value of at least five millions of dollars; but they were always wanting more. One gift their descendants are probably still enjoying—a pension of £5000 a year settled upon themselves and their heirs forever. The duke was a remarkably handsome man, and had manners of such wonderful grace and courtesy that they fascinated all who met him. His ability as a soldier has somewhat overshadowed his gifts as a statesman; but he was remarkable in both. All that he needed to make him truly glorious was a conscience and a heart.

After Marlborough's recall, the war dragged slowly on until it was ended by the peace of Utrecht (1713). Louis XIV. had so far gained his point that Spain and the West Indies were left in possession of his grandson, Philip V.; Anne was recognized as queen of Great Britain; England was to keep Gibraltar and Minorca (one of the Balearic Islands gained during the war) and received in addition the Island of Newfoundland in North America, together with Acadia (Nova Scotia), and a tract of land about Hudson Bay. This war is known in American history as "Queen Anne's War," and is only a repetition of the horrors of Indian massacre. The town of

Deerfield, in Massachusetts, was destroyed, and more than a hundred persons carried away prisoners. An additional article of the treaty gave to Great Britain the right, formerly possessed by the French, of importing annually for thirty years nearly five thousand negro slaves to America. Shameful to relate, this was the article of the treaty most urgently insisted on.*

Queen Anne died the year after the Peace of Utrecht, aged fifty years, after a reign of twelve years. Her death was undoubtedly hastened by the continual brawling of her ministers and Parliament. She dreaded a meeting of her cabinet, and it was while trembling in anticipation of one of these stormy sessions that the fit of apoplexy came on which ended her life. Her husband, Prince George of Denmark, had died some years earlier.

As a queen, Anne had little opportunity to show personal character, owing to the changed system of government in her day, for now Parliament was supreme. From that time, the saying is true that "the monarch reigns but does not govern." As a woman, she seems to have commanded both respect and affection. She was very generous, not only to her favorites, but to others who needed help; and "Queen Anne's Bounty," a fund for poor clergymen, given from her own perquisites, still keeps her memory green. She was the last sovereign of Eng-

---

* It was after the peace of Utrecht that the expatriation of the French colonists in Acadia (Nova Scotia) took place, celebrated in Longfellow's "Evangeline." Against their will they were removed to other parts of the country, the larger part of them settling in what is now Western Louisiana, where to this day they retain their language (now greatly corrupted) and, to a large extent, their ancient customs, habits, and dress.

land to touch for the "King's Evil," as Edward the Confessor was the first; and the great Doctor Johnson faintly remembered being taken to a tall lady in a black velvet gown and a hood, whose magic touch, it was hoped, would remove the curse of scrofula.

The most brilliant statesmen of Queen Anne's reign were Harley (Lord Oxford) and St. John (Lord Bolingbroke). In science there was Sir Isaac Newton, whom Queen Anne had the honor of knighting; Pope was just beginning to be known as a poet, and Addison and Steele were busy with the "Spectator." The industrious Defoe had not yet written "Robinson Crusoe," nor had Dean Swift begun "Gulliver's Travels." The reign of Anne is regarded, next to Queen Elizabeth's and Queen Victoria's, as being the most brilliant period of our English literature.

The Electress Sophia of Hanover, who by the Act of Settlement was appointed the next in succession, died about ten days before the queen.

CHAPTER XLIII.

GEORGE I. INVASION OF THE PRETENDER. SOUTH-SEA BUBBLE. DEATH OF THE KING. GEORGE II.

EORGE I., Elector of Hanover and son of Sophia, was now king of England (1714). The people only half-liked the idea of receiving a German prince who could not speak English* and was

---

* He was obliged to speak with one of his ministers, Sir Robert Walpole, in Latin, as he knew no English and the Premier no German.

too old to learn (he was fifty-four), but anything was better than a Roman-Catholic Stuart. At first sight the English were prejudiced against him. He was awkward and undignified in appearance and uncultivated in mind, so that he seemed ill-fitted to come into a court which was one of the most witty and graceful in Europe. George I., however, had so many good qualities that he soon won the approval, though never the affection, of his subjects. He was truthful, business like, and just, and perhaps it was fortunate for Engand that his interest was largely in Hanover, so that he left his new kingdom to govern itself through its representatives. The family of Hanover, to which the Georges belonged, is often called the "House of Brunswick," the Electors of Hanover being at that time also Dukes of Brunswick.

George I. has left an amusing account of English customs in a letter written by him at this time. "This is a strange country," he says. "The morning after my arrival at St. James's, I looked out of the window and saw a park which they said was mine. The next day, Lord Chetwynd sent me a fine brace of carp out of my own canal; and I was told I must give five guineas to his servant for bringing me my own carp out of my own canal in my own park." The king was very economical, and would rather have bought his carp in the market at a much lower price.

"The tory party is gone," wrote Lord Bolingbroke after Queen Anne's death. George I. at once formed a whig ministry of which Lord Townshend was the head. The whigs began impeaching several of the most noted of Anne's ministers, among them Lords Oxford and Bolingbroke and the Duke of Ormond; but as the accusation was dictated only by party spite, nothing further came of it. Marlborough was reinstated in his position as captain-general of the forces. It was necessary, however, to keep a close watch upon him, as he was soon found to be in correspondence with the Pretender,* or, as he was more often called, the Chevalier of St. George. The latter lost no time in sending forth a manifesto asserting his right to the English crown, and the old struggle began once more, his friends in Scotland exciting an insurrection there in his favor.

Louis XIV. of France died in 1715, and the Pretender, who had looked for aid from him, was disappointed in his hopes. The Regent Orleans refused any open assistance, not wishing to go to war with England, and James was obliged to depend on his Scottish friends. The Earl of Mar, with some others, raised a force of five thousand men for his support, and was joined by the Duke of Ormond, one of the dismissed English tory leaders. The campaign was very ill-planned. Part of the army, under Mar, was defeated at Sheriff-Muir, near Stirling, by Argyle; another part, marching southward under command of a Mr. Forster, surrendered at Preston in Lancashire. These two defeats put an end to the Pretender's hopes in Scotland (1715). James Stuart himself was a most unsuitable person to be the centre of a rebellion. He was haggard and melancholy looking and so silent that some of the soldiers tauntingly asked whether he could speak; he was tame and spiritless, and when he did talk, it was to complain of his misfortunes. Abandoning his followers, he sailed se-

---

* The son of James II. "Pretender" in this sense means a claimant; not an impostor.

cretly with Mar for Paris, while many of his adherents were taken and executed. Lord Derwentwater and Lord Kenmure were beheaded on Tower Hill, while Lord Nithisdale escaped by changing clothes with his wife in the prison. After this, England had rest from the Pretender for thirty years. The regent of France allied himself with England, and James was obliged to seek an asylum elsewhere. He married the grand-daughter of John Sobieski, the late king of Poland, and thenceforward lived mainly in Rome.

An important law called the "Septennial Act" was passed by Parliament in the following year (1716). By this, the same Parliament was allowed to sit for seven years, though always retaining its right to dissolve itself at pleasure.

A bill had been passed in Queen Anne's reign forbidding the sovereign of England to leave the country without consent of Parliament. It was now repealed, leaving George I. free to go to his own dominions of Hanover whenever he pleased. His oldest son, George, Prince of Wales, was left in charge of the kingdom, though without the title of Regent, as he was not on good terms with his father.

During the premiership of Lord Stanhope, successor to Lord Townshend, England drifted into a war with Spain, brought about through a quarrel between Hanover and Charles XII. of Sweden on account of some disputed territory. To annoy the Elector, Charles agreed with Cardinal Alberoni, the Spanish minister, to proclaim James Stuart as James III. of England, which was done in Madrid, the Pretender having gone there for the purpose.

Holland and France now entered into an alliance with England against Spain, and this being afterward joined by the emperor, is known by the name of the Quadruple Alliance. The death of Charles XII. (1718), and the defeat of the Spanish fleet by Admiral Byng (1719), put an end to the war.

The event occupying most attention in England in this reign, was the famous South-Sea Bubble*—an attempt to pay off the national debt, which now amounted to £53,000,000, by means of a stock company organized to trade with the Spaniards in South America (1717). The government gave its sanction to the scheme by allowing its stock to be exchanged for the Company's stock. Speculation ran wild; the stock rose to 900 per cent. A similiar scheme, originated by John Law, was at the same time running the same mad career in Paris; and the thrill of it even reached America, and was felt in Kaskaskia and Fort Chartres in Illinois, as well as in New Orleans. At last the bubble burst; the stock could no longer be sold at any price, and many of those who had invested their all in it were ruined. The king and the ministry were severely blamed for the countenance they had given to this unfortunate mania. Lord Stanhope, the premier, fell a victim to the excitement. Being violently attacked on the subject in Parliament, and defending himself with equal vehemence, he was seized with a fit of apoplexy and died on the following day (1721). For the next twenty-one years, the real head of the government was Sir Robert Walpole.

Walpole's policy was one of peace. He said, "The

---

*The Southern Atlantic Ocean was then often called "The South Sea" as the Caribbean Sea was called "The Spanish Main."

most pernicious circumstances in which this country can be, are those of war; as we must be losers while it lasts and can not be great gainers when it ends." He was equally a lover of quiet at home. His aim was to avoid everything that would lead to variance, and to conduct all affairs with the least possible friction. He is charged with saying, in actions if not in words, "Every man has his price," not always in money, but in something which the man wants; and he did not scruple to employ bribery to accomplish his ends. Such an administration can have but little history.

Some disturbance took place in Ireland which, under a less skilful minister, might have led to an insurrection. As small coin there was exceedingly scarce, a contract was granted to a man named Wood to coin half-pence and farthings to a certain amount, his profit to come from the labor employed on them. The Irish, excited by factious politicians, were furious at this measure, which they fancied was intended in some way to impose upon them. Their anger was increased by a series of letters signed M. B. Drapier, written for political purposes by the celebrated Dean Swift; and although the government had Wood's half-pence tested, and found them fully up to the standard, the unreasoning rage of the people was so great that Walpole thought it best to annul the contract, giving Wood a compensation in money.

George I., like William III., was more attached to his native country than to England, and made frequent visits there. On one of his journeys, he was attacked with apoplexy, while in his traveling-carriage, and, refusing to stop on the road, was taken to his brother's palace at

Osnabrück. When the carriage reached its destination, King George was dead. His wife, Sophia Dorothea of Zell, had never been in England. This unfortunate lady had been for nearly twenty years a prisoner, on account of conduct which may have been nothing more than imprudent. She died a few months before her husband, and a story was long current that a paper had been thrown into his carriage, purporting to be a letter from her, summoning him to meet her within a year and a day. The shock of this, it is said, brought on the apoplexy which ended his life.

George II. was taking his afternoon nap when Sir Robert Walpole, booted and spurred from a hasty ride, came into the room and insisted on waking his majesty to tell him the news. The new king did not believe it at first, and when he was at last made to understand the fact, the minister asked his wishes in regard to summoning a council. "Go and get your directions from Sir Spencer Compton," answered the king, bluntly, the inference being that he meant to select the person named, as his prime minister. Sir Spencer Compton, who had been the prince's treasurer during George III.'s lifetime, was a dull, plodding man, always ready to do his best, but with no genius for government. He had not the faintest idea of what he ought to do, and asked Sir Robert to write a speech for him to give to the king to read in the Council. The ex-premier readily did this, and the new one took it to the king. The latter made some objection to it, and Sir Spencer was obliged to have recourse to Walpole again, for he did not know how to alter the document. Queen Caroline, George II.'s wife, a handsome woman of great wit and spirit, observed to her husband that it was a pity to choose a man for minister in whose own judgment his predecessor was the fittest person to perform the duties of the office; and as the king was ruled by her in everything, Sir Robert was soon reinstated. The latter and the queen remained firm friends, and really governed the country between them; while they managed the ignorant little king so well that he thought all the while he was doing it himself.

George II. was now forty-four years old. He could speak English fluently, though he did it incorrectly and with a vulgar accent. He had a violent temper, but possessed the manly virtues of courage and a love of justice.

In 1732 (the year of George Washington's birth), General James Oglethorpe procured a patent from the king for colonizing a strip of country in North America, between the Savannah River and the northern boundary of Florida, the latter country belonging to Spain. His object was to found an asylum for imprisoned debtors* and other helpless poor, where they might, by thrift, retrieve their fortunes. The expedition left England the next year (1733), and the territory, named Georgia in honor of King George II., was the last settled of the thirteen English colonies in America.

---

*The cruelties inflicted upon debtors in the Fleet and Marshalsea prisons are almost beyond belief, and we could not credit them but that they were proved by government investigation.

CHAPTER XLIV.

WAR WITH SPAIN. AUSTRIAN SUCCESSION. YOUNG PRETENDER. QUEBEC.

THE Spaniards had been from the first jealous of the new settlement of Georgia, which they thought would interfere with their trade, and they began to search English ships for prohibited goods, as the English themselves after the Revolution searched ours for British sailors. A story told by a man named Jenkins increased the popular ill-feeling. He said that a Spanish vessel overhauled his schooner, and the captain, not finding anything contraband, tortured him in various ways to make him tell what he had hidden away, and finally tore off his ear and gave it to him, saying that he would have served the king just so if he had caught him. Jenkins carried the ear about with him, wrapped in cotton, and although some persons believed that he had lost it in the pillory, the assertion helped to increase the anger against Spain. The war was carried on mostly by the navy. Admiral Vernon took Porto Bello, on the Isthmus of Darien, while Commodore Anson captured many prizes at sea, and in the course of his voyage sailed around the globe (1740-4).

While this war was going on, England became engaged in another, contrary to the advice and wishes of Sir Robert Walpole, who in consequence resigned his office (1742). Queen Caroline had died five years before. The country had grown rich and prosperous under Walpole's peaceful administration, and the king parted from him with sincere regret, creating him at the same time Earl of Orford.

The new quarrel was called "The War of the Austrian Succession," and turned on the question whether or not Maria Theresa, the daughter of the late emperor Charles VI., should reign over his hereditary dominions of Austria and Hungary. He had provided for this, as he thought, by an agreement called the "Pragmatic Sanction," which had been signed by the chief powers in Europe; but Louis XV. of France, disregarding this promise, supported the Elector of Bavaria as successor to Charles VI., and was joined by Frederic II. of Prussia (Frederic the Great), who began his aggressions by taking from Maria Theresa the province of Silesia. England sided with Austria, and as the Hungarian queen pacified Frederic II. by giving up her claim to Silesia, the latter retired from the war, leaving England and Austria to fight it out with France and Bavaria. The French were defeated by George II. at the battle of Dettingen, the last at which an English king ever fought in person. King George, however, showed such partiality for his Hanoverian troops and officers, that he lost favor with the English, and the cry "No Hanoverian king!"* began

---

* The people had previously objected to his spending so much time in Hanover, and during one of his absences the following notice was stuck up on the gate of St. James's Palace: "Lost or strayed out of this house, a man who has left a wife and six children on the parish. Whoever will give any tidings of him shall receive four shillings and sixpence reward. N.B.—This reward will not be increased, nobody judging him to deserve a Crown." (The English "crown" is a coin worth five shillings). A popular caricature represented the Hanoverian White Horse, in a cocked hat and jack-boots, riding the British Lion.

to be frequently heard. Two years afterward, the king's second son, the Duke of Cumberland, was defeated by the French under Marshal Saxe in the battle of Fontenoy (1745). He was recalled to England on account of a new danger. France once more took up the cause of the exiled Stuarts, and another Jacobite invasion was planned, this time to be led by Prince Charles Edward, son of the Old Pretender. The latter was still living, but was more spiritless than ever, and it was thought that his son, now twenty-five years old, would have better success in rallying the friends of the cause. Charles Edward sailed for Scotland with a few followers, and on his arrival there was joined by several Highland chieftains, among whom was the celebrated Cameron of Lochiel.* The "Young Chevalier," as his friends loved to call him, was the very reverse of his father. Well formed and extremely handsome, with fair hair which curled in natural ringlets, and the blue eyes of the Saxon, he had, in addition to these gifts of appearance, a manner winning though dignified, and a romantic sense of honor. The more prudent among the Scots felt that he was destined to fail, and hesitated to join him; but he moved resolutely on with such forces as he could command, and at first met with brilliant success. He took several towns, and caused his father to be proclaimed at Edinburgh under the name of James VIII. of Scotland. He also gained a victory over Sir John Cope at Preston Pans, after which the Highlanders left him and went home with their booty, and he spent some time in recruiting his army. Having collected what he thought a sufficient force, he invaded England, marching as far south-

---

* See Campbell's poem, "Lochiel's Warning."

ward as Derby. Here the Scottish army insisted on retreating, alleging that there had been neither an English uprising nor an invasion from France, on both of which they had counted; and the prince, after trying in vain both entreaties and threats, was obliged to return with them to Scotland.

The English were at last aroused to a sense of their danger, and sent a force to Scotland under the Duke of Cumberland (son of George II.) which met that of the Young Pretender on Culloden Moor, near Inverness, and inflicted on it a crushing defeat (1746).* Charles Edward escaped, and remained in concealment for five months; and though a reward of £30,000 was set upon his head, and several hundred persons knew of his hiding places, he reached France in safety. One of those who took care of him in his concealment was Flora Macdonald, celebrated in Sir Walter Scott's novel of "Waverley," under the name of Flora MacIvor. (She is said to have come to America, and to have died in North Carolina within this century.)

The Duke of Cumberland stained his military reputation by the most revolting cruelty after the battle of Culloden. He had his prisoners shot in cold blood, and allowed his soldiers such inhuman license that he was long remembered in Scotland under the title of "The

---

* The romantic aspect of this uprising in the view of the Jacobites may be judged from this stanza of a popular song, "The Scottish Cavalier:"

He was the first to draw the sword when the standard waved abroad:
He was the first to charge the foe on Preston's bloody sod:
And ever in the van of fight the foremost still he trod,
Until on bleak Culloden's height he gave his soul to God;
Like a fine old Scottish Cavalier, all of the olden time.

Butcher." When he returned to London, however, there was nothing but praise for him; he received a pension of £40,000 a year, in addition to his other revenues, and the thanks of numerous bodies of citizens. Such of the unhappy participants in the rebellion as had escaped "The Butcher" were speedily brought to trial, and about eighty of them, including Lords Kilmarnock, Balmerino, and Lovat, were executed with all the barbarities of the usual sentence for high-treason (1746).

The future fortunes of Charles Edward, "The Young Chevalier," were not in harmony with this beginning. Being obliged to leave France, he wandered from place to place, becoming constantly more dissipated and disreputable. He was married to the Countess Louise von Stolberg, whom he treated so ill that she was obliged to separate from him, and at last he closed his discreditable life in Italy, a poor, despised drunkard. His brother Henry entered the Romish Church, was created by the pope, Cardinal York, and died at Rome a very old man, in 1807. With him ended the male line of the Stuarts.

As usually happened when there was war going on in Europe between France and England, a "sympathetic" war took place between the French and English colonies in America. The one which corresponded to the War of the Austrian Succession was called here "King George's War." Its main incident was the taking (1745), by a few regiments of New-England militia under Governor Shirley, of the fortress of Louisburg, a place so strong that it was called "The Gibraltar of America." The Peace of Aix la Chapelle (1748) closed the war, and all conquered places were returned. The indignation of the New Englanders at having the fortress of Louisburg, which they had purchased with their blood and treasure, taken away from them by a stroke of the pen, was so great that the day of its surrender was called "a black day," not to be named without a feeling of disgrace.

England had now another breathing-spell of peace. After the retirement of Sir Robert Walpole, the most prominent names among English statesmen are those of William Pitt (afterward the great Lord Chatham) and Lord Chesterfield. The latter introduced in Parliament one of the most important bills of the century—namely, that of the reformation of the calendar. Until the sixteenth century, the calendar prepared by order of Julius Cæsar, called the "Julian year," had been everywhere used. Pope Gregory XIII., knowing that it was ten days out of the way, had reformed this (1582), and the new reckoning had been accepted by all Continental Europe except Russia and Sweden. By the middle of the eighteenth century, the error had grown to eleven days, and it was arranged in England that the second day of September, 1752, was to be counted as the fourteenth,* in order to bring the calendar into harmony with the correct time. The lower classes of people, thinking that they had been cheated, thronged the streets crying out, "Give us back our eleven days!" and threatening violence, but were pacified without bloodshed. By the same Act of Parliament, the beginning of the legal year was changed from April 25 to January 1. Sweden followed the example of England the next year,

---

* This seems to make a change of twelve days instead of eleven.

while in Russia the old style, now twelve days out of date, is still in use.

The American colonies, during all this time, had been gradually increasing in importance and prosperity, and in 1754, a convention of delegates met at Albany to consider a plan proposed by Dr. Benjamin Franklin of Pennsylvania, for a union of the thirteen colonies for mutual protection and defence. The plan was adopted by the convention and submitted to the colonial assemblies and to the British cabinet. It met with the usual fate of moderate measures; the colonies refused it because it left too much in the power of the king; the English government would not sanction it because it was too democratic. So the first effort at American union fell to the ground.

In the same year (1754), hostilities began between the French and English on this side of the Atlantic. The latter had made some settlements on the Ohio River; and as the French claimed all this part of the country, they resented the intrusion, and interfered with the settlers. General Braddock, who was sent from England to the assistance of the colonists, was surprised and defeated by the French and Indians near Fort du Quesne, in Pennsylvania (1755), where the British troops were saved from destruction only by the skill of George Washington, then a major of Virginia volunteers. The war dragged on for some years longer, there being no efficient commanders on the side of the English until the ministry of William Pitt put new vigor into the administration. Under General Amherst, Louisburg was retaken (1758) after a siege of seven weeks, and Fort du Quesne, being abandoned by the French, was occupied by General John Forbes, and named Fort Pitt, in honor of the statesman whose energetic measures had changed the course of the war. The fort fell into decay, but the city which grew up around it still keeps the name of Pittsburg. In the following year, the glorious victory of Wolfe on the Heights of Abraham, near Quebec, practically ended the war, though peace was not formally made until four years afterward. General Wolfe and the French commander, Montcalm, were both killed in the action.

The island of Minorca, it will be remembered, had been ceded to the English by the Treaty of Utrecht. Although there had been no declaration of war between France and England, the English had since made some piratical attacks on French vessels. In retaliation for this, the French attacked Port Mahon, in Minorca, which Admiral Byng had orders to defend. He sailed to this place, but thinking the French fleet superior to his own, resolved not to attack it, and left the island to its fate. The fort surrendered (1756) after making the best defence it could. The popular clamor against Byng was so violent that he was tried by court-martial and shot on the quarter-deck of his ship.

Among the influences now affecting the great body of Englishmen, who cared little for the foreign wars which brought them no profit and but a faint impression of sharing in the national glory, was the new impulse given to the religious life of the people by the preaching of John Wesley. He was afterward joined by his brother Charles and by George Whitefield, and both in England and America they tried to arouse a more earnest and personal interest in religion. They wished to raise it from dead formality to a true spiritual life; and when they were not allowed the use of churches in which to address their followers and fellow-laborers, they held meetings in the open air, where thousands at a time were brought under the spell of their eloquence. The poorer classes, especially, yielded eagerly to the emotions inspired by their fervor, and an electric thrill seemed to run through the nation. Wesley himself had no intention of separating from the Church of England; but his successors developed his plan for an organized religious life into the great movement now known as Methodism.

CHAPTER XLV.

SEVEN-YEARS' WAR. INDIA. DEATH OF GEORGE II. STAMP ACT. LETTERS OF JUNIUS.

EIGHT years after the Peace of Aix la Chapelle, France and Austria leagued together for the destruction of Prussia, against which each had some grievances. Russia, Saxony, and Sweden afterward joined this alliance. Frederic II., king of Prussia, having had private notice of their intentions, did not wait to be attacked, but acted on the offensive by seizing Dresden, the capital of Saxony. This was the beginning of what was afterward known as the Seven-Years' War (1756-63).

In such a condition of affairs, England naturally took part with Prussia. It was not only to preserve the balance of power and because the kings of the two countries were own cousins that she did so, but because the king was in danger of losing his electorate of Hanover. The Duke of Cumberland was sent for the defence of that country, but the French, entering it with a large army, compelled him to retreat and to sign the "Convention of Kloster-Seven" (1757), by which he agreed practically to disband his army. When the duke returned to England, his father treated him so coldly that he gave up all his employments and retired in disgust to private life.

In addition to her wars on the Continent and in America, England was carrying on a vigorous contest in India. That country was still largely under the control of native rulers, with whom the French allied themselves against the English. As early as 1751, Robert Clive, a young man in the East-India Company's service, had entered the army, and now, with a mere handful of Englishmen and a few Sepoys, he attacked and took the town of Arcot from the French, and gradually extended the English rule. In 1756 occurred the tragedy of the "Black Hole" in Calcutta. The nabob Surajah Dowlah, who had long been jealous of the English, seized Fort William in Calcutta, and shut up one hundred and forty-six prisoners in a loathsome dungeon so small that they could scarcely stand in it. Here he kept them through a hot August night. In the morning, after suffering untold torments, only twenty-three of them were left alive. The next year (1757) Clive, having collected a small army of English and Sepoys, retook Calcutta, and later in the year fought the memorable battle of Plassey, where with three thousand men he defeated Surajah Dowlah's army of fifty thousand.

When he returned to England, having laid the foundation of a vast empire, the conqueror was raised to the peerage under the name of Lord Clive, Baron of Plassey. In the same year, the victory of Sir Eyre Coote drove the French out of Pondicherry, thus giving the British control over the whole of Southern India.

In 1760, King George II. died suddenly, from a rupture of the heart. His son Frederic, Prince of Wales, had died nine years before, leaving a son who now became King of England as George III. The latter was at this time twenty-two years old, and was the first of the Georges who was born in England.

George III. succeeded to the throne when England was at a high pitch of national pride and self-satisfaction. The victories of Wolfe in America and Clive in India contributed to this confidence; and the nation felt safe under the administration of the "Great Commoner," William Pitt. The French, annoyed at their defeats, now entered into an alliance with Spain called the "Family Compact," the kings of both countries being Bourbons. As this bound Spain to take part with France against England, Pitt wished to be beforehand with her and declare war at once, thus taking her at a disadvantage; but the king refusing to do so, Pitt resigned his office and was succeeded by Lord Bute (1761).

In the same year, King George married Princess Charlotte of Mecklenburg Strelitz, a girl of seventeen, plain-looking but sensible. His attention was attracted to her by reading a letter she wrote to Frederic the Great, asking him to spare her country the horrors of war. It was a simple little letter, such as any well-educated school-girl might write, but George III. thought it admirable, and offered himself at once to the young princess. The marriage was a very happy one and the king proved himself a good husband—something so rare in his family that it is worth noticing.

Spain soon broke out into acts of open warfare, as Pitt had expected. The English captured the city of Havana in Cuba, and several of the smaller West-India Islands, besides taking Manilla, the capital of the Philippines. Notwithstanding these successes, Lord Bute, alarmed at the increase of the national debt, which now amounted to £132,000,000, was anxious to make peace, and a treaty at Paris (1763) ended the Seven Years' War.* By this, France gave up the whole of Canada to the British, and tacitly renounced her right to the great Northwest Territory, which included within its limits the Great Lakes and the Upper Mississippi Valley, and the present states of Ohio, Indiana, Illinois, Michigan, Wisconsin, and Minnesota. England gave back to Spain her recent conquests of Havana and Manilla, with several of the West-India Islands, receiving Florida in return. The treaty was extremely displeasing to the English, on account of these concessions, and Lord Bute became the most unpopular man in the country. People contrasted his weak measures with the energy of Pitt; and, to the surprise of every one, he resigned his office (1763). He was succeeded by George Granville.

Among the various ways in which the growing spirit of popular freedom showed itself was the desire for increased liberty of the press. A political paper called "The North Briton," edited by John Wilkes, had long

---

*The corresponding war in America (which, however, began there two years earlier) was called the French and Indian War.

been the vehicle for attacks on the government; and after an address of the king to Parliament in which he spoke of the peace as honorable to Great Britain, Wilkes published in his paper a violent attack on the minister, and, by implication, on the king. Wilkes was thrown into the Tower, but was released on account of his privilege as a member of Parliament. The Commons expelled him from his seat by a unanimous vote, and ordered his paper to be burnt by the hangman. He was reëlected by his constituents and after repeated expulsions, reëlections, fines and imprisonments, he was at last allowed to take his seat, and remained a member of Parliament for many years, the original question being entirely dropped. This was taken as a vindication of the right of free utterance both in printing and speaking, and, this right having once been established, it has been impossible since that time ever to violate it.

George III.'s policy differed in one respect from that of his two immediate predecessors. He was determined to govern. He was an honest man, though one of narrow views and an overwhelming idea of his personal prerogative. In the debates on the legality of Wilkes's arrest, General Conway, a distinguished officer and a fair-minded man, voted conscientiously against the government; upon which the king insisted on his being instantly dismissed from the army. "In this question, I am personally concerned," he wrote to Grenville. "I am not to be neglected unpunished."

But all ministerial and royal imprudences were thrown into the shade by Grenville's proposed bill for taxing the American Colonies. His excuse for this was that England had been at great expense for their defence in the French and Indian war, and that it was only right that they should bear their share of the burden. The tax took the form of a Stamp Act, requiring that all law documents should be written upon stamped paper, each sheet thus paying a duty to England.*

The measure passed (1765) with little opposition. Pitt was absent when it was voted on; and the only strong remonstrance was contained in a spirited speech by Colonel Isaac Barré. The character of this may be judged by a few extracts. Col. Barré said, referring to the Americans, "They, planted by *your* care! No; your oppression planted them in America. . . . They, nourished by *your* indulgence! They grew by your neglect of them. . . . They, protected by *your* arms! They have nobly taken up arms in your defence."

In the colonies, however, the resistance to the Act was forcible and instantaneous. "No Taxation without Representation!" was the cry. In the Virginia House of Burgesses, Patrick Henry uttered his cutting invectives against it. In Massachusetts, James Otis poured forth the burning words which made John Adams, another of our great orators, characterize him as "a flame of fire." A general Congress met at New York in

---

* Dr. Franklin had been sent to England by several of the colonies, when hints of the threatened taxation reached America, to use his influence against it. He writes to a friend at this time, "Depend upon it, I took every step in my power to prevent the passing of the Stamp Act. But the tide was too strong against us. We might as well have hindered the sun's setting . . . Frugality and industry will go a great way toward indemnifying us. Idleness and pride tax with a heavier hand than kings and parliaments. If we can get rid of the former we may easily bear the latter."

October, 1765, which put forth a declaration of rights, acknowledging allegiance to Great Britain, but protesting against illegal taxation and against the vexatious limitations which were imposed on trade by the navigation laws* and other similar enactments. A suggestion was made that the colonies should be asked to tax themselves for the purpose of assisting the mother-country, and if this had been followed out, the amount raised would probably have been far in excess of what was expected from the sale of stamps. No attention was paid to the proceedings of the Stamp-Act Congress, as it was called, and by the first of November, the day on which the law was to go into operation, there were no stamps to sell. The people of the colonies had destroyed them all; and the officers employed in their distribution were glad to get off with their lives.

Among the orators who spoke in the English Parliament against the Act was Edmund Burke, then as always, the friend of liberty. It was in one of his speeches on this subject at a later time that he brought in his famous simile of shearing a wolf. A man was resolved to shear a wolf. "But have you considered the resistance, the difficulty, the danger of the attempt?" "No; I have considered nothing but the right. Man has the right of dominion over the beasts of the forest, and therefore, I will shear the wolf!" William Pitt (now created Earl of

---

* By these laws the colonies were forbidden to sell their products except in England, nor could they buy European goods in any other country. No foreign ships were allowed to enter American ports. The Americans were not permitted to make iron-ware and woolen goods, and many articles which they made could not be sent from one colony to another.

Chatham) spoke to the same purpose. "I rejoice that America has resisted. Three millions of people, so dead to all the feelings of liberty as voluntarily to submit to be slaves, would have been fit instruments to make slaves of the rest. . . . It is my opinion that the Stamp Act should be repealed, totally, absolutely, and immediately." The Stamp Act was repealed (1766) but coupled with the bill for repeal was another declaring the power of Parliament "to bind the colonies in all cases whatsoever." This did not promise harmony, yet as the immediate point was gained, the colonies were quieted, and the usual accompaniment of bonfires and bell-ringing testified to the joy of the American people.

While the discussion over the Stamp Act was still going on, the king was attacked by an illness, the nature of which was kept secret, but which is now supposed to have been temporary insanity. On his recovery a Council of Regency was appointed, at his suggestion, in case of a relapse; and Grenville, having displeased him in some personal matters, was allowed to retire, his place being taken by Lord Rockingham.

In agreement with its declaration, Parliament now (1767) proceeded to lay taxes on tea, glass, paper, and painter's colors, more for the sake of asserting its rights than with an expectation of revenue. The duties on the last three articles were soon withdrawn, but the king insisted on retaining that on tea.

By an arrangement with the East-India Company, its merchants were enabled to send cargoes of tea to America, which, even after the duty was paid, could be sold at a lower rate than formerly. This, it was supposed, would be eagerly accepted by the Americans, it being assumed that they complained of the tax only because it affected their pockets. But the colonists desired, not cheaper tea, but the maintenance of the principle that there could be no taxation without representation; and the concession went for nothing.

In the midst of the excitement produced in England by the discussion of these subjects, a series of letters under the signature of "Junius" appeared in the newspapers, attacking the government, with violent personal abuse of its members, in which even the king was not spared. Every effort was used to discover the writer of these letters; but the authorship of "Junius" continued a mystery for several generations. It is only within the present half-century that evidence has come to light which makes it almost certain that the author of the "Letters of Junius" was Sir Philip Francis, a government official of some distinction.

CHAPTER XLVI.

WAR WITH AMERICA. PEACE OF VERSAILLES. WARREN HASTINGS.

THE tea-ships arrived duly in America, according to the provisions of the English government and the East-India Company; but no tea was sold here. In Boston, where the governor refused to allow it to be taken back to England, a company* of

---

*This orderly riot is called in history "The Boston Tea-Party." It curiously happened that the last survivor of it, David Kennison, was a soldier at Fort Dearborn (Chicago) in 1810. He died in Chicago, February 24, 1852, at a great age, and his bones lie in a grave, unmarked but not unknown, within the present limits of Lincoln Park.—"Fergus' Historical Series," No. 16.

men disguised as Indians boarded the ships, broke open the chests, and emptied the tea into the water (1773). In New York and Philadelphia, the vessels were sent back without unloading their cargoes. In Annapolis, a ship that had paid the duty was burnt in the harbor, with its cargo. In Charleston, the tea was intentionally stored in damp cellars, where it was soon spoiled. As Boston was considered the hot-bed of the rebellious spirit, Parliament as a punishment passed the "Boston Port Bill," which closed the harbor to all commerce, and removed the seat of Massachusetts government to Salem (1774). An attempt was made to quarter several regiments of British soldiers on the inhabitants of Boston, and vexatious alterations were made in the charter of the colony, all tending to restrict its liberty. A congress of delegates from the thirteen colonies met later in the year, and a Declaration of Rights was announced in reference to which Lord Chatham (William Pitt) said, "I must declare that for solidity of reasoning, force of sagacity, and wisdom of conclusion, under such a complication of difficult circumstances, no nation or body of men can stand in preference to the General Congress at Philadelphia." But George III. was incapable of learning anything. He had but one idea as to America, and that was, to crush down opposition by force. "The die is cast," he wrote to Lord North, the premier, when he sent General Gage with troops to Boston, "The colonies must either triumph or submit." The first alternative was clearly meant to be ironical.

The skirmish at Lexington, the seizure of Ticonderoga, the battle of Bunker Hill, the appointment of George Washington as commander-in-chief of the Continental

Congress, followed one another rapidly (1775), and early in the next year, General Washington's bold and masterly movements forced General Howe to evacuate Boston. On the fourth of July, 1776, the Continental Congress, assembled at Philadelphia, declared that the colonies were and of right ought to be, free and independent states. The Americans had continued to petition the king for redress of their grievances even after the effort seemed hopeless; but no notice was taken of their petitions, on the ground that the Congress was a self-constituted body, and in rebellion. Washington was defeated by General Howe (who had under his command a large number of Hessian troops hired by the British government) at Brooklyn Heights (August, 1776), and soon afterward was obliged to abandon New York City. Franklin and others had been sent as envoys to ask aid from France; and though Louis XVI. was not then prepared to go to war with England (which would have been the result of open assistance), he helped the Americans secretly with money, and connived at Lafayette's going to America on his own responsibility. The battles of Brandywine and Germantown, unfavorable to the Americans, were more than counterbalanced by the victories over Lord Burgoyne at Saratoga (1777), where the British general was taken prisoner, with his whole army.* This was the turning-point in the war, and is reckoned as one of the "Fifteen Decisive Battles of the World." The next year (1778), the indepen-

---

* One of Burgoyne's soldiers, John Whistler, entered the American service, rose to be a captain, and was the builder of the first Fort Dearborn (1803). His grand-daughter, Gwinthlean Whistler, widow of Robert A. Kinzie, now lives in Chicago (1891).

dence of the United States was recognized by France, and after three years more of intermittent fighting the American victory at Yorktown, where Lord Cornwallis surrendered with his army, practically closed the war.

Matters did not arrive at this pass without attempts on the side of Great Britain toward peace. Lord North brought in two bills (1778), one renouncing formally the right of the British Parliament to tax America; the other authorizing the king to send commissioners to treat with any person or persons whom the colonies might appoint, as a means of restoring peace. The effect of the reading in Parliament is thus recorded in the "Annual Register:" "A dull, melancholy silence for some time succeeded to this speech * * * Astonishment, dejection, and fear overclouded the whole assembly." Lord Chatham, very ill with the gout, was brought to the Parliament House, wrapped in flannels, and supported on either side by his son and his son-in-law, and there made his last speech. He protested against any measure that looked toward the surrender of the colonies. His voice had always been against taxation; it was now raised still more strongly against separation. While attempting to speak further, he fell back in convulsions, and was carried home insensible. He lingered a few weeks, and died, lamented by all except the king and his party, the tories. When George III. heard that the Commons had voted him a public funeral,* he wrote to Lord North that he was "rather surprised," but trusted that it would be merely an expression of gratitude for

---

* Parliament also decreed a monument in Westminster Abbey, an annuity of £4000, to his heirs, and a gift of £20,000 to pay his debts.

certain services which he specified. "This compliment, if paid to his general conduct," remarked his majesty, "is rather an offensive measure to me personally." The funeral honors were paid, and Chatham's name still rouses in the hearts of Americans as well as Englishmen, feelings of pride and veneration, while the best they can say of George III. is, "Poor man, he meant well!"

England had declared war against France as soon as the treaty of the latter country with the United States was made known, and it was not long before she was embroiled with Spain and Holland. Everywhere her powerful navy enabled her to hold her own. Gibraltar sustained successfully a three years' siege, and Admiral Rodney defeated a Spanish fleet off Cape St. Vincent and a French one in the West Indies. A small American squadron under John Paul Jones captured two British vessels, the "Serapis" and the "Scarborough," off the coast of Scotland.

The year 1780 was long remembered in England on account of the "No popery!" riots in London. Extremely severe laws against Roman Catholics had been in force all through the century. Priests who performed mass or became teachers were liable to be imprisoned for life; and all Catholics were declared incapable of owning landed property, which, in case of inheritance, was given to the nearest Protestant relative. The repeal (1778) of these disgraceful laws enraged the bigoted masses, and Lord George Gordon, a weak, vain, and restless young man, drew together a great mob, which for a few days seemed to have possession of London. The rioters broke open Newgate Prison, liberated three hundred prisoners, and burned the costly building to the ground. They then rushed through London and the suburbs, destroying houses and Roman Catholic churches, and burned the fine residence of Lord Mansfield, chief-justice of England, with the valuable law-library which he had spent fifty years in collecting. Lord George Gordon was accused of high treason, but was acquitted, and afterward died insane. A large number of the rioters were executed.*

Although the capture of Lord Cornwallis and his army at Yorktown in 1781 had virtually ended the American war, the final treaty of peace was not signed until two years afterward. Approaches were made to Dr. Franklin at Paris, on the part of the British government, and as he refused to treat on any other terms than a recognition of American independence, the negotiations were somewhat delayed. In November, 1782, however, a preliminary treaty was signed, yielding all that was demanded by the United States, including permission to fish on the banks of Newfoundland. Early in the next year, peace was made at Versailles with France and Spain, several of the West India Islands changing hands again, and Florida being once more given back to Spain. On September 3, 1783, the definite treaty was signed with the United States. The king's first speech in Parliament after the signing of the treaty was in a manly and generous tone. After stating the facts, he said that he had sacrificed every consideration of his own to the wishes and opinions of his people, and added, "I make it my humble and earnest prayer to Almighty God that Great Britain

---

* A spirited account of these riots is found in the opening chapter of Dickens's "Barnaby Rudge."

may not feel the evils that might result from so great a dismemberment of the empire, and that America may be free from those calamities which have formerly proved in the mother country how essential monarchy is to the enjoyment of constitutional liberty. Religion, language, interest, affections, may, and I hope will, yet prove a bond of permanent union between the two countries." Two years later, when John Adams, our first minister to England, was presented to him, he said that though he had been the last to consent to a separation, he would be the first to meet the friendship of the United States as an independent power.

In the same year with the acknowledgment of American independence, the Prince of Wales became of age. By his extravagance of living, his losses at the gaming table, and the alterations he was making in Carlton House, which had been given him as a residence, he was so deeply involved that at one time he had a sheriff's process for debt in his house. His father refused to assist him, and for a time he reduced his expenses. Then, the opposition drawing attention to his notorious debts and threatening to make them public, the king consented, on condition of his reforming, to allow him (from the public funds of course) £10,000 a year additional income, £161,000 to pay his debts with, and £20,000 to spend on Carlton House.

We must now turn to British affairs in India. Lord Clive had returned there after a few years spent at home, and had employed his great talents in reforming abuses and in consolidating the splendid empire which he may almost be said to have given to England. Returning home (1767) in ill-health, with enormous wealth, he was accused by General Burgoyne (the same who was afterward defeated at Saratoga) of misconduct in India, and an investigation was held (1773). Acts of oppression and deceit toward native chiefs were proved against him (he was always faithful to his own government) and he was censured for these, while at the same time his "great and meritorious services to his country" were recognized. The mortification broke his heart. Being of a melancholy temperament, which was increased by a life of inaction, and suffering from illness, he killed himself (1774) at forty-nine years of age.

After Clive's last return from the Indian peninsula, the old corruption and mismanagement began there again, and Warren Hastings was sent out as governor-general of India, being the first person who bore that title. He was an able and vigorous ruler, surrounded by difficulties which taxed his powers to the utmost. Hyder Ali, king of Mysore, the most enterprising of the native chiefs, invaded the Carnatic (a district on the eastern coast of India) with 90,000 men, led by French officers, and after inflicting great injury on the English, was defeated by Sir Eyre Coote at Porto Novo, with the effect of establishing their power more firmly than ever.

To satisfy the grasping demands of the East-India Company, Hastings practised such extortions on the native princes as have left an indelible stain on his memory. Exorbitant fines, seizure of vast amounts of property under false pretences, employment of torture to force the giving up of treasures, bribery of officials, all these things dim the glory of the man who had done more than any other to secure the great empire which had been conquered by his predecessors, and to this day remains a monument of English prowess. His genius for administration, his foresight, his knowledge of the springs to be touched in dealing with men, place him in the very front rank of England's great colonial governors. But when he returned home (1785), expecting rewards and applause, he was met by an impeachment which, from the magnitude of the interests involved and the station of the accused, led to one of the most famous state trials of history.

Once more the grand old hall of William Rufus was crowded. The greatest orators of the day were arrayed against the prisoner; Burke, Fox, Sheridan, all famed for impassioned eloquence, for convincing reasoning, did their utmost to prove him guilty. On his side, the counsel were men of great legal ability, but of lesser note. One of them, Law, was afterward chief-justice of England. The court was crowded during its first sessions with the rank and fashion of England, both men and women, all eagerly taking one side or the other as if their own fate depended upon the result. The trial lasted for seven years. There were long recesses of the court, during which Hastings was released on bail; but not until 1795, was the verdict given—not guilty!

That Warren Hastings was guilty of great crimes against humanity can not be denied. That he derived no benefit personally from those crimes is equally true, for he did not come home a rich man; whether his great services to the country justified his acquittal for wrongs done was the question for the court to decide, and it was decided in the affirmative.

Though justice was not done, as it now seems to us, the objects of the trial were accomplished. It has become impossible, since that day, for any English officer to repeat the cruelties which fill our souls with horror; and the poor Hindoo pariah is, in theory at least, as much under the protection of law as his fellow-subjects in England.

CHAPTER XLVII.

THE FRENCH REVOLUTION. NAPOLEON IN EGYPT. IRELAND.

IN 1783, the office of prime minister of England was conferred upon William Pitt, a man only twenty-four years old, second son of the great Lord Chatham. When he began, the country was exhausted by a long war, and public discontent was freely vented in abuse of the administration. Within a few years all this was changed. The debt was reduced by ten millions sterling, and people trusted the government, for it was perceived that there was a strong hand at the helm. As long as he held the office, Pitt enjoyed the confidence of the king without sacrificing his own independence.

The year 1789 was a crisis in the history of two nations with whom the fortunes of England were closely connected. The United States of America, which had been up to that time a loosely-joined confederacy, with no central bond to hold the members together, became really united by the adoption of its constitution and the organization of a centralized government. It was no longer "one nation to-day and thirteen to-morrow," as Washington had described it. It was a consolidated country, which for the first time commanded the respect of the world. England marked her sense of the change by sending a resident minister to represent her interests in America, which before she had disdained to do. From the 30th of April, 1789, the day of Washington's inauguration as president, the United States took its place among the family of nations.*

Five days after this event, the meeting of the States-general at Versailles, near Paris (May 5, 1789), marked the opening of that great convulsion called the French Revolution.† At first, English sympathy was largely on the side of the Revolutionists. People saw, or thought they saw, an effort toward a constitutional government, which was to replace the old arbitrary tyranny; and they rejoiced for the sake of humanity. But it was not long before they began to see the cloven foot of the worst form of tyranny—the tyranny of the many—under the sweeping robe of progress, and those who had been most eager in praise of the movement turned with loathing from its excesses. The first effect in England was to make more marked the division of party lines, and friends were separated who had before stood in close alliance. Burke and Fox, in particular, became political opponents, the latter, a man less clear-sighted and well-balanced than his friend, supporting the revolutionists,

---

* As England refused to give up certain forts which she held in our western territory and continued to interfere with our commerce, it was found necessary to make another treaty with her (1794), which was negotiated by John Jay, afterward chief-justice of the United States. By this treaty everything was settled for ten years.

† See "A Short History of France," chapters XXIX-XXXII.

those "architects of ruin," as Burke called them. In the violent language of the time, those who opposed the Revolution were despots—those who defended it were Jacobins.*

The execution of Louis XVI. in 1793 filled England with horror; and when the French National Convention declared war against her within two weeks afterward, under pretext of helping the party in England who wished to make that country a republic, the national spirit burst forth like a torrent. A fleet sent to assist the royalists in the defence of Toulon (1793) was driven away by a force under the direction of Napoleon Bonaparte. This was his first military action, and he did not again come into direct collision with the English until they met in Syria (1798).

A coalition was formed by Great Britain, Holland, Russia, and Spain, to restore the monarchy in France; but the immense armies, mad with enthusiasm, sent into the field by the republic, baffled all their efforts. The navy, however, was successful in several quarters, Nelson, Howe, and Hood, keeping up the honor of the English flag at sea.

In Holland, the French were successful, and the Stadtholder (the Prince of Orange) fled to England. The authorities left in Holland now joining the French, England seized the Dutch dominions in the East and West Indies. Demarara and the colonies in South America, the Cape of Good Hope in Africa, and Ceylon, Ma-

---

* Be careful to distinguish between "Jacobite" and "Jacobin." The former denoted the followers of James II. and his descendants, the latter the most violent and radical party of the French anarchists.

lacca and other Dutch possessions in Asia were taken (1795).

In England, those who sympathized with the Revolution did their best to stir up ill-feeling among the lower classes; and a bad harvest, making high prices, increased the excitement. The king was hooted and pelted in the streets, and his coach, after he had left it, was broken to pieces by the mob. The Bank of England was obliged to suspend specie payments (1797), and its notes had to be taken instead of gold and silver.

It was during this year that Nelson, supported by Admiral Jervis, gained a great victory over the Spanish fleet off Cape St. Vincent. In the heat of the action he exclaimed, "Westminster Abbey or victory!" This time it was victory. A few months afterward, Admiral Duncan defeated a French fleet at Camperdown.

Napoleon Bonaparte, who had reappeared on the scene in "The Day of the Sections" (1795) and the campaign in Italy (1796-7), now undertook an expedition to Egypt (1798) to break the English power in that country and prevent communication with India through the Red Sea. Landing at Alexandria with an immense army, he soon afterward defeated the Mamelukes (Egyptian soldiers) in the Battle of the Pyramids. Admiral Nelson, however, vanquished the French fleet in Aboukir Bay with great loss.* For this he was made "Baron Nelson of the Nile." Only four of Napoleon's ships were able to escape to France. Meanwhile, Bonaparte, marching into Syria, undertook to conquer that country from the Turks. At Acre he found the latter supported

---

*This was the famous "Battle of the Nile," where took place, the incident celebrated in Mrs. Hemans's "Casabianca."

by the English admiral, Sir Sydney Smith, and after a siege of two months was forced to retire. On returning to Egypt from this most disastrous expedition he deserted his army and secretly embarked for France, where, by a change in the government, he was made first consul (1799).

Sir Ralph Abercrombie, who was sent to Egypt to attack the French army left there by Bonaparte, gained a victory near Alexandria, but was mortally wounded in the action. General Hutchinson, who now assumed the command, defeated the French general Menou, and agreed that the French troops in Egypt should be transported to France at the expense of England. The *savans* (learned men) who went with Napoleon had collected an enormous quantity of Egyptian manuscripts and antiquities of all sorts, including the famous "Rosetta Stone,"* which they were now obliged to give up to the English, retaining only their private papers.

A rebellion in Ireland was the natural consequence of the revolutionary successes in America and France, and an association called "The Society of United Irishmen" was formed there in 1793. It was begun by Protestants under the leadership of Theobald Wolfe Tone, but was soon largely joined by Irish Catholics. For some years their movements and intentions were kept secret, but in 1798 the project of an insurrection was betrayed to the English government, and some of the leaders were arrested. Martial law was proclaimed in Ireland, and

---

* On this stone is engraved an inscription in Greek, ancient Egyptian, and hieroglyphics, by means of which it became possible to decipher all Egyptian picture-writing. It is in the British Museum.

many acts of violence were committed on both sides. Lord Edward Fitzgerald was killed in defending himself, and Thomas Addis Emmet was confined for three years.*

By the efforts of Pitt (which included unscrupulous bribery of its members) the Irish Parliament passed a vote agreeing to union with England (July, 1800). The scene, as described by a member of this last Parliament, was very impressive. "The speaker, with an eye averted from the object which he hated, proclaimed, with a subdued voice, 'The Ayes have it.'" When the House adjourned, the speaker was followed to his residence by forty-one members, walking bareheaded, and in profound silence. He bowed to them before entering his house, and then "the whole assemblage dispersed, without uttering a word."

Having now reached the last year of the eighteenth century, we may properly look back and see what that century had accomplished in England. Politically, the press had been made free, and the debates in Parliament, previously most jealously kept secret, were reported from 1771. England had gained Canada and lost the thirteen colonies; the latter after all a real gain to her, although an apparent loss, for independent America has been of far more value to her than colonial America ever could have been.

---

* Emmet was released (1802) on condition of leaving England forever. A few years later he came to New York, and ended his life there as a prosperous lawyer. His brother, Robert Emmet, was concerned in a rebellion in 1803, and was hanged in Dublin. Two of Thomas Moore's exquisite poems were written in memory of him and his lady-love: "Oh, breathe not his name," and "She is far from the land where her young hero sleeps."

She had established an empire in India to which mankind has seen no parallel in modern times, and there is no quarter of the globe where her dominion was not increased. Captain Cook added to the world's knowledge by his discovery (1778) of the Hawaiian Islands (called by the English Sandwich) and his investigations of the resources of Australia led to the establishment of a penal settlement in New South Wales (1788).

In science, the application of steam to practical purposes had begun, and was constantly widening, James Watt extending and applying what Newcomen had begun. His partner, Boulton, said triumphantly to Boswell, when the latter visited his manufactory: "I sell here, sir, what all the world desires to have—POWER!" Franklin had tamed the lightning; Herschel, with his powerful telescope, brought a new planet into sight. The Duke of Bridgewater devised, and, with the help of Brindley, the great engineer, carried out the project of connecting the industrial districts by a chain of canals. Wedgwood invented a method of making pottery which soon rivalled the work of France and Holland. A quarter of the surface of England, marsh, waste moor, and forest, was reclaimed during this century, and ten thousand square miles of land added to what was already cultivated.

It is strange that a nation claiming so high a degree of civilization as England, should so long have tolerated the unspeakable horrors of the slave-trade; but though the matter was in agitation for twenty years, with all the influences that could be brought to bear upon it, the detestable traffic was not suppressed until the nineteenth century. The bill passed the Commons repeatedly, but was always thrown out by the House of Lords. John

Howard brought the frightful condition of the prisons before public attention, though the system of laws which punished with death the stealing of articles from a shop to the value of five shillings, still continued in force.

The discovery of a preventive of small-pox, belongs to the eighteenth century. This disease had long been the scourge of Europe, taking its victims from high and low alike, when Lady Mary Wortley Montague, the spirited wife of the ambassador to Turkey, brought home with her from that country the practice of inoculation. While the unreasoning prejudice against it was still great in England, Queen Caroline had the good sense to allow two of her children to be inoculated; and the remedy became a recognized one. In the latter part of the century, however, the discovery by Dr. Jenner of the process of vaccination provided a milder treatment, equally effectual, and infinitely less dangerous.

In art, William Hogarth, a painter who satirized the faults and follies of common life, was most noted in the middle part of the century. Later, Reynolds and Gainsborough were celebrated, each in his own line, as painters, and sculpture was represented by Flaxman. Sheridan was the great play-writer, and Garrick the great actor of plays in those days.

When we try to name the men of letters of the last half of the eighteenth century, we have a long task before us. There were Hume and Gibbon and Robertson, the historians; Richardson, Fielding, and Smollett, the originators of our system of modern romance-writing; Thomson, Young, and Gray, the poets; Johnson and Goldsmith (who also wrote in many other styles), the essayists; Adam Smith, founder of the science of political economy; Lady

Mary Wortley Montague and Horace Walpole, the inimitable letter-writers; Frances Burney, novelist and diarist; Watts and Wesley and Newton, the writers of so many of our familiar hymns. Last on the list come the two poets of humanity, Robert Burns in Scotland and William Cowper in England, the latter dying in 1800, and so finishing the century.

CHAPTER XLVIII.

UNION WITH IRELAND. TRAFALGAR. ORDERS IN COUNCIL. PENINSULAR WAR. WAR OF 1812. WATERLOO. ST. HELENA.

THE opening year of the new century saw the assembling of the first Parliament of Great Britain and Ireland (1801). At the same time the vain words "King of France" were dropped from the royal title and the *fleur de lys* blotted out from the royal arms. The Irish Parliament ceased to exist; a hundred Irish members were added to the House of Commons in England and thirty-two peers, including four bishops, to the House of Lords. Pitt made a strong effort to procure the admission of Roman Catholics to Parliament, but the king opposed it from conscientious motives, and Pitt resigned the premiership, which he had held for eighteen years. Mr. Addington took his place and formed a new ministry (1801).

The right of searching the vessels of other nations for contraband goods had never been given up by Great Britain, and the northern countries, Russia, Sweden, Denmark, and Prussia formed a league to protect their commerce from the encroachments of the English. Sir Hyde Parker and Lord Nelson were sent to Copenhagen with a fleet, and a deadly fight took place. Nelson said afterward, "I have been in more than a hundred engagements, but that of Copenhagen was the most terrific of them all." Several of the ships ran aground, and the admiral, Sir Hyde Parker, gave the signal to withdraw; but Nelson put his spy-glass to his blind eye so that he could not see it, and went on fighting. The Danish fleet was destroyed, and he sailed away for the Baltic to find the Russians. When he arrived off Cronstadt he learned that the emperor, "Mad Paul," had been assassinated; and as Alexander I., his successor, was disposed to make peace, there was no difficulty in putting an end to the league. Soon afterward a treaty was made with France at Amiens, and for a moment the world seemed quiet again.

The peace did not last long. The English refused to give up Malta, as stipulated in the treaty, because the French army was kept up; and Bonaparte, who was still First Consul, ordered all English residents or travellers in France to be thrown into prison (1803). A French army took possession of Hanover, while the English seized the French and Dutch colonies in the West Indies. A great number of soldiers, called the "Army of England," were assembled at Boulogne, and Bonaparte reviewed them there; but as he had other work on hand, and the British fleet swept the channel unremittingly, the army of England never sailed.

In 1804, Bonaparte proclaimed himself emperor under the name of Napoleon I. At the same time,

Addington resigned, and Pitt again became prime minister. A year later, Nelson fought the battle of Trafalgar (1805). The order for the day was, "ENGLAND EXPECTS EVERY MAN TO DO HIS DUTY." Every man did his duty, and the English won a glorious victory; but Nelson was killed. Admiral Collingwood, the second in command, succeeded him.

In 1806, England lost another of her greatest men. William Pitt died in January, on the twenty-fifth anniversary of the day on which he first entered Parliament, worn out at the age of forty-six by care and anxiety. The usurpations of Napoleon filled him with dismay and dread. "Fold up the map of Europe for twenty years!" he exclaimed in despair, after the battle of Austerlitz. His rival, Fox, survived him only a few months. They are buried near one another in Westminster Abbey.* Nelson is buried in the centre of the crypt under the great dome of St. Paul's, London.

It is impossible, in writing the history of any country in Europe during the first fifteen years of this century, to avoid constant references to the name of Napoleon. Having beaten Austria and Russia at Austerlitz and Prussia at Jena, he entered Berlin in Triumph, and from that place issued the "Berlin Decrees," which have made his visit there so famous. By them he declared the British Islands in a state of blockade (on paper), and forbade all other countries to hold any commercial intercourse with England or her colonies. The English government, fearful that Napoleon would press into his service the fine Danish fleet, sent to demand of Den-

---

* "Drop upon Fox's grave a tear
'Twill trickle to his rival's bier."—Sir Walter Scott.

mark that it should be given up to them. This being indignantly refused, a force was sent to bombard Copenhagen, which was forced to surrender, and the whole Danish fleet was carried to England, with immense quantities of naval stores and artillery (1807). This arrogant act must always remain a blot on the escutcheon of England. The island of Heligoland* was seized at this time, and several of the Danish West-India Islands were captured.

A more honorable action was the abolition of the African slave-trade, which took place in 1807 through the long and continued efforts of Wilberforce, Clarkson, and Granville Sharp.

Napoleon's Berlin Decrees brought on the Peninsular War, in which Sir Arthur Wellesley (afterward Duke of Wellington) made himself a splendid name. It was not the first time he had been heard of, for the battle of Assaye, in India (1803), where Wellesley defeated 30,000 natives with less than one-sixth of their number, had already shown his generalship. Napoleon's troops, under General Junot, had invaded Portugal, because that country refused to submit to the Berlin Decrees. Wellesley gained the battle of Vimeira (1808), but by the "Convention of Cintra," between England and France, he was obliged to leave the country. Sir John Moore was killed in the battle of Corunna;† his soldiers defeated the enemy, but were glad afterward to escape to England. Wellesley defeated the French at Talavera (after which he was made Viscount Wellington), Busaco,

---

* This island has recently (1890) been given to Prussia.

† The poem beginning, "Not a drum was heard, nor a funeral note," was written to commemorate this event.

Albuera, Salamanca, and Vittoria (1809-1813), and having driven them across the Pyrenees into their own country, pursued them as far as Toulouse. Then he returned to England, was created Duke of Wellington, and took his seat in the House of Lords.

The king's old malady, insanity, by which he had several times before been attacked, came upon him hopelessly in 1810, after the death of his beloved daughter, the Princess Amelia. From this time to his death in 1820, George III. is a cipher in the history of his country. His oldest son, the Prince of Wales, afterward George IV., was appointed regent.

The second quarrel of the United States with England, commonly called the War of 1812, was preceded by several years of "strained relations" between the two countries. In 1807 Great Britain, in retaliation for Napoleon's Berlin Decrees, issued "Orders in Council," forbidding ships of any nation to trade with France, and assuming the right to capture any vessels violating this prohibition. The Americans were now between two fires. England had long claimed the right of searching their ships and taking from them by force any sailors born on British soil. In pursuance of this claim, the English ship Leopard lay in wait for the U. S. frigate Chesapeake, out of Norfolk harbor, and demanded certain men stated to be British subjects. The American Commodore Barron refused to give them up, whereupon the Leopard opened fire on the Chesapeake, which, being unprepared for fighting, was obliged to strike her flag and surrender the men. Outrages like this at last became so intolerable that war was declared, June, 1812, under President Madison's administration. The war was conducted mostly by sea and on the Great Lakes of America, where the United States' navy obtained many successes. By land it was carried on languidly, and without great credit to either party. The wanton burning of public buildings at Washington (the Capitol, President's house, etc.), without even the pretence of military necessity, seemed more like the action of savages than of the representatives of a civilized nation. Both parties being tired of the war, peace was made at Ghent (Dec. 24, 1814) without any mention of the original matter in dispute—the claim of a right of search. Nevertheless, that claim has not been asserted since then. The battle of New Orleans (Jan. 8, 1815) was fought two weeks after the treaty was signed, the news of the peace not having then reached this country. In this battle the British were defeated with the loss of two thousand men, including their general, Pakenham, while the Americans, under General Andrew Jackson, lost only a handful.

The feature of this war which is of greatest interest to Northwestern Americans, is the fact that in prosecuting it in the West, the British repeated the cruel, unpardonable course which had, in revolutionary times, brought disgrace upon their statesmanship and their arms. They made allies of the savage Indians, and again the tomahawk, the scalping-knife, and the torch became British weapons through their use by their friends the red men. One of the very first occurrences of the war was the "Chicago Massacre" of August 15, 1812. News was brought to Captain Heald, commandant at old Fort Dearborn, that war had been declared, and that he must evacuate his fort and withdraw to Fort Wayne with all his men, together with settlers and their families. He was told that the Indians would fall upon them mercilessly as soon as they left the protection of the fort; but he first tried to engage their services as guards by distributing among them a large quantity of goods, and then started out. Before they had gone two miles the savages attacked them and killed all, men, women, and children, except a score or so whom they held, some for torture and some for ransom. Next day they burned the fort, and Chicago was without inhabitants for four years.

In 1814, Napoleon, having wearied out humanity with his inordinate ambition, accompanied by its frightful destruction of human life, was forced by the allies, who had been fighting him under different coalitions for many years, to abdicate and retire to the island of Elba. To their utter astonishment he escaped, and reappeared in France the next year at the head of an army. A congress was sitting in Vienna for the purpose of reëstablishing the boundaries he had deranged, when the news was brought to them. The Duke of Wellington, who was present, hastened home to impress upon Parliament the necessity of proceeding against Napoleon as a common enemy. The Parliament responded to his appeal, an enormous sum was voted to carry on the war, and a combination of the principal European powers was formed to dethrone the emperor, who had again assumed the sceptre, the Bourbon king, Louis XVIII., fleeing before him.

Now for the first time the two greatest generals of Europe were to be personally opposed to each other. Napoleon was confident of success. He is reported to have said, "Enfin, je vais me mésurer avec ce Vilainton."*

---

* "At last, I am going to match myself with this Wellington." (In French "vilain" means "low, bad, villainous.")

Each laid his plans with the utmost skill. Wellington intended to join the Prussian general, Blucher, and attack Paris; Napoleon aimed to meet and defeat them separately. He marched toward Brussels, drove Blucher from his position at Ligny, and sent Marshal Grouchy after him to prevent his union with Wellington. The English army made a stand at Waterloo, a place about twelve miles from Brussels. Here Napoleon attacked them (June 18, 1815), and a long day's struggle ensued, both sides fighting with desperate valor. Toward nightfall, Napoleon gathered up all his strength for a last charge; the "Old Guard," who had been his companions on many an eventful field, rushed forward only to meet, at the hands of the English, their first defeat. Already the detachment of Prussians under Blucher, who had out-marched Grouchy, had appeared upon the scene. The French columns broke and fled, pursued by the victorious allies; Napoleon just escaped capture as he drove furiously away in his carriage; the battle of Waterloo was over; his standard fallen, never to rise again.

The allies marched at once to Paris, where Louis XVIII. was again set upon his throne. The emperor, after a vain attempt to escape to America, went voluntarily on board the British ship Bellerophon, saying that he wished to throw himself upon the protection and hospitality of England. But he was too dangerous an enemy of society to be let loose again to destroy the peace of Europe; and, the Regent refusing him permission to set foot on English ground, the allies decided that he should be sent to St. Helena, a lonely, rocky island in the Atlantic Ocean west of Africa, there to remain a prisoner in the hands of the British. He lived six years longer, strictly guarded, at St. Helena, and died in 1821, in the fifty-second year of his age.

CHAPTER XLIX.

DEATH OF GEORGE III. GEORGE IV. CATHOLIC EMANCIPATION. WILLIAM IV.

GREAT distress followed the sudden change from war to peace. The suspension of trade lessened the demand for labor, and the numbers of soldiers and sailors suddenly disbanded increased the trouble. Food became so dear as to threaten a famine, and many riots took place in the manufacturing districts, where the newly invented machinery for saving handwork threw many persons temporarily out of employment. Meetings were called, loudly demanding reforms of various kinds, and at one of these, held at Manchester (1819), several persons were killed.* The popular orator Henry Hunt, and the political economist William Cobbett, boldly advocated the cause of the workingman, and were fined and imprisoned in consequence.

In 1815, the Algerine pirates (who had been put down by our own Decatur in 1805) were again rampant, and Great Britain sent an expedition against them which, in connection with a small Dutch squadron, destroyed the fortifications of Algiers and many of the piratical vessels. More than a thousand Christian slaves were liberated and nearly that number of men lost by the English in the action.

---

* This occurrence went by the name of "Peterloo."

King George III. died in 1820, at eighty-two years of age, after a reign of sixty years, the longest in English history. The last ten years of his life were passed in darkness. Blind and deaf, as well as insane, he was a sorrowful spectacle, and death came as a welcome relief. His faithful and excellent wife, Queen Charlotte, was carried to the grave only a few months before him. His son, George IV., had long been Prince Regent. The little grandchild who was to take possession of his throne seventeen years later as Queen Victoria, was born the year before his death; her father, the Duke of Kent, died a week before the king.

In his private character, George III. was amiable and upright, and by his homely simplicity endeared himself to the common people. As both he and Queen Charlotte were economical even to niggardliness, they were not popular with the court circle, who would have preferred greater hospitality. In his public life the king was undoubtedly honest and conscientious, but his narrow mind and unconquerable obstinacy were the cause of great injury to the nation. His ideas of the kingly prerogative were almost as absurd as those of the Stuarts, but his faults had this advantage: they made it impossible for any subsequent English sovereign to repeat his mistakes.

The regency of the fourth George had lasted nine years before his father's death (1811-1820), so that no change was perceptible in the government when he took the name of king. A plot, called the Cato-Street Conspiracy, was formed by the radicals to assassinate the cabinet ministers, who were disliked as representing the aristocracy. It was discovered, and the ringleaders, who were led by a person named Thistlewood, were executed.

The beginning of the new king's reign was disgraced by a prosecution of his wife, Queen Caroline, whom he had married only for her money, and had always disliked. Accusing her of misconduct, he subjected her to the ignominy of a public trial, in which she was defended by the popular statesman, Lord Brougham,* and honorably acquitted. The Commons showed their goodwill to her by voting her an annuity of £50,000. Not being a person of great delicacy of feeling, she tried to force her way into Westminster Abbey as a spectator on the occasion of the king's coronation; but her unfeeling husband had given orders that she should be excluded. The mortification caused by this repulse threw her into an illness, of which she died in less than three weeks afterward (1821). Their only child, the Princess Charlotte, married to Leopold of Saxe Coburg (afterward King of the Belgians), had died some years before.

George IV. was a traveling king. Soon after his coronation he visited Ireland, where he was welcomed as the first English king who had ever gone there in peace. Afterward he went to Hanover, and still later made a tour in Scotland. While he was away on this latter trip, his prime minister, Lord Castlereagh,† committed suicide, and was succeeded in his post by George Canning, a distinguished orator and statesman (1822).

Some outrages committed in India by the government of Burmah furnished an excuse for annexing a part of the territory belonging to that country (1826). The

---

* Pronounced Broom. † Pronounced Castleray.

next year, England entered into the war which Greece was carrying on with Turkey. The naval battle of Navarino, in which the combined English, French, and Russian squadrons destroyed the Turkish fleet, ended the war, and made Greece an independent kingdom. Prince Otho of Bavaria accepted the crown, which was not a coveted one, several princes declining it. Otho was deposed after a reign of nearly thirty-five years, and Prince George of Denmark, brother of the present Princess of Wales, was elected king in his place. Lord Byron, the great English poet, who was deeply interested in the welfare of Greece, spent the last months of his life there, dying at Missilonghi in the midst of the struggle for liberty (1824).

England was now entering upon an age of reform. Though conservative by nature, when the mind of the people is firmly set upon doing away with old abuses, the removal of these follows, notwithstanding occasional drawbacks and disappointments. Mr. Huskisson, president of the Board of Trade, was active in promoting a spirit of commercial liberality tending toward free-trade, which gradually developed into that system which has made England so prosperous. Taxation was reduced; England had never seemed so thriving; but the excitement produced by this state of things led to over-speculation, and a panic ensued which reduced the country nearly to the verge of bankruptcy (1825). Many of the banks stopped payment, and the government was barely able to save its own credit. A great number of business failures followed; and it was long before a feeling of security was restored.

Of all English laws, those for the punishment of crime

were the most opposed to common sense and to Christianity. Nearly three hundred offences, ranging from pocket-picking up to high-treason, were punishable with death; and this frightful severity, instead of suppressing crime, seemed only to increase it. By the unflagging exertions of Sir Samuel Romilly, these laws were very much mitigated; and since then they have been gradually modified, until at the present day the death-penalty is inflicted only in cases of wilful murder or high-treason.

The time was now ripe for the repeal of the Corporation and Test Acts, which had been on the statute-book since the reign of Charles II. This measure, passed in 1828, was the forerunner of a more important one; the Catholic Relief Bill, which restored to Roman Catholics those rights of which they had been deprived since 1673.

This was brought about largely by the efforts of Daniel O'Connell, a famous Irish orator and agitator, who, being elected to the House of Commons as member from Clare, was refused admittance to it on account of his religion. After the passage of the bill, he took his seat in Parliament and continued to represent his country there for many years.

The Catholic Emancipation Bill, as it is commonly called, was the last one of importance passed during the reign of George IV., who died in 1830, at the age of sixty-eight, after a reign of ten years. Of the character of this monarch there is little to be said, except that it was contemptible. He was a man of good abilities, but selfish, cold-hearted, and utterly without principle. His private life was a scandal to the nation, and he had no public virtues. Fortunately the time was past when the individual character of the ruler could do harm, except in the way of example.

A few months after the death of George IV., the first steam railway for the conveyance of passengers was opened in England. Five years before, the bill of the Liverpool and Manchester Railway had been passed, against violent opposition, the objection being that with the best engine that could be found, the rate of progress was but little more than three miles an hour. When some of the committee expressed an opinion that it might be possible to attain a speed of fifteen, or even twenty miles an hour, the statement was called a gross exaggeration, and the remark was made, that even if this rate of speed could be attained, the danger of bursting boilers would be so great that people would as soon allow themselves to be fired off from a rocket as to trust their lives to such a machine. The genius of George Stephenson, a self-trained engineer, was soon employed in proving to the world that the so-called visions were sober facts. Other inventors were at work to lessen human toil and increase human comfort. Arkwright, Hargreaves, and Crompton made improvements in machinery; Sir Humphrey Davy invented the safety-lamp for miners' use, and MacAdam taught the English how to make good roads. Gas had been introduced, not only into the streets but into the houses, though with great opposition from the whale-fishing interest. It was thought a very garish and unbecoming light for domestic use, although its value in preventing crime in the streets was considered beyond question.

If we look at the list of writers in the first thirty years of the century, their number astonishes us, their brilliancy dazzles us.* When we have written the names of Walter Scott, poet, novelist, essayist, historian; Byron, Wordsworth, Coleridge, Southey, Campbell, Moore,* and many others, poets; Lamb, Hunt, Landor, De Quincey, Wilson, Sidney Smith, and Jeffrey, essayists and reviewers, and feel that the list is only begun, we stop short, discouraged. The literary history of the time is in itself so full of interest that it will well repay careful and extended study. As a help toward this, read Mrs. Oliphant's "Literary History of England," which treats of this period.

George IV. left no descendants. His next brother, the Duke of York, died three years before him; and the third of George III.'s sons, the Duke of Clarence, succeeded him as William IV. He had been bred to the navy, and is called the "Sailor-King."

CHAPTER L.

PARLIAMENTARY REFORM. ABOLITION OF SLAVERY. VICTORIA.

FOR a long time the question of Parliamentary reform had been agitating the king, the Parliament, and the people. The boroughs—election districts we should call them here—were represented just as they had been hundreds of years before, no notice having been taken of the fact that some had grown more populous and others less so in the mean time. There were actually some districts in which not

---
* Pronounced More.

one voter lived, where the rich men who owned the land sent such persons to Parliament as they chose; while several large cities which had become great manufacturing centres were without a representative of their own. Added to this, voting was restricted to people who owned property, or paid large rents, thus leaving an immense number of citizens without the right of suffrage. The Duke of Wellington, who was William's premier as he had been George's, was the determined enemy of reform, and found himself so unpopular that he resigned his office (1830). Lord Grey, an advocate of the proposed change, succeeded him.

The Reform Bill found its most bitter enemies among the nobility. It was passed more than once by the Commons, and as often thrown out by the House of Lords, who considered it a direct attack on the aristocracy. Even in the House of Commons, the bill, when first read by Lord John Russell, was received with shouts of laughter. Sidney Smith's* famous illustrations of "Mrs. Partington" was made in a speech on this occa-

---

* After ridiculing the idea that the House of Lords could prevent a reform in Parliament, he said: "I do not mean to be disrespectful, but the attempt of the Lords to stop the progress of reform reminds me very forcibly of the great storm of Sidmouth and the conduct of the excellent Mrs. Partington on that occasion. A great flood had set in at the time; the tide rose to an incredible height; the waves rushed in upon the houses, and everything was threatened with destruction. In the midst of it all, Dame Partington was seen at the door of her house with mop and pattens, trundling her mop, squeezing out the sea-water, and vigorously pushing away the Atlantic Ocean. The Atlantic was roused. Mrs. Partington's spirit was up; but I need not tell you that the contest was unequal. The Atlantic Ocean beat Mrs. Partington. She was excellent at a slop or a puddle, but she should not have meddled with a tempest."

sion. It seemed impossible to believe that any Englishman could seriously vote for curtailing the privileges of the upper classes.

Whatever was the determination of the aristocracy, the people were equally resolute. During the time when the measure was in suspense, riots broke out in many places, public buildings were destroyed, lives were lost, and confusion and apprehension prevailed everywhere. The populace shouted madly, "The bill, the whole bill and nothing but the bill!" Frightful disturbances in Ireland accompanied the agitation of this question. Tax-collectors were murdered, property burned, and so many excesses committed that it was found necessary, for a time, to place some districts under martial law (1832). After years of struggle, the long-contested bill was passed, the king giving a hearty consent to it, June, 1832.

The three main provisions of this act (which has been called the greatest revolution experienced by England since that which placed William and Mary on the throne, 1689), were: 1. The withdrawal of the right of sending members to Parliament from small districts, commonly called "rotten boroughs;" 2. The bestowal of the same right on cities and districts with two thousand inhabitants and upward; 3. The giving the franchise in towns to all persons occupying houses worth in rent £10 a year, and in the country to persons owning land worth £10 a year, or who paid a yearly rent of at least £50. With these concessions the nation was perfectly satisfied, and it was not until 1867-'68 that laws were passed further extending the franchise. Now it embraces not only householders paying rent, but also lodgers.

In the midst of the excitement attending the passage

of the Reform Bill, the Asiatic cholera broke out for the first time in England (1831). Terrible as was this visitation at the time, it proved a blessing in the end, calling public attention to those sanitary precautions which before had been strangely neglected, and causing improvement among the body of the people in habits of cleanliness and comfort.

The year 1833 witnessed one of the great moral triumphs of the century — the passage of the law for abolishing slavery in the British colonies. William Wilberforce, who had been since 1789 spending his life in trying to bring about this object, lived just long enough to see the bill become a certainty, dying before it went into operation, which took place Aug. 1, 1834. The sum of £20,000,000 was awarded to the planters as payment for the loss of their "property." Nearly three-quarters of a million of human beings were set free by this measure.

In the following year (1834), Lord Grey, the premier, under whose administration the reform bills had been carried through, resigned, and was succeeded for a short time by Sir Robert Peel, who soon gave place to Lord Melbourne. The latter remained in office, except for a short interruption, until after the accession of Queen Victoria. At the same time, the tory party assumed the name of "Conservatives." At a later day, the whigs took the name of "Liberals," and the old appellations have almost dropped out of use.

King William IV. died June 20, 1837, after a reign of almost exactly seven years. He was a man of many good qualities, among which sincerity, fairness of mind, a strong sense of justice, and great zeal and industry in the public service were conspicuous. From the obstinacy of his father, King George III., he seems to have been quite free; and his use (or misuse) of the royal prerogative was so slight compared with that of his father and elder brother, that he approached the ideal of a constitutional king. The full realization of this ideal, however, was reserved for the next reign.

Besides the statesmen who have already been mentioned, there were in this period Sir Robert Peel, afterward renowned for his opposition to the corn-laws; Lord Brougham, noted for his brilliant and versatile talent, and for his efforts in the cause of reform; and Lord Palmerston, the advocate of Catholic emancipation, afterward prime minister. Mr. Gladstone first took his seat in Parliament in 1832 (as a Conservative), at twenty-three years of age.

Alexandrina Victoria, daughter of George III.'s fourth son, the Duke of Kent, became queen on the death of her uncle, William IV., when she was just eighteen years of age. It had long been known that she would occupy that position, and she had been most carefully trained by her mother for its duties. Her manners were simple and girlish, though dignified, and she had a strong sense of duty and of the responsibilities of her office. Her way of glancing at Lord Melbourne, the premier, for instructions, when she presided at the first meeting of the privy council, is said to have been peculiarly modest and graceful. As the crown of Hanover could descend only to a male, the sovereigns of England ceased to have any connection with that country at the death of William IV., and that kingdom passed to his next oldest surviving brother, the Duke of Cumberland.

An interesting incident in the annals of this period is the election of Mr. Moses Montefiore, a Jew, to be sheriff of London. The queen knighted him, and we have read within a few years of his celebrating his one hundredth birthday, and of his death not long afterward. It is pleasant to know that the honors at which he arrived were due, not to his great wealth, but to his noble and life-long charities.

The first political event in her majesty's reign was a rebellion in Canada, in which some adventurers from the United States took part, but which was soon put down. Upper and Lower Canada were afterward joined in one (1840), and both were at length merged in the "Dominion of Canada," which united the British possessions from the Atlantic to the Pacific under one government (1867). There were not wanting statesmen at the time of the first revolt who advised letting Canada go. They thought the time had come when a peaceful separation would be for the interest of both parties; but they were overruled, and our northern neighbor still lives under the British flag.

As China refused to allow the carrying of opium (a source of profit to English merchants) into her territory, a war with that country was the consequence (1839), which ended in the storming and taking by British troops of several Chinese cities, including the capital, Pekin. The empire was forced to pay £21,000,000 for the expenses of the war, to open five ports to English commerce, and to give up the island and city of Hong Kong forever to the English. Of the morality of this triumph it is scarcely necessary to express an opinion.

In 1839 occurred the first great "Chartist" demonstration. A huge petition, signed by more than a million of people, was rolled into Parliament like a hogshead. The petitioners demanded universal suffrage, annual Parliaments, vote by ballot, abolition of any property qualification for members of Parliament, and the payment of these members, who get nothing in return for their time and labor, except the honor of serving their country. None of these things were granted at the time, the subject having been too recently set at rest by the Reform Bill to make it worth while to reöpen it; and finding that they could accomplish nothing, the Chartists gradually calmed down.

In 1840 Queen Victoria married her cousin, Prince Albert of Saxe Coburg Gotha—a man whose sterling qualities of mind and heart quickly endeared him to the English people. He was indeed a model prince. Enlightened, large-minded, conscientious, and highly accomplished, his influence was always exerted on the side of right, while his private character was without reproach.

Almost simultaneous with this happy marriage was the introduction into England of the system of penny-postage, brought about by the persistent efforts of Sir Rowland Hill (1840). At the same time originated the practice of affixing stamps for prepaying postage, which has now become universal in the civilized world.

The English, having interfered in the domestic affairs of Afghanistan, were expelled from the city of Cabul, of which they had taken possession, by an insurrection of the natives (1841), and almost the entire army of 17,000 men perished from cold and hunger and the attacks of their enemies in the dreadful retreat across the mountains into India. The next year Lord Ellenborough, the governor-general of India, destroyed the fortifications of Cabul, and then abandoned the country to the natives. A war in India followed; Sir Charles Napier conquered Scinde *(Sind)* 1843, and the Punjaub, a great country in northern India, was annexed, after fierce fighting, to the British dominions. This gave the English the control of the entire peninsula of Hindostan.

It was by the interposition of the English government in the affairs of Egypt that that country was made practically independent of Turkey (1841). Mehemet Ali, who had taken possession of Syria (also a province of Turkey), was obliged to withdraw his forces and to confine himself to Egypt, the latter being yielded to him as a virtually independent monarch, with the title of "Hereditary Viceroy."

CHAPTER LI.

BOUNDARY TREATIES. CORN-LAWS REPEALED. CRIMEAN WAR.

THE Treaty of Ghent (1815) following the war of 1812, had left unsettled the northwestern boundary of the United States, the territory on the Pacific coast seeming at that time too unimportant to be worthy of mention. For many years, a joint occupation of the tract now comprising our states of Oregon and Washington and the territory of British Columbia, had been agreed upon; but by 1846, immigrants were pouring in so rapidly to the great country watered by the Columbia, that a treaty was made, fixing the boundary at 49° of latitude, which divided very fairly the land in question. The "Webster-Ashburton" treaty had settled the long-disputed question of the north-eastern boundary of our country four years before (1842).

Of all the unpopular laws ever passed in England, few have caused such bitterness of feeling as the Corn-law of 1815, which forbade the importation of foreign wheat* until the price at home reached 80 shillings a quarter—almost starvation point. This measure, intended to benefit the land-owner at the expense of the consumer, was, like other laws enacted in favor of the privileged classes, upheld by the whole force of the wealthy land-holding interest; and its repeal was bitterly denounced as an attack upon the rights of property. A strong Free-Trade party had been for a long time growing in England, and an "Anti-Corn-Law League" had been formed in 1839. Sir Robert Peel, who had at first been in favor of protective legislation, now gave his whole support to the movement for repeal. Richard Cobden and John Bright were on the same side, urging the abrogation, not only of the Corn-Laws, but of all others that conflicted with the principles of free-trade, including the old navigation laws, which were still in force. After frantic opposition the bill for repeal was passed (1846).

Sir Robert Peel, who had been prime-minister since 1841, resigned his office in the same year in which the Repeal was carried to its triumphant conclusion. The ostensible cause of trouble was his failure to carry a bill for putting down disturbances in Ireland; but the real difficulty was the anger felt by the Conservatives at his change of policy in respect to free-trade. Lord John

---

* In England "corn" is the general name for all grain.

Russell became premier, and Mr. Disraeli (afterward Lord Beaconsfield) first came into notice as a leader of the Protectionists. There were some indications of Sir Robert Peel's returning to power, when he was killed by a fall from his horse (1850).

In 1848 (called the "year of revolutions," from the upheaval of many of the ancient tyrannical governments of the continent), a new demonstration of the Chartists took place. They demanded the same changes that had been asked for in 1839, and had made preparations for enforcing their demands by arms; but the Duke of Wellington took such efficient precautions against a breach of the peace that the agitation was quieted without the loss of a life.

The first "World's Fair," or exhibition of the industry, products, and art of all nations, was held in Hyde Park, London, in 1851. Prince Albert conceived the grand idea of thus bringing together the nations of the world on common ground, and the example has been followed by other countries. The exposition to be held in Chicago in 1893 is the latest of the many which have sprung from this precedent.

The attempted encroachments of Russia on Turkish territory induced England and France (the latter being then under the rule of Napoleon III.) to combine against the Czar in what is known as the Crimean War (1854-6). After an unsuccessful attempt to attack the Russian fortress of Cronstadt, in the Baltic, the English fleet under Sir Charles Napier, joined the French one under Marshal St. Arnaud, and both proceeded to blockade the harbor of Sebastopol, in the Crimea. A combined force of English and French landed on the coast, and, after defeating the Russians at the crossing of the river Alma, attacked the strongly fortified town of Sebastopol. The Russians made desperate efforts to raise the siege, in the course of which the battles of Balaklava and Inkermann were fought. At the former of these occurred the mistake commemorated in Tennyson's "Charge of the Light Brigade." The sufferings of the English army during the ensuing winter were terrible; partly on account of the loss, in a terrible storm, of many vessels loaded with supplies, but still more because of the wretched arrangements prevailing in the English army for the distribution to the troops of the necessaries of life. Men perished in the camps and hospitals by thousands. The country was a sea of mud under the terrible storms of a Crimean winter. Horses fought each other for the few and scanty rations that were served out to them, the cavalrymen and artillerymen each trying to fight off the animals of the other from devouring their miserable supply. At one time, the entire transport corps had dwindled to less than a dozen living beasts, while the carcasses of the dead lay unburied by hundreds about them. The French suffered immensely, though not so much as the English, because their military system had been more perfectly maintained during the preceding years. Cholera broke out in both armies, and more deaths resulted from it than from all other causes put together. Of the 24,000 English soldiers who died during the progress of the war, scarcely one-sixth died in battle or from wounds received.

After Parliament became aware of the state of things in the Crimea, a vote of censure was passed against the ministry, and Lord Palmerston was called to office in place of Lord Aberdeen, the former premier, who had succeeded Lord John Russell a few years before.

When the sickness caused by hardship and exposure was at its height, Miss Florence Nightingale, an English lady who had made hospital-work the subject of many years of study, went to the Crimea, taking with her a supply of nurses and of things which sick men need, and the whole aspect of things began to improve. She went among the sick and wounded like an angel of light, and from that time forth, an English writer has said, there was at least one department of the business of war which was never again a subject of complaint. Longfellow's "Santa Filomena" was suggested by Miss Nightingale and her work:

> "Lo! in that house of misery
> A lady with a lamp I see
>   Pass through the glimmering gloom,
>   And flit from room to room."

Meantime, the siege of Sebastapol went slowly on. Lord Raglan, a survivor of the Peninsular War and the battle of Waterloo, and who had been at the head of the army since its first arrival, died in 1855. The first French commander, Marshal St. Arnaud, had died the year before, and been succeeded first by General Canrobert, and later by General Pelissier. Lord Raglan's successor, General Simpson, remained through the war. The Russian emperor, Nicholas, also died in 1855, and his son, Alexander II., carried on the war until September of the same year, when, the allied armies having destroyed one after another the magnificent fortifications of the town, the place was evacuated by the Russians, who did their best to make it another Moscow. In the peace of Paris which followed (1856), Russia* gave up all claim to the provinces on the Danube which she had tried to seize from Turkey; vessels of war of all nations were excluded from the Black Sea, except a few under each flag to serve as a sort of armed naval police; and the Christian subjects of Turkey were declared to be under the protection of all the contracting powers.

A terrible mutiny in India (1857) next engaged the attention of England. The Enfield rifle, for which it was necessary to use greased cartridges, had been introduced into the army, and the Sepoys (native troops), whose religion forbids their using certain kinds of meat, revolted, because they were forced to bite off the ends of the greased cartridges. At Delhi, Cawnpore, and Lucknow, insurrections took place, accompanied by frightful cruelties on the part of the natives. The rebellion was crushed only after a two years' struggle, Sir Henry Havelock, Sir Colin Campbell (afterward Lord Clyde), and Lord Lawrence being among the many distinguished officers who succeeded in bringing it to a conclusion. The atrocities which the natives (particularly those of a company led by a wretch called Nana Sahib) inflicted on all English, especially women, are such as to defy description. The English, taking advantage of the fact that is a part of the Hindoo belief that the body must be kept intact in order that the soul

---

* "It is not Sebastapol which we have left to them," said Prince Gortschakoff, the Russian general, "but the burning ruins of the town which we ourselves set fire to, having maintained the honor of the defence in such a manner that our great-grandchildren may recall with pride the remembrance of it, and send it on to all posterity."

may enjoy immortality, inflicted a punishment which was supposed to have a peculiarly terrifying effect on the minds of the natives. Such as had been convicted of any personal share in the outrages were bound to the muzzles of loaded cannon, and blown to pieces and scattered to the winds by the discharge.

The Sepoy rebellion having shown the incapacity of the East-India Company to manage the affairs of a mighty nation, the company was dissolved, and the administration of its affairs transferred to the crown (1858). A royal viceroy took the place of the governor general; and a new office, that of Secretary of Indian affairs, was created, the holder of which has a seat in her majesty's cabinet. At a later time, Queen Victoria was formally proclaimed Empress of India (1877).

In 1861 Prince Albert died, a loss not only to his own family but to the nation. It was the year of the breaking out of our Civil War, and the prince, with his right feeling and good judgment, had thrown his influence altogether on the side of preserving kindly relations. The English government had, with what seemed unwarrantable haste, recognized the Confederate government as a belligerent,* without even waiting until our minister, Mr. Charles Francis Adams, could have time to arrive in England and represent the matter. This action, under the circumstances, created much ill-feeling in this country, which was increased when, at a later time, Great Britain allowed the Confederacy to build and equip steamers in her harbors for the purpose of destroying our commerce. On the other hand, an American naval officer, Capt. Wilkes, took by force from the

---

*A power entitled to make war on another.

British steamer Trent, two ambassadors from the Confederate states, sent to England and France respectively. This unjustifiable action caused great excitement in England, but on the demand of Great Britain, the ambassadors were given up. "Right of Search" was no more.

After the close of the War for the Union, the United States demanded reparation for injuries inflicted on our commerce by the Alabama and other Confederate cruisers built and equipped in England. Commissioners from both countries met at Washington (1871) and signed a treaty by which it was agreed to refer the matter to five arbitrators, to be appointed respectively by England, the United States, Italy, Brazil, and the Swiss Confederation. These met at Geneva, in Switzerland (1872) and decided that the British government should pay to the United States the sum of $15,500,000, to be given to its citizens for losses incurred by the depredations on the high seas of the English Confederate cruisers.

A disputed question as to the ownership of the island of San Juan, in the straits between Vancouver Island and our Territory of Washington, was referred to the Emperor of Germany, William I. He decided that the American claim to the island was a just one, and the last question of boundaries between the United States and the Dominion of Canada was settled by the evacuation of the island by Great Britain, November, 1873.

After the death of Lord Palmerston in 1865, the leading men in the British government were Earl Russell (formerly Lord John Russell) and Mr. Gladstone, liberals; and Mr. Disraeli (Lord Beaconsfield) conservative.

CHAPTER LII.

TREATY OF BERLIN. EGYPT. THE QUEEN'S JUBILEE.

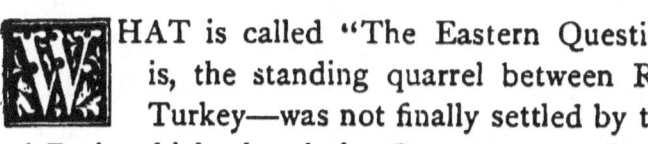HAT is called "The Eastern Question,"—that is, the standing quarrel between Russia and Turkey—was not finally settled by that Treaty of Paris which closed the German war. Twenty years later the Eastern countries were again fighting each other, and as British interests were involved in the war, Lord Beaconsfield, the prime-minister of England, acted as arbitrator between the contestants. The negotiations were closed by the Treaty of Berlin (1878) and the island of Cyprus was placed under English rule and occupation as a security for the fulfilment by Turkey of her part of the treaty. This transaction reflected great honor on the Earl of Beaconsfield, who continued to be prime minister until the defeat of his party caused him to retire, whereupon Mr. Gladstone formed a new ministry (1881).

During the last twenty years England has been gradually acquiring more and more control in Africa. In 1875 the government purchased from the Khedive (the ruler of Egypt) all his shares of the Suez Canal stock, in order to secure control of that route to India. In spite of the relief afforded by this payment, the Egyptian government became so deeply indebted to foreign nations as to bring about an interference in its affairs by several European countries, which resulted in a sort of joint protectorate over it. This state of things produced great discontent in Egypt, and an insurrection broke out in the army, headed by an officer named Arabi. The Khedive being unable to restore order, the rebels gradually grew bolder, and in 1882 attacked the European population of Alexandria, massacring several hundred of them, and Arabi took possession of the fortifications. Admiral Seymour, commander of a British fleet in the harbor, bombarded the stronghold, and Arabi and his troops fled. Sir Garnet Wolseley was now sent to Egypt with a force of 25,000 men, and fought the battle of Tel el Kebir with Arabi, in which the latter was defeated and made prisoner. He was tried for rebellion and sentenced to death, but the penalty was commuted to banishment.

The next year another rebellion against the Khedive called for the intervention of England. An adventurer calling himself the Mahdi, or redeemer of the Mohammedans, had excited the people of the Soudan (an immense district including the Upper Nile, subject to Egypt), to rise against the Egyptian government. The British military occupation of the country had been continued, and General Hicks, an English officer leading Egyptian troops, was sent against the Mahdi, but was defeated and slain, together with his whole army (1883).

Great Britain, having determined to abandon the Soudan and treat with the Mahdi, sent General Charles Gordon, an officer who had distinguished himself in the Crimea and in China, to settle the terms and withdraw the British troops from the country. In 1884, he went to Khartoum, in Nubia, where he proposed and proclaimed terms which the Mahdists treated with contempt. Not being provided by the home government with a sufficient military force to return across the desert, he was besieged by the Mahdi in that place, and, before the force sent to his rescue by Lord Wolseley could reach him, he was assassinated. The British operations in the Soudan proved a failure. The lives of many officers and men were sacrificed, and the whole army retired in 1885, though British occupation of Egypt went on.

Africa has been the scene of various other interventions on the part of England. In 1868 the king of Abyssinia in Eastern Africa ill-treated some English residents in that country, upon which Sir Robert Napier stormed and took his capital, Magdala, and the king killed himself. In a war in Western Africa with the Ashantees (1872), their town of Coomassie was burned by an army under Sir Garnet Wolseley. In 1877 a war with the Boers of the Transvaal Republic, in South Africa, ended in the defeat of the British, who abandoned the country. In 1879 a British force in Zululand (South Africa) was attacked and almost destroyed by the savages. In return Sir Garnet Wolseley burned their towns, defeated and captured their king, Cetewayo, and forced a speedy peace. The son of Napoleon III. (the Prince Imperial) who had accompanied the English army as a volunteer, was killed in a skirmish with the natives.

At the same time with these operations in Africa, a war brought on by English jealousy of Russia was going on in Afghanistan. The Ameer (ruler of the natives) refused to receive an English embassy, though he had already admitted one from Russia. The English thereupon invaded the country and forced it to accept a British resident minister at Cabul, the capital. The resident and his suite having been murdered, General Roberts entered the city with his forces and inflicted severe punishment on the Afghans. After much fighting the latter were subdued, and matters were arranged to the satisfaction of the English, who then withdrew from the country (1881).

Of the great British possessions of Australia and the neighboring islands, nothing has yet been said. By right of discovery and early exploration, they belonged to the Dutch, and until the beginning of the present century Australia was called New Holland. The Dutch, however, did not follow up their discoveries by making settlements, and it was reserved for English enterprise to transform the wastes of the great islands into populous countries. Captain Cook visited them several times from 1769 to 1777, and did much toward drawing attention to their capacities for development. Other explorers followed him, and about twenty years after his first visit a penal settlement was established at Port Jackson, in New South Wales (1782). The exportation of criminals from England practically ceased in 1839, although many still remained who were serving life-sentences, or sentences for a term of years. In 1851 the discovery of gold in Australia by a miner from California, caused a rush to that continent, of adventurers, many of whom became permanent settlers. The gold-fever abated after a while, having run its usual course; but the prosperity born of enterprise and industry is ever increasing. Enthusiasts look forward to some day in the far future when the empire of the world shall be transplanted from the North Atlantic to these regions, its exact antipodes.

In 1880 the Liberal party were again in the ascendant. Lord Beaconsfield, conservative, who had been in power since 1874, resigned, and Mr. Gladstone became prime minister for the second time. The great struggle in Ireland against the alleged oppression of tenants by landlords was then going on; and an Irish Land-Bill was passed, which, though making great concessions, failed to give satisfaction to the malcontents. The leader of the agitators, Mr. Parnell, was president of a "Land League" for the promotion of the interests of tenants, which league also demanded "home-rule" (the reëstablishment of the Irish Parliament); a question not yet settled (1891).

The disestablishment of the Irish Church (which relieves the Catholic Irish from the support of the Church of England in Ireland), went into effect Jan. 1, 1871.

The reforms demanded by the Chartists first in 1839 and again in 1848, long continued a subject of discussion in Parliament. After many years of altercation, certain changes were made by the efforts of Mr. Disraeli (1867), which for the present have laid the vexed question to rest. The property qualification for members of Parliament has been abolished; Jews have been admitted into that body (1859); voting by closed ballot instead of by the old method (a show of hands) has been adopted, and a great extension has been made of the class possessing the franchise (right to vote).

The great subject of education has, within the last quarter of a century, engaged the attention of Parliament. Something approaching our common-school system has been established, and many societies have been founded for promoting the enlightenment of the common people.

In literature, no period has been of such varied richness as the nineteenth century. The authors of the first third of that time have already been noticed. Since then we have, among poets, Tennyson and the Brownings; among novelists, Dickens, Thackeray, and George Eliot; among historians, Macaulay, Grote, Hallam, and Dr. Arnold; among essayists, Matthew Arnold, Carlyle, and Ruskin; among men of science, Darwin, Huxley, and Herbert Spencer. This list may serve as a mere suggestion of the vast number of writers who have contributed to each of the branches indicated, as well as to other departments of literature which have flourished during this brilliant and fruitful period.

In 1887, Queen Victoria celebrated her jubilee—the completion of a reign of fifty years. She has now (1891) occupied the throne for a longer time than any other sovereign in English history except Henry III. and George III., and can look back with pleasure over a reign marred by fewer faults than that of any of her predecessors.

Such are the outlines of the story of Great Britain; its beginning, its advance, its development into splendid maturity. No place, no age, no race, whether past or present, can compare in interest with that island, its twenty centuries, its sturdy people. If not the birthplace of human freedom, it was its nursery, school, battlefield, and forum, and is its home. If not the fountain of letters, it has been the channel wherein their course has found freest and strongest flow. The tree of the knowledge of good and evil has grown and flourished in Anglo-Saxon soil, and its fruit is a system of morality and piety, not perfect, but more near to perfection than the fruitage of any other growth, ecclesiastical or political, in all the world.

Through much tribulation has England come to glory. There were epochs of awful blackness, frightful oppression, heart-breaking cruelty; but by setting the points of survey far enough apart, a steady progress must be perceived. Things often seemed to be going to ruin, but whenever they got to the extreme of hopelessness, hope dawned—a thunderstorm, an earthquake, a cataclysm burst forth—and the light slowly or suddenly returned.

The firmness of fibre in the race is directly traceable to the fearful struggles by which its freedom and its advancement have been gained. America is essentially the child and heir of England; we enter into the inheritance of her riches of knowledge and power. Everything she has gained we enjoy. Our peril is to be found in the fact that we come to the rich legacy almost as a free gift, not having for so many centuries worked for it, fought for it, died for it, as did our forefathers in the older country. If we keep clear of the peril, it will be because with the gift we also inherit the industry, truth, courage, firmness, virtue, and patriotism, which history associates indissolubly with the name of Englishman.

LIST OF SOVEREIGNS.

SAXON KINGS:

EGBERT,	827— 836
ETHELWOLF,	836— 858
ETHELBOLD,	858— 860
ETHELBERT,	860— 866
ETHELRED,	866— 872
ALFRED,	872— 901
EDWARD (the Elder),	901— 925
ATHELSTAN,	925— 941
EDMUND (the Magnificent),	941— 946
EDRED,	946— 955
EDWY,	955— 959
EDGAR (the Peaceable),	959— 975
EDWARD (the Martyr),	975— 978
ETHELRED II. (the Unready),	978—1016
EDMUND II. (Ironside),	1016—1016

DANISH KINGS:

SWEYN,	1013—1013
CANUTE (the Great),	1016—1035
HAROLD (Harefoot),	1035—1040
HARDICANUTE,	1040—1042

SAXON KINGS (RESTORED):

EDWARD (the Confessor),	1042—1066
HAROLD II. (Godwin),	1066—1066

NORMAN KINGS:

WILLIAM I. (the Conqueror),	1066—1087
WILLIAM II. (Rufus),	1087—1100
HENRY I. (Beauclerc),	1100—1135
STEPHEN (of Blois),	1135—1154

LIST OF SOVEREIGNS.

PLANTAGENET KINGS:

HENRY II.,	1154—1189
RICHARD I. (Cœur de Lion),	1189—1199
JOHN (Lackland),	1199—1216
HENRY III. (of Winchester),	1216—1272
EDWARD I. (Longshanks),	1272—1307
EDWARD II. (of Cairnarvon),	1307—1327
EDWARD III.,	1327—1377
RICHARD II. (of Bordeaux),	1377—1399
LANCASTRIAN KINGS: { HENRY IV.,	1399—1413
HENRY V.,	1413—1423
HENRY VI.,	1423—1461
YORKIST KINGS: { EDWARD IV.,	1461—1483
EDWARD V.,	1483—1483
RICHARD III.,	1483—1485

TUDOR KINGS:

HENRY VII.,	1485—1509
HENRY VIII.,	1509—1547
EDWARD VI.,	1547—1553
MARY,	1553—1558
ELIZABETH,	1558—1603

STUART KINGS:

JAMES I.,	1603—1625
CHARLES I.,	1625—1648
(COMMONWEALTH),	1648—1660
CHARLES II.,	1660—1685
JAMES II.,	1685—1688
WILLIAM III., }	1689—1702
MARY II., }	1689—1694
ANNE,	1702—1724

BRUNSWICK KINGS:

GEORGE I.,	1714—1727
GEORGE II.,	1727—1760
GEORGE III.,	1760—1820
GEORGE IV.,	1820—1830
WILLIAM IV.,	1830—1837
VICTORIA,	1837—

www.ingramcontent.com/pod-product-compliance
Lightning Source LLC
Chambersburg PA
CBHW030604300426
44111CB00009B/1097